THE
HOMESELLER'S KIT SECOND EDITION

- Fix-up Tips
- Selling on Your Own
- Finding a Good Agent
- Tax Consequences

EDITH LANK

Dearborn
Financial Publishing, Inc.

While a great deal of care has been taken to provide accurate and current information, the ideas, suggestions, general principles and conclusions presented in this text are subject to local, state and federal laws and regulations, court cases and any revisions of same. The reader is thus urged to consult legal counsel regarding any points of law — this publication should not be used as a substitute for competent legal advice.

Publisher: Kathleen A. Welton
Acquisitions Editor: Patrick J. Hogan
Associate Editor: Karen A. Christensen
Senior Project Editor: Jack L. Kiburz
Cover Design: Tessing Design, Inc.

©1988, 1992 by Dearborn Financial Publishing, Inc.

Published by Dearborn Financial Publishing, Inc.

All rights reserved. The text of this publication, or any part thereof, may not be reproduced in any manner whatsoever without written permission from the publisher.

Printed in the United States of America.

92 93 94 10 9 8 7 6 5 4 3 2 1

Library of Congress Cataloging-in-Publication Data

Lank, Edith.
    The homeseller's kit : fix-up tips, selling on your own, finding a good agent, tax consequences / Edith Lank. — [2nd ed.]
        p.   cm
    Rev. ed. of: The complete homeseller's kit. c1988.
    Includes index.
    ISBN 0-7931-0396-7 (pbk)
    1. House selling.   I. Lank, Edith. Complete homeseller's kit.
II. Title.
HD1379.L325   1992
    333.33′8—dc20   91-45398
                                                                  CIP

Table of Contents

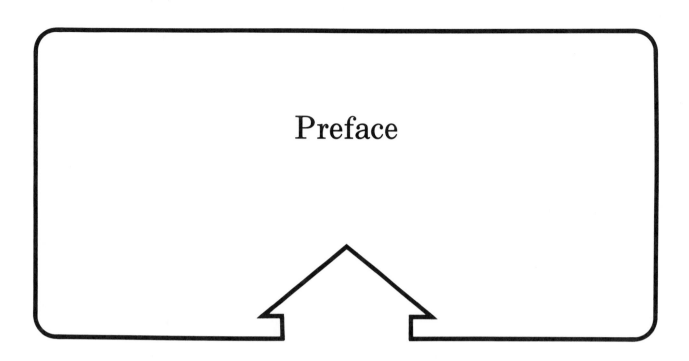

Preface

Thousands of letters have come in to my syndicated real estate column, radio and television shows from would-be home sellers, those currently involved in the process and others smarting from wounds received. (Those with happy, successful sales don't usually write to a columnist!)

So when my son and daughter-in-law put their first home on the market and sought to buy a larger one (grandchildren!), I had ample advice to give them, and that was the genesis of this book.

Everything I've learned is set forth to help you with the adventure. The book includes advice for selling on your own and unique information—found in no other book I know of—on making the best use of a broker if you do retain one.

One of the most frequent queries I receive concerns the income tax consequences of a sale, so the book concludes with a chapter on just that topic. The text guides you from the decision to sell to selecting a good agent (and dismissing a poor one); preparing, pricing and showing your home; negotiating a sales contract and making sure the buyer obtains financing; ensuring a smooth and timely closing and on through to an analysis of those tax ramifications.

If you are selling your home, you face changes in your life—sometimes exhilarating, sometimes worrisome. I hope this book smooths the way, and I'd enjoy hearing how it goes.

To Sell or Not To Sell

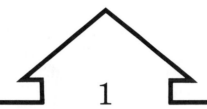

Statistics from telephone companies and van lines indicate that the average household in the United States moves once every seven years. How does this compare with your experience?

WHEN YOU HAVE NO CHOICE

You may have no choice in the matter. A corporation may couple a promotion with a transfer across the country. Or you yourself may decide that it is worth uprooting the family for a career opportunity in another area. If yours is a military family, you must accept the fact that you may often spend only two or three years in one place.

It may be a pleasant milestone that suggests your move: an increase in income, the marriage of your last single child, retirement. Or you may be forced to sell your home because of a dramatic life change: divorce or death in the family or debilitating illness.

Perhaps you are unable to carry your mortgage and are facing foreclosure. In this case, immediate action is essential as you will see at the end of this chapter.

But when your motivation is the need for more living space, you are faced with a choice: Should you add on to your present home or buy another?

IN FAVOR OF ADDING ON

If you presently enjoy a pleasant neighborhood with favorite friends and playmates, a helpful mail carrier, a school you have confidence in or a place of worship within walking distance, you may prefer to stay put. It's much easier to improve or expand the property you have now than to start all over again in a new locality. You can retain the rose bushes you've been nurturing, the kitchen you've wallpapered and your low-interest mortgage.

It is satisfying, also, to plan precisely the home improvements you have been wanting. In adding on, you can custom-tailor two small bedrooms for the twins, put the washer and dryer where most convenient for you or build a sewing nook into the new family room.

To make the decision on a practical basis, ask yourself: Is my present house a modest one compared to its neighbors? If so, an additional investment in it may be prudent.

Consider a neighborhood where houses sell for approximately $130,000. Your home, though, is a bungalow worth only $100,000. It is probably safe to spend $25,000 expanding your property. Then, if you have to sell, it should not be difficult to find a buyer willing to pay $125,000 (or at least $120,000) to live on that particular street.

IN FAVOR OF MOVING

Suppose instead that you own a particularly impressive house on a $125,000 street, property that would be worth more than $160,000 in another part of town. As it stands, the house might bring $130,000. Beyond that price, buyers with more to spend will look in more prestigious areas.

It is obviously ill-advised to invest money in improving such property. An extra $25,000 spent on additions would increase the price by only a few thousand dollars, if that, should you have to sell.

A given street, in other words, will support only a given price range. It is economically unwise to overimprove a house for the neighborhood.

Even in the most favorable circumstances, the expansion or improvement of a house seldom raises its value by the amount of money invested. (One exception, these days, is any form of energy-saving modification.) Installation of a swimming pool, for example, may even reduce the number of potential buyers. Some will have nothing to do with a pool; others may find it pleasant but refuse to pay extra for it.

One danger in adding on to a house is the factor called *functional obsolescence*. Appraisers lower their estimate of value for a house if its parts do not match. A new wing, for example, may turn a three-bedroom house into a five-bedroom house. If the original small kitchen is retained, however, the house may not serve the needs of a five-bedroom family.

Besides the possibility of not recouping investment costs on eventual sale, there is the consideration of your present outlay. Even with the expenses of selling and buying, you may find it costs less to move to a larger home. You might even pick up, at a bargain, a house that has been generously expanded by homeowners who cannot recoup *their* costs.

If you are trying to decide whether to add on, look at nearby houses that are on the market. Open houses, usually held on weekend afternoons, allow you to visit freely without making appointments. This preparation for your sale is valuable for

TABLE 1-1: Add on or Sell and Buy Elsewhere: Worksheet

	No. of Bedrooms	No. of Baths	Which is better in: Lot and Location	Garage	Sq. Ft.	Condition
Your House House No. 1						
Your House House No. 2						
Your House House No. 3						
Your House House No. 4						

several reasons. For now, concentrate on how your home compares with those presently on the market.

Table 1-1 will help you make your add-on-or-sell decision.

Although asking price is not relevant to this particular decision, it is helpful to make a note of that figure. Ask also how long the house has been on the market.

While you are viewing these houses, make notes on the salespersons and brokers you meet, observing their techniques if you intend to sell on your own, and estimating their capabilities if you intend to list with a brokerage firm.

FOR OLDER HOMEOWNERS

"My home is paid up and costs me practically nothing." Such a statement is infinitely comforting to someone who lived through the Great Depression. Many older persons feel safe in a house that is free and clear. This emotional satisfaction is valuable.

The drawback is that it may prevent you from selling a house that no longer serves your needs, for a paid-up house is actually as expensive as any other form of housing.

Because you paid $4,500 for your home before World War II, it can be difficult to understand what is implied when you are told that your property may be worth $150,000. You have never seen that money, but it is yours. If you sell your house, you can take the profit tax-free under the special provisions for homeowners aged 55 or older (outlined in Chapter 13). After selling expenses are subtracted, you might clear $140,000.

That $140,000, invested in long-term certificates of deposit or treasury notes, will yield many thousands of dollars per year. Add to that sum the amounts you presently pay for property taxes, homeowner's insurance and maintenance costs. You could probably sell your home and realize sufficient income for the rental of an apartment or other housing in a retirement or resort area.

This is not to say that every older homeowner must take that route. Those who are comfortable should, of course, remain where they are. The gardening and small repairs that bedevil some homeowners are satisfying activities for others. The emotional stress of uprooting can be a serious consideration for the elderly.

But it is important that you, as the owner of a paid-up home, realize that you do have an option. Each day that you remain in your home, you are making a decision to keep your money in the house instead of in an income-producing investment.

Another consideration is the advantage of moving before you are forced to do so. If you plan to move to a warmer climate or to a one-level house or apartment eventually, you will have the benefits of better decisions if you are not under pressure. You are more likely to receive full market value for your home if you have time to spruce it up for the market, show it at favorable months of the year and consider offers at leisure.

Your choice of retirement housing, also, will be more satisfactory if you are free to visit resort, retirement or other desirable areas before making your decision, house hunt or apartment hunt without haste and pick your own pace for moving.

WHEN TO GO ON THE MARKET

In a perfect market, supply and demand are in balance—just as many home seekers as houses on the market—and, in an ideal situation, plentiful mortgage money available at reasonable interest rates.

Perfection is rare in this world, though, and at any given time, your community is likely to have a *sellers' market* (not enough houses to satisfy demand) or a *buyers' market* (surplus housing stock on the market so that buyers can call the shots).

Where does your town stand at any given moment? Most real estate brokers know intuitively what sort of market prevails. To judge for yourself, look for statistics on:

- unemployment,
- days on market and
- relative prices.

When unemployment runs high (large local factory closed, oil-price crisis in an energy-dependent state), workers leaving the area may flood the market with houses, and the few buyers remaining are able to pick and choose.

Real estate brokers should have figures for *days on market* (DOM) showing the number of days elapsed between the time houses go on the market and the dates of contracts for sale. In a buyers' market, DOM runs several months or more.

Because many sellers have no option but to accept whatever price the buying public may offer, price levels falling near or even below those of the previous year signal a buyers' market.

Catching a Sellers' Market

If you are in no hurry to sell, you will certainly try to catch a sellers' market. Except in southern resort markets, spring and early summer usually yield the highest prices. More buyers are stirring then, as many families hope to move before the school year begins. Spring starts early in real estate; activity usually heats up as early as February.

No Point in Waiting

If you are selling one home and buying another, it doesn't make much difference where in the cycle you find yourself because you will have an advantage at one end or the other.

Although fewer buyers are looking in the depths of winter, those who do plow through bad weather are usually well motivated and ready to deal. If your circumstances dictate a winter sale, there is no need to worry.

When you have decided to sell your house, that is often the most favorable time to list it. Six months before you expect to move is almost a minimum for best results. Even if satisfactory buyers for your home appear promptly, the complicated paperwork involved in mortgage application, and the dovetailing of your needs and the buyer's, can result in problems if you are pressed for time.

If your house is not sold before you must move, you are thrust into the unenviable position of paying for two places at once. And because a vacant house seldom shows as well as one with furniture in place, your empty house may sell less readily or bring less money.

Although houses have certainly been transferred in less than a week, in unusual circumstances or with no new mortgage involved, it is best to allow three to six months when possible. You are most likely to receive the highest price for your house if you draw from the largest possible pool of buyers. An unhurried approach to your sale is the best guarantee of sufficient market exposure.

IF YOU ARE FACING FORECLOSURE

With many mortgages, a homeowner can technically be subject to loan foreclosure after even one late payment. But lending institutions are not eager to foreclose; most will work with a borrower who faces temporary problems.

Your first step, when trouble looms, should be to confer with your lender in person, if possible, or by phone (for starters) if your lender is an out-of-town institution. Often, temporary payment schedules (interest only, FHA intervention for as long as a year) can be arranged to help deal with the problem.

When you receive written notice that foreclosure is being instituted, the worst response is to ignore it and hope the problem disappears. Once the procedure gets too far along, considerable legal fees will have been incurred. Even if you could raise the money to pay the loan off and stop the process, you would be liable for extra costs.

Why not simply give up and wait to see what happens? Here are two very good reasons.

- If the house is sold at a foreclosure auction, the proceeds may not cover the outstanding loan, accumulated back payments and the load of legal costs. In that case, the lender is likely to seek a *deficiency judgment* against you personally. The judgment—money you still must pay—could cripple your attempts to get back on your feet.
- Once you have gone through foreclosure, it becomes almost impossible to place a mortgage again. From a lender's point of view, foreclosure is much worse than bankruptcy in an individual's credit history.

If real estate values have plunged in your area, the best move is to ask the lender to take your house back and forgive the debt ("deed in lieu of foreclosure"). Your attorney can explore this matter for you.

But if your house can be sold for a sufficient sum, prompt action is essential. Get in touch with a real estate broker and list the house immediately, at rock-bottom price, for quick sale. If called in early enough, the broker might persuade your lender to hold the foreclosure process in abeyance for a few weeks. Many investors are out there looking for bargains in just such situations. You might be able to salvage your credit reputation, avoid extra legal fees and even realize leftover equity, if any.

Anyone facing foreclosure has special need for an attorney even though, in such a situation, additional fees are a burden.

Agent or FSBO

2

What proportion of homeowners sell on their own, without using brokers? It all depends on whom you ask, but the figure appears to be one or two out of every ten. The National Association of REALTORS®, interviewing 4,000 homeowners, found that 81 percent bought their homes through real estate agents. At different times, lending institutions have estimated that nine out of ten mortgage applications involve brokered transactions.

This book, then, will offer advice at every stage on how to do it on your own, but will concentrate also on how to get the most out of a broker.

BECOMING A FSBO

As soon as you advertise your own home for sale, you become what is known in real estate circles as a FSBO (fizz-bo, "for sale by owner"). What motivates a FSBO? The stated objective is usually to sell a house at full market value and pocket the commission. Often, though, the seller is intrigued by the challenge of a new task. Many look forward to mastering a new skill and hope to do it better than many so-called professionals.

The majority of FSBOs do quit and list with brokers, usually within a month, as they begin to realize the study, effort

TABLE 2-1:   Doing It on Your Own

Do you have:	YES	NO
1. Leisure time for studying, preparing, answering phone calls, showing the house?	____	____
2. The ability to handle disappointment or rejection?	____	____
3. Extra time to explore the market before you must sell?	____	____
4. A good lawyer who specializes in real estate?	____	____
5. Some sophistication in financial matters?	____	____
6. A realistic, nonemotional approach to your home?	____	____
7. Access to credit bureau information?	____	____
8. The ability to ask prospects face-to-face about their assets, income and credit rating?	____	____
9. Good negotiating skills?	____	____
10. Patience?	____	____

Passing on the quiz is 70. Unless you answered "yes" to at least seven of the ten questions, seriously consider using a broker.

and expense involved in selling a house. Some tackle the job with zest, however, and carry through the whole transaction. Those who succeed are usually sophisticated in business and financial matters.

As a seller, you can eliminate the broker, but you cannot eliminate the expenses incurred and the work performed by the broker. You can provide some of the broker's services yourself; your attorney will probably do the rest. Without an agent, you must work extra closely with a lawyer. Ask in advance for advice, and never sign papers without showing them to your lawyer first.

Many people think the job of selling consists of finding someone who wants to buy your home, but that is just the tip of the iceberg. Ensuring that buyers are financially qualified, agreeing on a proper sales contract and seeing the transaction through all the paperwork down to final closing are the most important tasks.

Answer the questions on the "Doing It on Your Own" quiz, Table 2-1, before you decide to become a FSBO.

THE AGENT'S PITCH

A FSBO's first classified ad may bring more calls from real estate agents than from prospective buyers. Instead of cutting

TABLE 2-2: Agent Interviews

Keep a record of those agents you talk to; there's no telling where you'll be a month from now. It will help if you can recall some details about them.

Agent's Name _____   Firm Name _____
Address _____   Phone Number _____

	YES	NO
Called at a convenient time?	_____	_____
Identified self promptly as agent?	_____	_____
Sounded cordial?	_____	_____
Offered useful information?	_____	_____
Asked permission to call later?	_____	_____

Agent's Name _____   Firm Name _____
Address _____   Phone Number _____

	YES	NO
Called at a convenient time?	_____	_____
Identified self promptly as agent?	_____	_____
Sounded cordial?	_____	_____
Offered useful information?	_____	_____
Asked permission to call later?	_____	_____

Agent's Name _____   Firm Name _____
Address _____   Phone Number _____

	YES	NO
Called at a convenient time?	_____	_____
Identified self promptly as agent?	_____	_____
Sounded cordial?	_____	_____
Offered useful information?	_____	_____
Asked permission to call later?	_____	_____

Agent's Name _____   Firm Name _____
Address _____   Phone Number _____

	YES	NO
Called at a convenient time?	_____	_____
Identified self promptly as agent?	_____	_____
Sounded cordial?	_____	_____
Offered useful information?	_____	_____
Asked permission to call later?	_____	_____

off hopeful brokers, you can learn a great deal by chatting with them at leisure. If you feel you have sufficient sales resistance, remember that inviting a broker into your home involves no commitment on your part. You can obtain free information about the local market and educational pointers on what is involved in home selling. After each interview with an agent, note your impressions on Table 2-2.

Expect a classic "listing presentation," which will make some or all of the following points:

The ability to handle tension, complications and disappointment is one of the prime requisites for a good real estate agent. Every transaction is different, posing new challenges. Your agent should protect you from as much headache as possible, using expertise to anticipate, head off and absorb many of the problems in your sale. Your agent can also save some of your lawyer's valuable time. Although not allowed to practice law, brokers do perform many services and check on details that might otherwise require the attorney's effort.

Selling a home involves emotional tension. It can be difficult to free yourself of sentimental ties, view your house dispassionately and regard it simply as a piece of merchandise. Thus (your would-be agent will argue) many homeowners employ brokers for much the same reason surgeons prefer not to operate on their own relatives.

Every agent has heard stories of how "my brother-in-law sold his place himself for full price the first day," and the broker refrains from mentioning that a house that sells within a few hours must be severely underpriced. There isn't much satisfaction in saving a six percent commission if you lose ten percent of the true market value—unless, like the brother-in-law, you are blissfully unaware of what has happened.

The buyers who deal with a FSBO are taking on their own challenge, forgoing many of the services of an agent, in hopes of picking up a bargain. They expect the saved commission to be passed on to them. Why else would they expend the extra effort of locating the property, negotiating the contract and arranging financing on their own?

WHY USE AN AGENT?

Some of the classic reasons for using an agent, which you will hear as soon as you start interviewing them, include the following (see Chapter 3).

- Out-of-towners and relocated executives, especially when short of time, usually search a new community with brokers.
- The agent deals with a pool of buyers and acts as a matchmaker. Fewer than five percent of buyers purchase the house they first call about. Your one classified ad is fishing with a single hook; the agent is fishing with a net. Prospects are sorted out and the appropriate ones directed to your home.
- The agent tries for 24-hour coverage of the telephone and expects to work weekends and evenings when buyers need service. When the agent is unavailable, backup service is usually arranged. This means that you won't be tied down.
- The agent screens prospects. Everyone who comes to your house will be looking for property like yours, capable of buying it and accompanied by the agent.
- Buyers are even more nervous than sellers. They find agents' expertise soothing, speak to them more frankly than to homeowners and believe them more readily because they have more than one house to sell.

What the Agent Does

Some of the services you will be offered include:

Market Analysis.   Pricing your house properly is half the job of selling. The agent will perform research, often before your initial interview, so that you will have the data needed to arrive at the proper listing price.

Information.   At the time your house is listed, the agent will collect detailed information about the property. The material will be used not only for assisting possible buyers in choosing which homes to view, but for writing advertisements, drawing up a purchase agreement and arranging the eventual transfer of title.

Fixup Advice.   It can be difficult for you to view your home with an impartial eye. Being skilled in looking at houses as buyers see them, the agent can offer valuable suggestions for showing your home off at its best.

Interim Services.   If you must leave town for a vacation or move before the house is sold, you can expect a real estate agent to supervise the property, pick up papers, arrange for lawn care or snow removal and check for vandalism or fire. Neighbors seeing anything suspicious usually call the number on the For Sale sign and the agent is available in an emergency.

Advertising.   These costs are usually borne by the real estate firm, which decides on the size and frequency of advertisements. You may be asked for suggestions, but you'll find that the agent is experienced in writing ads.

Qualifying Prospects.   Unless each house hunter who visits your property is financially capable of buying it, then you, the agent and the prospects themselves are just spinning wheels. The agent has an established technique for judging buyers, and will obtain information about income, assets and credit rating within the first few minutes of conversation. The process is called *qualifying* the prospect.

Matchmaking.   "Buyers are liars" is a catchphrase in many real estate offices. The implication is not that buyers deliberately tell falsehoods, but rather that they are motivated by many subtle influences of which they themselves are unaware.

A family explains to an agent, quite sincerely, that they are interested only in a four-bedroom colonial in Sunny Meadows. For three months, the agent shows them every four-bedroom house that comes on the market. Finally, when yet another one is listed, the agent calls to give them first chance at it, only to be told, somewhat apologetically, that they bought a house the preceding week. They had been out on a Sunday, visited an open house and fallen in love—with a three-bedroom ranch in Hidden Valley. They liked the big trees! Buyers are liars, concludes the agent.

The agent develops skill, therefore, in reading between the lines, listening carefully and helping people find out more about their motivations than they themselves know. A large part of the work involves skillful dovetailing of buyers' needs with available homes. The agent's filing system or computer terminal will contain the names of appropriate prospects for your particular house.

Appointments To Show.   You can expect your agent to clear appointments with you in advance, accompany all prospects and conduct the actual showing of your home. The material in

Chapter 8 will examine in detail all the reasons, if at all possible, why you should not be present. An overzealous owner can jinx a sale. Every good broker has developed a skilled, professional technique for showing property to best advantage.

Open Houses.   For the same reasons, your agent may recommend that you leave the property during an open house. This period, usually a weekend afternoon, is advertised as a time when the public is welcome to visit the house. Special signs invite all comers, and the agent will devote several hours to your property that day.

Reports on Progress.   While your home is on the market, you should receive periodic calls from your agent. You will appreciate these even if the agent only reports that nothing is happening. In this case you can expect suggestions for improving your home's appeal.

Negotiation of Contract.   The agent's tact and diplomacy are most directly displayed in the process of bringing you into agreement with the qualified buyer who wants your property. Knowledgeable in finance and law, with the experience of past transactions to call upon, the agent serves as a buffer between buyer and seller, skillfully smoothing the path to a satisfactory agreement.

After the Contract.   With all-cash buyers scarce, the agent faces increasingly difficult challenges in helping to arrange financing for your purchaser. As the mortgage market becomes more complex, expertise in finance is often the major factor in your successful sale. The agent should guide the purchaser to the most favorable lender, help with the mortgage application and supervise the complicated paperwork. During what constitutes a nervous time for all, particularly the buyer, the agent continues to serve as liaison, also staying touch with lawyers and escrow or title company.

Transfer of Title.   In the matter of final settlement, local customs differ widely. In some areas, real estate brokers run the closing session; in others the agent is not even present.

After the Sale.   The broker will keep all papers dealing with your sale readily available for a period of years.

IF YOU ARE SELLING ON YOUR OWN

Don't pay much attention to the broker who has "just the buyer" for your property; that may simply be an attempt to get a foot in your door.

Finding a Good Agent

3

If you are selling on your own, you can safely skip this chapter, although it might be helpful to read over the material on the differences among agents, brokers, salespersons and REALTORS®. Take a look also at the final section of this chapter: the matter of lawyers.

THE AGENT

Every business or profession makes subtle distinctions in rank. The difference between an *associate* professor and an *assistant* professor, for example, has considerable meaning in the academic world. So it is with real estate. Before starting your search for the best of all possible agents, you should know the significance of the different terms you will encounter.

An *agent* is one who is empowered to act for another. A *real estate agent* is a limited agent, retained by you for a single purpose, to find a buyer for your property. It is worth noting that the person you hire is *your* agent and not the buyer's. Real estate agents are licensed in two general categories: broker and salesperson; their licenses are issued by the state.

THE SALESPERSON

An entry-level license is issued to a *salesperson*. The salesperson is in an apprenticeship position, closely supervised by a specific broker who agrees to take legal responsibility for the salesperson's acts. Obtaining a salesperson's license usually involves study and an examination; further standards are set by the various states. It is a mistake to assume that a salesperson is necessarily an uninformed beginner. Often an expert agent chooses to remain associated with a broker rather than to establish a separate office.

THE BROKER

Only a broker may collect commissions from the public. These fees are then shared with the salesperson according to a prearranged schedule; a 50/50 division is common. The salesperson provides the legwork on a transaction, and the broker furnishes supervision, backup resources and office expenses. The salesperson must work for one specific broker and may not receive fees from any other person. Because of the irregularity of their income, most salespersons are not strictly employees, but rather independent contractors who receive no salary or benefits, and who arrange their own social security, income tax and retirement programs.

THE Realtor® OR REALTIST

A *Realtor®* is a broker who chooses to join a private organization, the National Association of Realtors®, and usually a local Board of Realtors® as well. Although the state licenses brokers and salespersons, the decision to become a Realtor® (the word is capitalized and trademarked) is a personal choice. The Realtor®'s salespersons may join as Realtor-Associates®.

The Realtor® subscribes to a Code of Ethics that goes beyond state regulations. A local multiple-listing service (MLS) is usually associated with a Board of Realtors®. A smaller, similar organization, the National Association of Real Estate Brokers, designates its members as Realtists, who also subscribe to a strict code. Some agents belong to both organizations.

The coined and trademarked word *REALTOR*® has become only too successful with the public. The national association, eager to keep its exclusive use of the word (like the owners of Xerox and Coke), was distressed to find in a recent survey that more than half of the people questioned thought any real estate agent was properly referred to as a REALTOR®.

FINDING AN AGENT

Your selection should be based upon:

- whether the agent is currently active in your area,
- how skilled and successful the agent has been and
- how comfortable and confident you feel with him or her.

A logical first choice is the person who sold you your home. If you were impressed with the service you received, by all means get in touch with that agent. Repeats are the most gratifying source of business, and you should receive a cordial welcome and a particularly conscientious job. If you bought your place 20 years ago, however, ask how active the agent is now and in which neighborhoods.

Referrals from friends, relatives, your lawyer or banker, coworkers or neighbors are good sources of possible agents. All are in a position to tell you what sort of service they received.

Remember, though, that the agent who did such a great job for your aunt will be of little value to you if he or she operates on the other side of the county. Agents specialize, and no one can be expert in too large a geographic area. You want someone who deals every day with buyers looking in your locality, who has on hand a complete inventory of neighboring houses on the market and who remembers prices, problems and trends from several years back.

If you are involved in a company transfer or starting a new job in a strange town, your employer may help you find an agent. Company transfer arrangements, in fact, often include extensive assistance with real estate. Appraisals of your present house, guaranteed minimum price, payment of commissions and legal fees, carrying your old mortgage for some months, house hunting and moving expenses may be offered. Your employer may even subsidize some of the interest payment on your new house if the rate is much higher than it was on your old mortgage.

Although you may not be obligated to list your house with any particular agent, those recommended by your company are probably expert and eager to do a good job and to maintain their relationship with your firm.

Friends and Relatives

What about your friend Harry and cousin Delbert who are in the real estate business? The question is touchy. Several points should be considered:

- If Harry operates on the other side of town, or is in business only part-time, think twice before asking him to take on your house.
- Doing business with a close friend or relative can be a good way to jeopardize the relationship.
- Delbert may feel hesitant about taking money from you, and end up donating valuable time instead.

If you have confidence in your friend, you may want to go ahead with the listing. Should you decide not to, an explanation is in order. Feelings will be hurt if your decision is discovered when someone in the office scans the computer printout of new listings and says, "Hey, isn't this guy over on Marshall Parkway your cousin? Did you know he was listing his house?"

Instead, call your friend a few days before listing and explain that you want to deal with a firm nearer home. You might also ask his opinion of the company you plan to use. The courtesy of an advance explanation will ease the situation.

Ads and Open Houses

If you set out on your own to find agents active in your neighborhood, start with the weekend classified advertising section. You should be reading the ads regularly in any event, before listing your home, to familiarize yourself with the current market. Brokerage offices or individual salespersons who have several nearby listings are good candidates for your consideration.

Conduct a survey of For Sale signs in your area and pay attention to Sold signs. REALTORS® consider the latter to be their very best advertising, and with good reason.

On a weekend afternoon, drive through the neighborhood and visit open houses. You'll build a valuable background of information on property in competition with yours, and you can meet agents and judge their methods. The one who lounges in the living room smoking and watching television, and who waves you through the house by yourself, is a good candidate for your forget-it list. Use Table 3-1 to take notes on the agents you meet.

TABLE 3-1: Open House Impressions

Visit open houses and keep score on how agents behave.

Agent's Name and Firm:

1. _____
2. _____
3. _____
4. _____
5. _____
6. _____

Agent:

	1	2	3	4	5	6
Greeted you at the door						
Introduced self						
Offered a business card						
Asked your name						
Asked you to sign in						
Furnished a fact sheet on the property						
Showed you through in a professional manner						
Asked personal questions						

Although the last entry on the "Open House Impressions" table may not strike you as a desirable quality, it is. If you were a bona fide buyer, such questions would enable the agent to offer service.

A good agent will do more than simply try to sell that particular house. Open houses provide an excellent opportunity to meet prospects, and the agent may come prepared with information on similar properties and listings for the entire area, should the specific house being shown not interest the visitors.

When it becomes apparent that you are not interested in buying the house, a skilled salesperson, if not busy with other callers, will invite you to sit down and discuss real estate further. This is the time for you to explain frankly that you are trying to gather background information before putting a nearby house on the market. You won't have to guide the conversation after that!

Even if you are pleased with the first agent you meet, it is prudent to talk with at least three, allowing them to inspect your house and make their listing presentations. Call firms active in your area and ask them to send an agent to talk with you. You may ask for a specific salesperson whose name you have seen on signs. If you don't, either the broker in charge will assign the call or the agent on floor duty will handle the request.

An excellent way to meet prospective agents is to allow them to present themselves. Put a For Sale By Owner sign on your lawn for one day or place one or two small classified ads. You may hear from more agents than you do buyers. Each agent who calls is obviously interested in your neighborhood, enterprising and presently free to take on listings. You won't hear from those who are inactive or currently swamped with work.

You may also find yourself flooded with house hunters on that day, and even receive several written offers that evening. This means that you have mistakenly priced your house too low in your ad. Call your lawyer immediately for advice.

Your best bet is to set the price higher than you think appropriate; the ad is intended simply to see which agents will contact you.

HOW TO JUDGE AN AGENT

There is no simple answer to whether you will be better served by a man or a woman, salesperson or broker, young or old, small office or large, independent firm or one bearing a nationally franchised name. In the end, the decision comes back to your own feelings and the abilities of the salesperson you are considering. Nothing matters as much as the particular individual you choose.

Women earn as much as men in real estate for the number of hours worked, which makes it clear that they are equally effective. Either is capable of selling your home successfully.

A recent survey of home sellers ranked highest in importance the agent's ethics, fair treatment of all parties, knowledge of the community and mastery of financing techniques. Few considered the size of the firm important.

Your own feelings must guide you in the choice between an experienced older salesperson and an energetic young one. The enthusiastic beginner, if properly trained and supervised, can often turn in a superior job. The broker may accompany the beginning salesperson on a listing interview. Then you can judge whether the newcomer is receiving proper supervision and how the two work together. On the other hand, you may prefer an experienced broker with a proven track record.

Part-timer or full-timer? Many feel that only the full-time salesperson is worth trusting with a listing. The premise is that there is a greater commitment to selling real estate. On the other hand, the salesperson whose spouse is a department head at the university or a line worker with many acquaintances at the local factory often has contacts with newcomers who might want your property. Although the full-time salesperson is probably a better bet, there might be good reason for you to prefer a specific part-timer. In that case, ask the broker in charge of the office if help will be available to back up your listing agent when he or she is unavailable.

The question of an independent office versus one associated with a well-known franchise is impossible to answer. So is the problem of whether to list with a large agency or a small one. Independent and small offices continue to exist, and their success makes it clear that they are selling or they would not remain in business. Avoid those large firms that specialize in commercial properties, with perhaps only one or two salespersons in their residential department. Their services could be too limited.

What about the broker who is also a REALTOR®? Although many good independents choose not to join the National Association of REALTORS®, the fact remains that REALTORS® do subscribe to a Code of Ethics that goes beyond state regulations. Local boards have established complaint procedures and offer an opportunity for the client to submit differences to the REALTOR®'s peers. Most important, more than 80 percent of REALTORS® belong to local multiple-listing services, which are of great benefit to both buyers and sellers. If multiple listing is available in your area, look for a member of that system.

Tests To Apply

Identification. The well-trained, ethical agent always starts a telephone conversation or a visit to your house with "Hello, I'm Sal Salesperson of Bravo Brokers." If you suspect that some of the respondents to your one-day ad are salespersons who have not identified themselves, resolve never to do business with them.

Phone Calls. One early test of effectiveness is the agent's handling of telephone calls. This will show you how easily you can reach your lister, and more importantly, how prospective buyers will be treated. Most busy agents arrange for office coverage beyond normal business hours: an answering service or answering machine. Children answering the agent's home telephone should be trained to record each call politely and accurately.

How quickly should your calls be returned? Remember that even the most efficient agents can be involved in situations where it is impossible to return calls immediately. They may be working with out-of-towners, meeting them early, orienting them to the community all morning, taking them to lunch, visiting houses all afternoon and, because the visitors have no other business in town, even extending the house hunting far into the evening. If your calls are returned at ten o'clock at night, you may hear the explanation, "I was working with out-of-towners."

If a day or two goes by without your calls being returned, cross that agency off your list. You don't want potential buyers of your home to receive such treatment.

Preparatory Homework

When agents arrive for a listing presentation, that initial interview in which they try to sell you on their services, they should demonstrate some preparation. They may have verified your property tax figures and lot size. This is not an invasion of privacy but the use of public information freely available to those who ask. Agents might also have a record of what you paid for the house and a comparative market analysis detailing recent sales for comparable properties. Such groundwork indicates a professional approach to the job at hand. Agents are likely also to be armed with statistics on how many listings and sales they have had in your neighborhood.

Personal Questions

The agent who is interested in serving you must determine your needs. Questions such as "When do you need to move?" and "Where are you planning to go?" are not impertinent. Rather, they demonstrate the kind of information gathering that marks a skilled agent. You want someone who can ask similar questions of prospective buyers.

Recent Transactions

If the salesperson does not volunteer information on recent dealings, ask. Ask also about training and courses of study in real estate. You may eventually decide to go with a personable newcomer, but you should know how long your agent has been in the business and what kind of success has been achieved.

Price Recommendations

A knowledgeable homeowner has been known to mention a ridiculously high asking price just to test the reactions of potential listers. The agent is in a delicate position. He or she is torn at this point: sounding pessimistic about securing that price, the agent runs the risk of losing your listing. But a professional salesperson knows that an overpriced listing receives little attention, and merely wastes time and advertising dollars.

A good agent will try, as tactfully as possible, to talk you out of an unreasonably high price. While hesitating to criticize your house, an agent may be inclined to make suggestions for enhancing its appeal. Beware of the agent who agrees readily to your ambitious price and promises a sale within a week. Houses are not supposed to sell that quickly.

You do not, on the other hand, want to list with a person who demonstrates no enthusiasm for your property. An agent should not play on your fears or denigrate your house in an attempt to pick it up at a bargain. Of course, you may encounter someone who is by nature reserved and unenthusiastic. Unless that suits your own outlook, you are better off with an agent who gets reasonably excited about your house.

Educational Background

The beginning salesperson may have studied only the material required by the state for licensing. As time goes on, however, top agents are most likely to attend seminars, real estate conventions, training sessions and college courses in appraisal, finance or construction. There's no harm in asking during your listing interview about the agent's background. Don't be surprised if it is in teaching; many trained and experienced teachers end up in real estate.

Cooperation with Other Brokers

If no multiple-listing service is available in your area, ask whether the agent cooperates with other offices that might want to show or sell your house. Such arrangements must be made by the broker, not by the individual salesperson who may be speaking with you; office policy is well established in this matter. You should work with an office that will cooperate fully with others.

Rarely you may encounter a member of a multiple-listing service who intends to evade its rules by keeping your listing under wraps for a while. Some tipoffs are that: the broker discourages a sign on your lawn, "forgets" to date the listing you sign or suggests a price far above the figure you would accept, effectively keeping exclusive control. Other brokers will be unable to talk buyers into viewing your property, and your agent alone will know that you would take less for it. A broker who suggests that you stipulate that your agent must accompany other brokers who want to show the house may effectively block their efforts and sabotage the usefulness to you of the multiple-listing service.

If your home is eventually sold by a cooperating broker from another company, you are not normally responsible for any extra commission. Discuss this point, just to make sure. Ask what share of the commission will be offered to the subagent from another firm who might produce your buyer. In some communities a 50-50 split is common, but the listing brokerage can set its own figure. If not enough is promised to a cooperating firm, other agents in a multiple-listing system may not be motivated to work on your property, thus cutting down on the pool of potential buyers.

Ask also about your listing company's policy on buyer brokerage. If another agent is being paid by the buyers to represent them, will your company cooperate in showing the property and negotiating a sales contract? Will your company consider appropriate adjustments to commission?

Buyer brokers are a relatively new group, and some firms may not be accustomed to working with them. Old-time brokers should not feel threatened by this new arrangement, though, and neither should you.

Commissions

Cross off the list immediately any agent who tells you that commissions are set by law or by the local Board of REAL-TORS®. This just isn't so. Commission rates are completely negotiable between you and the agent, although a salesperson requires the broker's permission to change the office's customary rates. Guidelines in the matter of commission rates will be discussed in Chapter 4.

Competition

During the listing presentation, agents are eager to convince you that their service is the best you can find. Pay attention to the way they speak of other offices. REALTOR® ethics and general business standards suggest that they not knock the competition. If you have a sad story of someone else's ineptitude to tell, an agent might properly reply, "I'm sure I can handle this to your satisfaction; give me a chance to see what *I* can do." An agent who criticizes another's practices may later cut corners on something else.

TYPES OF LISTINGS

An explanation of the types of listing contracts open to you will be found in the next chapter. One arrangement, however, should trigger a red light. If an agent proposes to guarantee you a certain sum from your sale, in return for the chance to keep anything over that amount, you have been offered a *net listing*. This arrangement is open to so much abuse that it is illegal in about half of the states. You can view with suspicion any practitioner who suggests it.

At first, the net listing may sound seductive; you receive the agreed-upon sum from the sale of the property, and the agent assumes all the risk that the sales price is not higher. But any number of complications may arise. The agent might be tempted to block an otherwise attractive offer; although the law requires that you, as the client, must come first, the agent's own interests are paramount.

Of course, you will want to calculate what you might net from your sale, as explained in Chapter 6, but this is a different matter from entering into a net listing.

THE GUARANTEED SALE

In some circumstances, you need to know that you can count on a certain minimum sum by a given date. Some offices can offer you a guaranteed sale. In essence, it is a promise to buy your property at a discounted price if it has not been sold by your deadline. Any guarantee should be in writing, and you need assurance that meanwhile the office intends to market the property aggressively and to try for a higher price.

The broker is justified in offering a price well below market value. Remember that the broker buys your house at wholesale. It is worth much more to the home buyer who intends to live in it. Some of the broker's costs, if he or she does buy your house and then sells it again, include an average of three months' taxes, insurance, utilities and lost interest on the investment while the house is vacant. Legal fees for buying and again for selling, maintenance, emergencies and *points* (explained in Chapter 10 and in the Glossary) must all be considered. The broker will also include the lost commission on the eventual buyer, who might otherwise have been sold another house.

If a guaranteed sale is contemplated, the broker should explain these factors to you, and furnish an estimate of true market value. The broker should counsel you to price the house attractively in hopes of selling it at retail within your time limit.

NEIGHBORHOOD EXPERTISE

While you are interviewing agents, stay alert for the one who is familiar with special programs at the local grade school, serves on the Scout committee and knows why the fast-food operation was turned down for the spot on Main Street. Local expertise is vital to good service, and usually indicates an agent who is genuinely interested in real estate.

DO YOU NEED A LAWYER?

Yes. The law will not require you to have legal representation to sell a house. In many areas, local custom will not expect it either. Nevertheless, you are well advised to have your own lawyer from the beginning of the transaction, no matter where your home is located.

In many areas, sellers routinely expect to employ attorneys to help prove that they can furnish marketable title to the property, to draw up the deed that transfers the real estate and to represent them at closing. In other parts of the country, transfer may be effected by title companies or special escrow companies, which perform many of the same tasks. Even in those areas, though, prudent homeowners retain their own lawyers. You can explain to the attorney that you may be requiring only limited services to supplement those for which you will pay a title company.

It is always appropriate to discuss fees in advance. The law firm may charge a percentage of the sales price of your home, or bill you by the hour for services actually performed. Extra charges are acceptable if an unforeseen snag arises, but a lawyer should be able to estimate the cost of your transaction.

Remember that lawyers specialize, and that you want one who is active in real estate. Start your search with a lawyer who has performed other services for you; consider the one who represented you when you bought the house.

Beyond that, you can request a list of lawyers from your real estate broker. Your agent knows which attorneys are active in real estate work. You need not fear conflict of interest; the lawyer is well aware of fiduciary duty to you as a client.

Lending institutions can be a source of information in this matter. Call a local savings and loan office and ask about law firms that handle their own real estate transactions. This is a particularly good way to find the best attorney in a strange town.

The law does not forbid an attorney from representing both you and the buyer, although ethics discourage the practice. It is common in small towns where there may not be much legal talent to choose from. The lawyer must withdraw, however, if a conflict arises.

When you select your lawyer, preferably before starting to market the house, be frank about any problems, either with the property or in your own situation. Unpaid judgments, an impending divorce, an electric system that you know violates code—all represent exactly the sort of complications for which you want legal assistance. Attorneys spend much of their time heading off trouble. If you employ one and conceal your problems, it's like seeing a physician and concealing your symptoms.

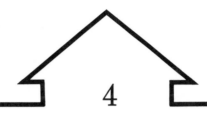

The Listing Process

4

The first part of this chapter deals with the process of formally listing your home for sale through a broker. Read it even if you are selling on your own, because without an agent, you will be listing the house with yourself, and your first task will be careful gathering of the information detailed in the second half of the chapter.

IF YOU INVITE AGENTS

The agents you have invited to your home for listing presentations have the task of convincing you that they are the right persons to handle your property. These initial interviews will cost you nothing, and you will not be obligated in any way. Even if you like the first agent who calls, it can be educational to talk with several others before making your decision.

The listing is an employment contract under which you agree to pay a commission to the broker for securing a purchaser who is ready, willing and able to pay the price and comply with the terms that you have specified. Strictly speaking, this contract might be enforceable by the broker even if you were not the owner of the property, and even if the transaction were never completed. In theory, the broker's function is completed when he or she finds a buyer who satisfies the requirements you have specified. In practice, the listing contract often contains provisions further regulating the payment of commission that protect both you and the broker. You may want your lawyer to review the contract before you sign it.

TYPES OF LISTINGS

Oral.   In approximately half of the states, a listing need not be in writing to be enforceable. Although the Statute of Frauds in all states requires that real estate contracts be in writing, a promise to pay a licensed broker a commission for aid in selling real property can be an exception. Even accepting the services of a broker, without any promise to pay commission, has sometimes been held by the courts as an implied contract of employment.

Net.   In a net listing, the sellers agree to a certain figure as their share of the selling price. Monies beyond that sum remain with the broker as commission. As previously pointed out, this type of listing is seldom in the seller's best interest, and it is illegal in many states.

Open.   On a country road, one may come across an isolated house with three or four For Sale signs in its yard, each bearing the telephone number of a different agency. This house is being marketed through open listings. The owners have promised a number of agents that they will pay a commission to the firm that produces a satisfactory sale. If the owners should sell on their own, no commission would be payable to anyone.

The open listing is often used in rural areas that lack multiple-listing arrangements, so that you may use the services of several agents in several nearby towns. Its simplicity is attractive, and it appears to be in your interest. Any particular agent, however, may lack the incentive to invest heavily in advertising or to spend time marketing your property. If a competing office effects the sale, the hours and money spent are not reimbursed in any way. It can be difficult to obtain maximum effort from those with whom you have open listings.

Exclusive. These listings fall into two categories, exclusive agency and exclusive right-to-sell. With the first, you retain the right to sell the property on your own, without owing a commission, and that constitutes the major difference between them.

Exclusive agency promises that the listing office will be your only agent. If anyone is to receive a commission, that firm will be the one. You retain the right, however, to sell the property yourself without paying a commission. In effect, you are in competition with your own agent.

Exclusive right-to-sell is promise of commission if the property is sold by anyone during the listing period. Even if you sell it yourself, you still owe a commission. With the protection this affords, a listing office is theoretically motivated to go all-out on the assignment. An example of an exclusive right-to-sell contract is shown in Table 4-1 (courtesy of the Greater Rochester Association of REALTORS®).

Multiple Listing

In a multiple-listing service (MLS), your agent shares the listing with a number of other brokers. If one of these finds the buyer, your original firm will receive a share of the commission, usually around 50 percent, depending on local custom. You will not be liable for any extra payment.

A listing that is thus shared might, in theory, be any of the types mentioned, but exclusive right-to-sell is the type most often required by a multiple-listing service. It is difficult to understand that you can sign an exclusive right-to-sell with hundreds of different offices; somehow that doesn't seem very exclusive. Each one becomes your agent, however.

Members of multiple-listing services are not prohibited from making individual arrangements for other types of listings, those that are truly exclusive to one firm. Although MLS is usually the most efficient way to market your property, you might prefer to deal with a single office. If you desire a *silent*

TABLE 4-1:   Exclusive Right-To-Sell Contract

GREATER ROCHESTER ASSOCIATION OF REALTORS® , INC.
EXCLUSIVE RIGHT TO SELL CONTRACT

THIS FORM IS FOR USE BY MEMBERS OF THE GREATER ROCHESTER ASSOCIATION OF REALTORS® , INC. ONLY FOR THE PLACING OF PROPERTY LISTINGS IN ITS MULTIPLE LISTING SERVICE.

REALTOR® EXCLUSIVE RIGHT TO SELL, EXCHANGE OR LEASE CONTRACT. COMMISSIONS OR FEES FOR REAL ESTATE SERVICES TO BE PROVIDED HEREUNDER ARE NEGOTIABLE BETWEEN REALTOR® AND OWNER. IT IS UNDERSTOOD THAT THE GREATER ROCHESTER ASSOCIATION OF REALTORS® , INC. (including its MLS) IS NOT A PARTY TO THIS LISTING AGREEMENT.

1. OWNERSHIP OF PROPERTY AND POWER TO SIGN CONTRACT. I am the Owner(s) of the property located at _____
_____ (the Property). I have complete legal authority to sell, exchange or lease the Property. I have not entered into any other agreement which would affect the sale, exchange, lease, or transfer of the Property; except as follows: (name or specify agreement.)

2. EXCLUSIVE RIGHT TO SELL, EXCHANGE OR LEASE. (Check and complete either (a) or (b)).
(a) _____ I hereby hire _____ (REALTOR®)
to sell or exchange the Property and I hereby grant to REALTOR® the Exclusive Right to Sell the Property for the price of $ _____ or any other price that I later agree to, and upon such terms and conditions as I may agree to or to exchange the Property upon such terms and conditions as I may agree to.

(b) _____ I hereby hire _____ (REALTOR®)
to lease the Property and I hereby grant to REALTOR® the Exclusive Right To Lease the Property for a rent of _____ per _____ or any other rent that I may later agree to, and upon such terms and conditions as I may agree to.

3. MULTIPLE LISTING SERVICE. I authorize REALTOR® to submit the information contained in this listing agreement and the applicable Greater Rochester Association of REALTORS® , Inc. Profile Sheet relating to the Property to the Multiple Listing Service of the Greater Rochester Association of REALTORS® , Inc. (MLS). REALTOR® will submit such information to the MLS through REALTOR® 's MLS terminal (or by first class mail or telecopy if REALTOR® does not have a MLS terminal) **within 48 hours** of my signing this Contract, excluding Saturdays, Sundays and holidays. REALTOR® shall retain this listing agreement and the Profile Sheet for at least six years.

4. PAYMENT TO REALTOR® . (Check and complete either (a) or (b), or both).
(a) _____ I will pay REALTOR® a commission of _____% of the sale price of the Property as set forth in the purchase and sale contract that I sign, or $ _____, or a commission of _____ if the Property is exchanged.

(b) _____ I will pay REALTOR® a commission of _____% of the gross rent for the Property as set forth in the lease contract that I sign, or such other compensation arrangement as is agreed upon in writing, a copy of which is attached.

5. AUTHORIZATION REGARDING OTHER BROKERS. I authorize REALTOR® to cooperate with other brokers, including brokers who represent buyers (with the understanding that such "buyers' brokers" will be representing only the interests of the prospective buyers), to appoint subagents, and to divide with other licensed brokers such compensation in any manner acceptable to REALTOR® , such other brokers and me. I understand and agree that if the commission provided for in Paragraph 4 is divided, it will be divided as follows: _____
_____.

6. PAYMENT OF COMMISSION. I agree to pay to REALTOR® the commission set forth in Paragraph 4 on the "closing date" specified in the purchase and sale contract or when I sign a written agreement to exchange the Property or when I sign a lease for the Property. I will pay this commission to REALTOR® whether I, REALTOR® , or anyone else sells, exchanges or leases the Property during the life of this Contract. REALTOR® has earned the commission when I am provided with a written purchase offer which meets the price and other conditions I have set or when the purchase and sale contract becomes a binding legal commitment on the buyer, or when I sign a written agreement to exchange the Property, or when I sign a lease for the Property. At the closing of the sale of the Property, my representative (such as my attorney) is authorized to pay to REALTOR® the commission agreed to in Paragraph 4 from the proceeds of the sale of the Property.

7. DUTIES OF REALTOR® AND OWNER. REALTOR® will bring all offers to purchase, exchange or lease the Property to me. I agree to refer all inquiries about the Property to REALTOR® . I agree to cooperate with REALTOR® in showing the Property to possible buyers or renters at any reasonable hour. I agree that REALTOR® may photograph the Property listed for sale, exchange or lease.

8. SUBMISSION OF OFFERS TO PURCHASE.
I agree that any offers to purchase, exchange or lease the Property shall be submitted through:

Check One

_____ the listing broker _____ the selling broker

FOR SALE, FOR RENT SIGN. Authorization to install a "for sale" or "for rent" sign placed on the Property:

_____ Yes _____ No

10. LOCKBOX. Authorization of the use of a lockbox. I understand that neither REALTOR® , any cooperating broker, the Greater Rochester Association of REALTORS® , Inc. nor its MLS shall be responsible for any theft, loss or damage attributed to the use of a lockbox.

_____ Yes _____ No

11. PROPERTY CONDITION DISCLOSURE. I have completed and delivered to REALTOR® a Real Estate Transfer Property Condition Disclosure Statement concerning the condition of the Property:

_____ Yes _____ No

LIFE OF CONTRACT; SALE, EXCHANGE OR LEASE OF PROPERTY AFTER CONTRACT ENDS TO A PERSON WHO WAS SHOWN THE PROPERTY DURING THE LIFE OF CONTRACT. This Contract will last until midnight on _____, 19_____. However, if I sell, exchange or lease the Property within _____ days after this Contract ends (the "Effective Period") to a person who was shown the Property by Owner(s), REALTOR® , or anyone else during the life of this Contract, I will pay REALTOR® the same commission agreed to in Paragraph 4 of this Contract. I will not owe any commission to REALTOR® if such sale, exchange or lease occurs during the life of a Greater Rochester Association of REALTORS® , Inc. MLS Contract I enter into after this Contract ends but before the expiration of the Effective Period.

TABLE 4-1: (Continued)

13. PUBLICATION OF PROPERTY DATA. I agree that REALTOR® may provide MLS with information, including the selling price, about the Property upon final sale of the Property. I further agree that REALTOR® may provide MLS with information, other than price, prior to final sale of the Property.

14. INFORMATION ABOUT PROPERTY. All information about the Property I have given REALTOR® is accurate and complete, and REALTOR® assumes no responsibility to me or anyone else for the accuracy of such information. I authorize REALTOR® to obtain other information about the Property if REALTOR® wants to do so. REALTOR® will use sources of information REALTOR® believes to be reliable, but is not responsible to me for the accuracy of the information REALTOR® obtains. I authorize REALTOR® to disclose to prospective purchasers and any other persons including other brokers any information about the Property REALTOR® obtains from me or any other source. I understand that New York law requires me to give certain information about heating and insulation to prospective purchasers if they ask for it in writing before a purchase contract is signed.

15. NON-DISCRIMINATION. I understand that the listing and sale, exchange or lease of the Property must be in full compliance with local, state and federal fair housing laws against discrimination on the basis of race, creed, color, religion, national origin, sex, familial status, age or disabilities.

16. RESPONSIBILITY OF OWNER(S) UNDER THIS CONTRACT. All Owners must sign this Contract. If more than one person signs this Contract as Owner, each person is fully responsible for keeping the promises made by the Owner.

17. RENEWAL AND MODIFICATION OF CONTRACT. I may extend the life of this Contract by signing a renewal agreement. If I renew this Contract, REALTOR® will notify MLS of the renewal. All changes or modifications of the provisions of this Contract must be made in writing, signed by Owner(s) and REALTOR® .

18. LIST OF BROKERS. I hereby certify that REALTOR® has provided me with a list of names and addresses of all MLS member companies.

19. OWNER'S LIABILITY FOR CONTRACT TERMINATION. In the event this Contract is terminated prior to the time specified in Paragraph 12 for any reason other than REALTOR® 's fault, I will be liable for and agree to pay all damages and expenses incurred by REALTOR® , including without limitation costs for advertising the Property.

20. ATTORNEY'S FEES. In any action, proceeding or arbitration arising out of this Contract, the prevailing party shall be entitled to reasonable attorney's fees and costs.

21. NOTICE TO HOMEOWNERS. The Secretary of State, State of New York, requires that the following explanation be given to homeowners and acknowledged by them in the listing of property:

EXPLANATION:

An "exclusive right to sell" listing means that if you, the owner of the property, find a buyer for your house, or if another broker finds a buyer, you must pay the agreed commission to the present broker.

An "exclusive agency" listing means that if you, the owner of the property find a buyer, you will not have to pay a commission to the broker. However, if another broker finds a buyer, you will owe a commission to both the selling broker and your present broker.

Owner(s) understands that this Contract grants REALTOR® the exclusive right to sell the Property.

Acknowledgement of Explanation:

_____   _____
OWNER(S) SIGNATURE   OWNER(S) SIGNATURE

In consideration of the above, I accept this Contract and agree to its terms and conditions.   Date: _____

_____   _____
OWNER(S) SIGNATURE   OWNER(S) SIGNATURE

_____   _____
Print Owner(s) Name   Print Owner(s) Name

In consideration of the above, REALTOR® agrees to use best efforts to find a purchaser.   Date: _____

_____   _____
Print Name of REALTOR*   Print Name of Broker or Salesperson

R
REALTOR

_____
Signature

9/91

SOURCE: Greater Rochester Association of REALTORS®, Inc.

TABLE 4-1:   (Continued)

BOARD OFFICE COPY

MLS# □□□□□   BROKER CODE □□□□ | □□□□   PROSPECT NUMBER □□□ | □□□
LISTING NUMBER   OFFICE   BRANCH   3 INITIALS   3 NUMBERS

GREATER ROCHESTER ASSOCIATION OF REALTORS, INC.
SINGLE FAMILY RESIDENTIAL PROFILE SHEET
CLASS 1

EQUAL HOUSING OPPORTUNITY   **1** RESI

FUNCTION CODE □□   TRANSACTION □□□□   AREA □□□□
AL, CS   BUY SELL RENT   AREA NUMBER OR ALPHA CODE

KEYWORDS: Fill in the boxes for each Keyword. Enter information as prompted by the computer. (R)'s denote required entries for adding a listing.

PROPERTY INFO

AD: (R) □□□□□   LN: □□□□
HOUSE #   STREET NAME   LOT NUMBER

SD: □□□□□   ZC: (R) □□□□□   LS: (R) □□□□   NA: (R) □□□□
SUBDIVISION NEIGHBORHOOD   ZIP CODE   APPROXIMATE LOT SIZE   NUMBER OF ACRES (APPROXIMATE)

SQ: (R) □□□□   SC: (R) □□□□   YR: □□□□   NS: (R) □□□□
SQUARE FEET (APPROXIMATE)   SCHOOL DISTRICT   YEAR BUILT   NEAREST CROSS STREET

1F: (R) □□□   2F: (R) □□□   B3: (R) □□□□   NR: (R) □□□
#BD #BA #PWD   #BD #BA #PWD   #BD #BA #PWD B OR 3   NUMBER OF ROOMS
FIRST FLOOR   SECOND FLOOR   BASEMENT OR 3RD FLOOR

FINANCE INFO

LP: (R) □□□□□   MB: □□□□□   2M: □□□□□   EQ: ⊠⊠⊠⊠⊠⊠⊠
LIST PRICE   MORTGAGE BALANCE   2ND MORTGAGE BALANCE   EQUITY (LP LESS MB LESS 2M)

IR: □□□□   MH: □□□□   MN: □□□□□   YD: (R) □□□□   MP: (R) □□□□
INTEREST RATE   MORTGAGE HOLDER   MORTGAGE ACCOUNT #   YEAR DUE MATURES   MONTHLY PAYMENT (PI. PIT. PITI)

AV: (R) □□□□   TT: □□□□   TA: □□□□□
ASSESSED VALUE   TOTAL TRUE TAX   TAX ACCOUNT #

OFFICE INFO

LA: (R) □□□□□   RP: (R) □□□ - □□□□   AP: (R) □□□ - □□□□
LISTING AGENT (LAST NAME FIRST)   REALTOR PHONE   ASSOCIATE HOME PHONE

ON: (R) □□□□□   OP: (R) □□□□□
OWNER NAME (LAST NAME FIRST)   OWNER PHONE

MONTH ABBREVIATIONS
JA FE MR AP MY JN
JL AU SE OC NO DE

LD: (R) □□□ □□ □□□   XD: (R) □□□ □□ □□□   CO: □□□□□
MONTH DAY YEAR   MONTH DAY YEAR   COMPENSATION TO COOPERATING BROKER
LISTING DATE   EXPIRATION DATE   I% OR DOLLAR AMOUNT OF GROSS SELLING PRICE

FEATURES: For adding a listing underline the appropriate feature selection(s). Features with an (R) are required and must have at least one selection underlined.

(R) A. TYPE	(R) B. STYLE	(R) C. BEDROOMS	(R) D. BATHS	E. KITCHEN/DINING FACILITIES	F. KITCHEN EQUIP./ APPLIANCES INCLUDED	(R) G. EXTERIOR	(R) H. BASEMENT
1. Existing	1. Cape Cod	1. One	1. One	1. Eat in Kit.	1. Refrigerator	1. Brick	1. None
2. New Build	2. Colonial	2. Two	2. Two	2. Breakfast Rm.	2. Oven/Range	2. Stone	2. Crawl Space
3. To Be Built	3. Ranch	3. Three	3. Three	3. Dining "L"	3. Oven/Range Built in	3. Stucco	3. Slab
4. Seasonal	4. Raised Ranch	4. Four	4. Four or More	4. Liv./Dining Combo	4. Jennaire Type	4. Wood Siding	4. Partial
5. Mobile	5. Split Level	5. Five	5. Plus½ Bath	5. Kit./Family Rm. Combo	5. Range Hood/Exhaust Fan	5. Alum/Steel/Vinyl Siding	5. Full
6. Modular	6. Contemporary	6. Six or More	6. Plus 2 Half Baths	6. Formal Dining Rm	6. Dishwasher	6. Composition	6. Unfinished
7. Carriage House	7. Cabin/Cottage	7. Studio	7. Master Bedroom Bath	7. 2nd Kitchen	7. Microwave	7. Concrete Block	7. Finished
8. Historic	8. Victorian	8. First Floor Master	8. Roughed in Bath	8. Breakfast Bar	8. Disposal	8. Brick & Frame	8. Walkout
9. Rehab Needed	9. Tudor	Bedroom	9. Other	9. Pantry	9. Trash Compactor	9. Stone & Frame	**ATTIC**
10. Other	10. Med./Spanish	9. Other		10. Other	10. Washer	10. Log	9. None
	11. A-Frame/Chalet				11. Dryer	11. Other	10. Crawl
	12. Other				12. Smoke Detector—Battery		11. Partial Attic
					13. Smoke Detector—Hard Wired		12. Full Attic
					14. None		13. Unfinished
					15. Other		14. Finished
							15. Fan

I. INTERIOR FEATURES	J. INTERIOR FEATURES (CONT.)	(R) K. GARAGES	(R) L. STORMS/SCREENS/ INSULATION	(R) M. SEWER/WATER	(R) N. HEATING/COOLING SYSTEM	(R) O. FUEL FOR HEAT	(R) P. PRESENT MORTGAGE
1. Hardwood Floors (Some)	1. Fireplace/Woodburning	1. One Car	1. Combination (Some)	1. Sanitary Sewer Avail.	1. Forced Air	1. Gas	1. VA
2. Wood Floors (Some)	2. 2 or More WBFP's	2. Two Car	2. Wood Storms (Some)	2. Sanitary Sewer Conn.	2. Hot Water/Steam	2. Electric	2. FHA
3. Ceramic Tile Floors (Some)	3. Woodburning Stove	3. Three or More Car	3. Wood Screens (Some)	3. Septic	3. Gravity Hot Air	3. Coal/Wood	3. ARM
4. Resilient Floors (Some)	4. Gas Fireplace	4. 1/2 Car	4. Thermopane (Some)	4. Well	4. Baseboard	4. Propane	4. Conventional Fixed
5. W/W/C (Some)	5. Artificial Fireplace	5. Attached	5. No Storms	5. Public Water Avail.	5. Central AC	5. Oil	5. SONYMA
6. Natural Woodwork (Some)	6. Wet Bar	6. Detached	6. No Screens	6. Public Water Conn.	6. Radiant Heat	6. Solar	6. FMHA
7. Stained Glass (Some)	7. Dry Bar	7. Carport	7. Other	7. Other	7. Heat Pump	**WATER SYSTEM**	7. Private
8. Leaded Glass (Some)	8. Central Vacuum System	8. No Garage	**INSULATION**		8. Wood/Coal Stove	7. Gas Hot Water Tank	8. 2nd Mortgage
9. Cathedral Ceiling	9. Water Softener Owned	**DRIVEWAY/PARKING**	8. Wall (Some)		9. Wall Furnace	8. Elec. Hot Water Tank	9. Balloon
10. 220	10. Water Softener Leased	9. No Driveway	9. Attic (Some)		10. Electronic Air Filter	9. Propane Hot Water Tank	10. Free and Clear
11. Circuit Breakers	11. Security System	10. Dirt/Gravel/Stone			11. Humidifier	10. Oil Hot Water Tank	11. Other
12. Electrical Fuses	12. Intercom System	11. Blacktop			12. Multi Zone Heating	11. Solar	
13. Copper Plumbing (Some)	13. Wall/Window AC Unit(s)	12. Concrete			13. Clock/Set Back Thermostat	12. Other	
14. Window Blinds (Some)	14. Cedar Closet	13. Common			14. Municipal Electric		
15. Drapes (Some)	15. Other	14. Circular			15. Other		
		15. Other					

TABLE 4-1: (Continued)

(R)
O. POSSIBLE FINANCING
1. Assumable
2. Assumable w/Lender's Approval
3. FHA
4. VA
5. Conventional
6. OWTB-1st
7. OWTB-2nd
8. Wraparound
9. Land Contract
10. Lease Option
11. Private
12. Exchange/Trade
13. Cash Only
14. Other

(R)
R. SHOWING
1. Lockbox
2. Lockbox-Call First
3. Call Lister for Showing/Key
4. Call Owner/Tenant
5. Thru Lister only per Letter in B.O.
6. Bonus Information

(R)
S. OCCUPANCY
1. Before Closing
2. At Closing
3. After Closing
4. To be Neg.
5. Tenants Rights
6. Leases
7. Other

(R)
T. PHOTO INSTRUCTIONS
1. PRC Take Photo
2. Photo Sub. by Lister
3. Line Drawing Sub. by Lister
4. No Photo Required

(R)
U. LOT LOCATION
1. Preservation District
2. Waterfront
3. Beach Access
4. Cul-de-Sac
5. Private Road
6. Primary Road
7. Neighborhood St
8. On Golf Course
9. Flood Insurance Area
10. Commercial Zoning
11. Home Office Zoning
12. Homeowners Assoc. Fees
13. Corner Lot
14. Designated Wet Lands
15. Other

V. MISC. EXTERIOR FEATURES
1. Patio
2. Deck
3. Shed
4. Barn/Out Bldg.
5. Post Type Gas Grill
6. Partially Fenced Yard
7. Fully Fenced Yard
8. Tennis Court
9. Inground Pool
10. Above Ground Pool
11. Neighborhood Swim Club
12. Garage Door Opener
13. TV Antenna
14. Cable Avail.
15. Wheelchair-See Remarks

W. ADDITIONAL FEATURES
1. Great Rm.
2. Family Rm.
3. Den/Study
4. Office
5. Library
6. In-Law Quarters
7. Enclosed Porch
8. Screened Porch
9. Open Porch
10. 1st Floor Laundry
11. 2nd Floor Laundry
12. Foyer/Entry Hall
13. Basement Rec. Rm.
14. Workshop
15. Other

DIRECTIONS: Enter up to 156 characters, including spaces and punctuation, to detail directions to the property. Directions do not appear in MLS book.

LINE 1:

LINE 2:

REMARKS: Enter up to 234 characters, including spaces and punctuation, to specify additional information about the property.

LINE 1:

LINE 2:

LINE 3:

Receipt of this form is hereby acknowledged. Seller(s) has verified the above information and warrants that it is accurate to the best of his (their) knowledge.

OWNERS _____   Firm _____

(Signed) _____   By _____

©1989 Greater Rochester Association of Realtors, Inc. REV AU/89

SOURCE: Greater Rochester Association of REALTORS®, Inc.

sale (one that is not publicized), multiple listing is not for you, because the system widely disseminates information about your house.

WHAT TO NEGOTIATE AT LISTING TIME

Commission rates are always negotiable between you and the listing broker. Rates in a given community may cluster around six percent or seven percent. Some types of real estate commonly listed at higher rates are vacant land, farms, resort property, inexpensive parcels and property that is difficult to market.

In an area of expensive homes, on the other hand, you may be able to negotiate lower fees than a firm's usual rate. Before making any such arrangement, however, a number of factors must be considered. Will the contract be placed in a multiple-listing service where the lower commission rate won't motivate cooperating brokers? Does the broker who operates below usual rates have a sufficient budget for advertising? Are you being offered limited, *unbundled* services? Find out exactly what is involved and which tasks you may be asked to perform for yourself.

Sellers have been known to make separate agreements with members of a multiple-listing system in this manner: "If you have to share the commission with another office, I'll pay six percent. But if you sell it yourselves, and receive the whole commission, let's settle for five percent." This sort of proposition is more attractive to brokers when it is linked to an expensive house.

The duration of a listing is also a matter for discussion. One month is too short a period for the agent's protection; some of the marketing techniques will just be getting under way. One year, on the other hand, is unfair to the seller, unless rural property is being marketed. In general, property that is correctly priced should sell within three months, except in depressed markets. The agent may ask for a six-month period instead, or even write in a six-month expiration date without asking your permission. Remember that the length of time is at your discretion, and that you want the contract to contain an *expiration date* with no automatic renewal. Check all of these points before you sign the listing contract.

DETAILS TO DISCUSS

You and the agent will discuss many items relating to your house besides the terms of the listing contract. For example, may a For Sale *sign* be placed on your property? You must give permission. Do so by all means. The sign is one of the best advertisements your home can have. It will give the firm's name and telephone number, and may also state "by appointment only," so that you will not be bothered by unexpected callers. A sign should not be placed, however, if the neighborhood is overloaded with property for sale, if local regulations forbid signs or if you have an overriding need for privacy regarding your sale.

Will the broker hold *open houses?* The proper time to discuss this possibility is at listing time. Sellers don't realize that few sales result from open houses but, if you want the broker to schedule them, talk about it now.

Hours for showing must be discussed. It is wise to place as few restrictions as possible. You may not want your house shown on certain days of the week, or while an invalid or shift worker sleeps. You may prefer that no one visit during the children's naps, or when you are eating dinner. Some sellers request 24 hours' notice before a showing.

Every one of these restrictions, however, limits your chances for finding the right buyer. Out-of-towners in particular are often under rigid time limitations. They may need to find a house in one day, and those homes that can be viewed promptly stand the best chance of being chosen.

What about a *key?* Do not hesitate to leave one with your lister's office for use when you are not at home. The lister will notify other brokers that the key is available and keep careful track of who borrows it. If you dislike giving out the key permanently, do so at least when you go on vacation or leave town for the weekend; otherwise, your home is effectively off the market for those periods.

In some areas, it is common to use *lockboxes* for properties whose owners are often absent. The lockbox is a gadget attached to your door, with your door key inside it. The box is opened with a special key carried by cooperating brokers; it is then a simple matter to show your house when you are away.

If potential buyers spot the sign and want to see your house, the agent can show it without an appointment.

Although the lockbox system works well, many prefer to limit its use to vacant houses. Customs differ by locality. A lockbox on the door has helped sell many a home because of the ease and spontaneity it adds to house hunting.

Pets on the premises are sometimes mentioned in the comments accompanying a multiple listing, so that other offices are aware of the large dog in the basement or the cats shut up in the garage. Special showing instructions can also be included: please turn down heat, back door must be slammed, leave lights on over those funny plants in the cellar.

FINANCING INFORMATION

Financing possibilities may be detailed in the listing information. You will be asked to set the price you want, a topic that deserves a chapter all its own (see Chapter 6), and the terms on which you will sell. It is simplest to start with "all cash," for you can always accept different terms later. If you are willing to *take back financing* (hold the mortgage yourself), or if you have an assumable mortgage, these selling points should be broadcast at the outset.

Try to learn about the mortgage situation in your area, and on your specific house. Your agent may need your mortgage number, and perhaps your specific authorization, to obtain information on your present loan.

If you are selling on your own, investigate for yourself. Talk with your mortgage holder to determine not only the present balance on the loan, but whether it will be of any value to the next owner of your house. Some old Federal Housing Administration (FHA) and Veterans Administration (VA) loans may be taken over (assumed) exactly as they stand by any buyer.

Newer VAs and FHA mortgages, and some conventional loans, particularly adjustable rate mortgages, might be "assumable with lender's approval." This means the buyer must meet bank standards and possibly pay a higher interest rate than you do. Find out whether your present mortgage is assumable in any fashion, and what closing costs (usually a small amount) would be involved.

Ascertain at this point whether you will be subject to a prepayment penalty if your old loan is paid off in full before the end of the term.

Find out from your agent whether new FHA and VA loans are available in your area and whether loan limits would cover your house. If so, they may be useful to many potential buyers. If these government-backed loans are available, you do yourself an injustice by stating that you do not want to see offers involving such mortgages. Although you might have to pass a more stringent bank inspection or pay more *points,* your house is more easily sold when FHA or VA financing is possible.

Your agent should discuss at the time of listing whether you are likely to be asked for specific *repairs* by a buyer's prospective lender. These potential costs should be considered from the start. A further explanation of repairs will be found in Chapter 6.

OTHER TOPICS TO DISCUSS

In some localities, you may be asked to furnish a *certificate of occupancy* for certain properties, particularly multiple dwellings. Your broker can explain what is involved. If this certificate is required, the listing should state clearly whether you agree to furnish it.

Your agent will probably use a standard listing form, which may include a *carryover stipulation.* This states that if the property is sold after the listing has expired to someone who first saw it while the listing was in force, a commission will be due. The provision protects the agent from exerting effort and investing money in your property while you wait out the listing, make a private deal with one of the firm's customers and cut the agent out of a commission. The number of days this provision remains in effect can vary; 60 days after expiration of the listing is probably long enough to protect the agent.

Appointments through lister. If you are using a multiple-listing service, you may have specific reasons for preferring not to talk with numerous brokers: a sick person in the house, perhaps, or a general dislike of telephone conversations. You may stipulate that all appointments be made through your listing office, or that your own agent accompany everyone, even other brokers with their customers. Such restrictions, however, limit your chances of selling. If your agent is not available when another broker is ready to show the property, your home may be ignored.

ACCURATE INFORMATION

Because other people will be making important financial decisions based on the information contained in your listing, it is essential that the details be as accurate as possible. Your lister should check *lot size* against your deed or survey, which will also yield a legal description of the property. Lot size can also be verified with the taxing authorities, who will furnish the *true tax figures.* Your tax bill may be misleadingly small (in some localities) if you are a veteran or a senior citizen, or are affiliated with a religious organization. It may be inflated, on the other hand, because of special assessments or unpaid municipal water bills.

Unless you are sure about the *square footage* of your home, it's best to measure before putting the house on the market. Use outside measurements, not counting basement or attic space. While you're outside, show the agent your *property lines.*

The old rule of *caveat emptor,* let the buyer beware, no longer has the force it once did in the sale of real estate. You and the agent can both be held responsible for misrepresentation. Not only must you answer questions truthfully, but you must volunteer information on any hidden defect or major problem, particularly if it involves health or safety.

A hidden defect is one that is not readily apparent in a normal prudent inspection. You are not required to say, "Come back here, you didn't notice the big crack in the living room ceiling," because the prospects could have noticed it for themselves. You should point out, however, that the septic tank is inadequate for the size of the house and requires frequent attention. If you do not do this, you may be storing up trouble for the future.

State laws vary in this matter, ranging from old-fashioned *caveat emptor* (on its way out) to California's elaborate disclosure form required of all sellers, which is reprinted in Appendix III.

In many areas, you are required to have past *utility bills* available to buyers. If you haven't kept them, your fuel supplier will furnish copies.

At the time of listing you should reveal all *liens* (financial claims) against your property. Your mortgage or trust deed is probably the largest lien. Others may include back taxes, mechanic's liens (filed perhaps for that driveway work you refused to pay for) or personal judgments. Your agent and your lawyer will investigate problem areas.

You must also disclose, at the time you list the property, all you know about *easements* (the neighbor's right to use your driveway), *code violations* (you know the plumbing isn't up to standards) and *zoning variances* (the house isn't really zoned for an attic apartment, but the city hasn't bothered you). If you are involved in a boundary dispute with a neighbor, mention it now.

CHATTELS AND FIXTURES

All property is divided into two classes: *personal* and *real*. *Real estate* consists of the land and whatever is attached to it. *Personal property* (chattels) is movable. The tree growing on your land is part of the real estate. When it is cut into lumber, it becomes personal property that can be carried away.

In the opposite manner, chattels can become part of the real estate. A bathtub in a store is personal property that can be loaded into your station wagon. Take it home and hook it up to your plumbing system and it becomes part of the real estate. It becomes, in fact, a *fixture*, which is a special term for chattels that have become real property.

You need to know this because many disputes in real estate transactions center around what does and does not remain with the property. In general, chattels may be taken away, fixtures must remain. To avoid argument, remove certain items before anyone views the property. If you plan to keep the large mirror in the hall, or—most commonly—the special dining-room chandelier, the simplest solution is to replace these items before the house is shown. What they don't see, they can't want. If you are not going to do this, state clearly in writing, at the time you list, that you reserve the right to remove the rosebushes, the window air-conditioner or anything else the buyers might assume stays with the property.

Items that most often give trouble are lighting fixtures, drapes, satellite dishes, basketball backboards, swing sets and wood stoves. The law holds that the items should remain that are permanently attached, are adapted to the use for which they were installed and were intended to remain. It's best to forestall arguments.

Carpeting usually remains if it is attached to the floor. Appliances are removable unless they are built-in. Even if you are willing to leave free-standing appliances, do not mention them in your listing; they may come in handy as bargaining tools later.

If you try to sell the house with its furniture, you are eliminating many potential buyers. Offer the house alone, noting that you would sell it with furnishings if so requested. You can always hold a professionally run tag sale for the furniture later.

SUPPLEMENTARY FACT SHEET

Besides the information on the listing form, other data can be of value to house hunters. Your agent may prepare a standard *information sheet*. If not, you can help put one together.

If you are selling on your own, an information sheet is essential, and will contain the same information that an agent's listing contract would include. Putting one together is a fascinating desktop-publishing project for the owner of a personal computer.

Room sizes and floor plans can be noted on your fact sheet. Mention carpet and tile colors. Describe the insulation, which is of ever-increasing interest. Utility bills should be summarized, noting nonrecurring expenses ("the water bill is high because we filled the pool twice").

This is the place to describe particular features you are proud of and to list nearby schools, bus lines, shopping centers and places of worship. Unless your neighbors would regard it as an invasion of their privacy, tell who they are, where they work and the ages of their children.

Use the sample listing fact sheet, Table 4-2, as your guide for preparing the fact sheet.

TABLE 4-2: Sample Fact Sheet

Address: _____   Price: _____

Style: _____   Taxes: _____

Entry: _____   Lot Size: _____

Living Room: _____

_____

Dining Room: _____

_____

Kitchen: _____

_____

Family Room/Den: _____

_____

Bedrooms: _____

_____

_____

Bath: _____

_____

Basement: _____

Garage: _____

Special Features: _____

_____

_____

_____

Schools: _____

_____

Financing: _____

_____

Offered by: _____   Phone: _____

This information is believed to be accurate, but is subject to errors, omissions, prior sale or withdrawal.

POSSIBLE EXCEPTIONS TO COMMISSION

When you list the property, you may have in mind a couple who have expressed an interest in your house. You may even delay listing with an agent, losing valuable time waiting for their decision. There are two ways to handle this situation. You can turn their names over to the listing agent, or you can request a statement that no commission will be due if the property is sold to this couple. Many brokers will honor a request to exempt specific purchasers from the listing contract.

The listing contract should be signed by all owners of the property, and in some states, this may include a spouse who is not an owner. A salesperson also signs the listing contract on behalf of the broker with whom you are entering into the contract.

It can be instructive, at this point, to make a list of the reasons you originally chose this particular house. Perhaps you bought because of the nearby bus line; then you bought a second car and haven't thought about public transportation since. But your original reasons may influence other buyers. Think back and write the list in Table 4-3 below.

TABLE 4-3: Your Reasons for Buying

I chose this house because . . .

1. _____

2. _____

3. _____

4. _____

5. _____

6. _____

7. _____

Keep these features in mind when you write your advertisement, or give the list to your broker.

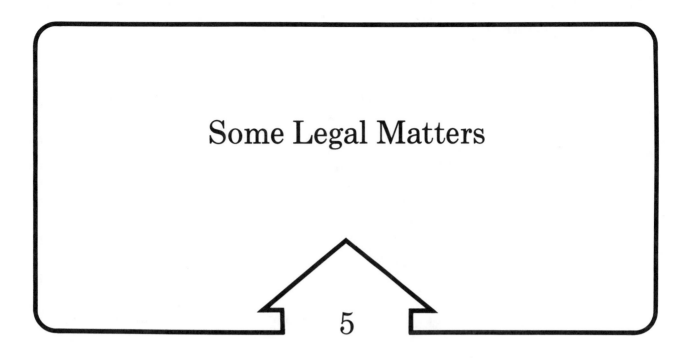

Some Legal Matters

5

Even if no broker is employed, most home sales are covered by the Federal Fair Housing Law, and sellers must be aware of the regulations involved.

This chapter also discusses the special legal obligations between principal and agent. Too few sellers are aware of these obligations.

FAIR HOUSING REGULATIONS

Both you and your broker must comply with a number of civil rights acts that are intended to protect the public from unfair discrimination in the sale of real estate.

The most sweeping, the *Civil Rights Act of 1866,* forbids discrimination on the basis of race or color. The law contains no exceptions, and it is clear that refusal to deal evenhandedly with a member of a minority race lays the seller and the broker open to severe penalties. Complaints are handled in federal courts.

More complex is the *Federal Fair Housing Act of 1968.* With some exceptions, this law forbids discrimination on the basis of race, color, religion, country of origin, sex, handicap and the presence of children in a family. Any complaint receives prompt investigation.

In addition, your state might forbid discrimination based on other grounds: age, marital status, record of convictions, government assistance as a source of income or political affiliation.

These prohibitions against discrimination apply not only to selling real estate, but also to granting credit and renting living space.

Old-fashioned restrictive covenants that are contrary to these laws, such as a deed restriction forbidding the sale of property in a certain area to Italians, are now illegal. Any such covenants remaining cannot be enforced.

LAW OF AGENCY

The law sets up a special set of duties and responsibilities between you and the broker with whom you have listed your home. Legally, the broker owes you a *fiduciary duty,* and you are known as the *client,* or *principal.* (Where the word "broker" is used in this book, it also applies to salespersons under the broker's direction and to cooperating offices in a multiple-listing service. All of these are subagents of the broker and bear exactly the same responsibility to you as does your listing broker.)

Primary to the fiduciary relationship is a requirement that the broker put your interests above everyone else's, including the broker's own. The broker owes you first loyalty; anything short of that is considered a breach of duty.

Note that buyers are not clients. Law requires that the broker be trustworthy in dealing with buyers, and a good one will know the buyers well and identify with their needs. Nevertheless, legally speaking, buyers are merely *customers,* and when push comes to shove, the broker's first loyalty is due to you, the client.

Responsibilities of the Broker

The specific responsibilities that this fiduciary duty entails include the following:

Obedience. The broker must obey instructions, except when asked to do something illegal (concealing a hidden defect, for example, or discriminating against buyers of a certain race).

Information. You may be enlightened enough that you have few questions on real estate matters. Still, your broker must inform you of any facts, figures or trends that may be helpful. Conversely, if you are innocently ignorant of the market and plan to list your house at a figure well below its true worth, the broker cannot take the listing as a quick and easy sale or, even worse, buy the house through a cousin. The broker's duty is to inform you of the present state of the market, and to suggest a price closer to the proper value. Similarly, if your agent has knowledge of the shaky financial situation of a prospective buyer, those facts must be volunteered even if you do not request them.

Not To Buy. Brokers are specifically prohibited from buying real estate listed with them unless they disclose their interest in the transaction. They may not purchase through a dummy corporation or a relative. If you do sell property to a broker, you may well find the notification spelled out in the purchase contract itself: "It is understood that the buyer is a licensed real estate broker."

Present Offers Promptly. The broker is not permitted to screen or block offers but must present any written offer to you immediately. When the seller says, "Don't bring me anything under $100,000," and an offer comes in for $95,000, the broker faces a conflict between obeying instructions and presenting all offers. Unpleasant as the confrontation might be, most brokers would convey the offer.

Confidentiality. The broker may not divulge confidential information that is not in your best interest. The broker may not suggest an offering price under your listed figure without your authorization, or reveal the figure at which you have confided that you might sell. Although many people don't realize it, this duty of confidentiality does not extend to the buyer.

Accounting.   The broker is required to maintain a separate escrow account in which the buyer's deposits are kept until time of transfer. You have the right to know the amount and form of any deposits. In the event of dispute, the broker should not return deposits to the buyer without your authorization. The broker also owes you continuous bona fide efforts to obtain a satisfactory purchaser for your house. This duty implies advertising, which is usually paid for by the broker, and showing your property.

State Requirements

Real estate licenses are issued by the various states, and each state has set up additional regulations for brokers. Some of the more common ones are these:

Reveal Extra Profits.   If the broker is receiving any fee in connection with your sale from an insurance company, mortgage broker, escrow company, home warranty insurer or the like, your broker should reveal the amount of money involved.

Furnish Copies.   You and other parties to a real estate transaction are entitled to receive immediately duplicate originals of anything you sign. The first such document will probably be your listing contract, which may be in duplicate or triplicate form for this purpose. You shouldn't have to go to bed that night wondering just what it was you signed.

No Directed Appraisals.   Appraisers' ethics forbid a directed appraisal, which is specifically mentioned in some state laws. A directed appraisal is one elicited by instructions such as "See if you can come in at a high price," or "Remember that there's a contract to buy this place for $97,000."

Legal Advice Forbidden.   Brokers walk a tightrope in this respect, for they accumulate a certain degree of expertise in narrow fields of law as they apply to real estate. Constantly alert to avoid the practice of law without a license, brokers may refer you to your attorney even though they know the answer to your question. In negotiating the purchase contract, brokers should refuse to draft an unusual provision, even when they know exactly what the wording should be.

Paying Unlicensed Person. It is illegal for the broker to pay any unlicensed person for help in a real estate transaction, and it is also illegal for anyone who is not licensed to receive a share of the commission. In some states, this prohibition against kickbacks includes even you, as the person who is paying the commission. If there is any adjustment or concession to be made, the broker may suggest, instead of turning back funds to you, that the commission rate be renegotiated to reflect the discount.

Commingling. The term refers to mixing the broker's own funds with those in the escrow account, and the practice is strictly forbidden.

Representing Both Parties. On rare occasions, a buyer will offer to pay a broker for securing property. The buyer thus becomes a client, and the broker has a conflict of interest. The broker may not accept commissions from both parties, with one exception: If you and the buyer each know about the situation and agree to it, preferably in writing, the broker may then represent both of you.

Concealing Facts. Even under your direction, the broker may not conceal relevant information about your property. As the principal, you assume a certain amount of legal responsibility for the broker's acts, and you could be held liable for any misrepresentation on the broker's part.

Do you understand the agent's fiduciary duties? See Table 5-1 for a quiz.

YOUR AGENT'S DUTIES

You can expect an agent to *accompany all showings* of your property to potential buyers. Only in an emergency is it acceptable to send an unescorted visitor. You might, in such a case, receive a hurried phone call:

"Those doctors I showed through yesterday are considering putting in an offer, and they'd like to go through the house again. I'm tied up here holding an open house, and we probably shouldn't delay them. Would you mind if they came over now? Please try to avoid any discussion of price or terms. Just smile and refer all questions back to me; that's safer at this point."

Unless your property is in a hard-to-find or distant location, you can reasonably expect a good agent to show every prospect through personally. At times, another salesperson from the same office may take over.

Communication is one of the agent's chief responsibilities, and the one most often neglected. You would like a report after each showing, or at least a call once a week. A report every other week is probably the agent's goal, and it is easy to overlook this duty when things get busy.

Nevertheless, you want to hear how often the house is being shown. (Cooperating brokers from other offices who enter while you are away should leave identifying cards on your kitchen counter.) You want to know what potential buyers say about your property, and what other brokers say. (At least, you think you want to know; actually, you may be bothered by some of their comments.)

You are entitled to these reports even if only to learn that nothing is happening. A top agent will have suggestions to make in that case—ways to enhance your home's appeal. You may hear a tactful plea that you not participate in showings. Where price is the problem, the agent may suggest meeting with you to discuss steps that may be taken. If price is not the issue, you may eventually want to offer a bonus of a few hundred dollars to the successful salesperson. This news, disseminated through the multiple-listing system, calls attention to your property, and occasionally achieves better results than lowering your asking price by the same amount.

If you are not receiving regular reports of progress, never hesitate to call and ask. Agents who furnish a home phone number are used to receiving calls in the evenings and on weekends and will not resent them.

Keep yourself available. If you leave town on a vacation, alert your agent to keep an eye on the house. Make sure the property can be shown, and leave your temporary phone number with the agency. An offer can be communicated by telephone and fax when quick action is needed.

Your agent will probably not bring you any oral offers. In every state, contracts for the sale of real property must be in writing. An idle question about whether you'd take $5,000 less than you are asking is of no value and can be harmful to you if answered. The agent would probably respond, "Let's put it in writing and I'll see what they say." All written offers, on the other hand, must be presented to you immediately. The agent must be scrupulous about expediting offers from cooperating offices.

TABLE 5-1: Quiz on Fiduciary Duties

	YES	NO
Does the agent have the right to:		
1. Tell buyers nothing about your defective septic tank?	_____	_____
2. Screen buyers for those who would be ethnically comfortable in your neighborhood?	_____	_____
3. Conceal relevant factors about your financial difficulties from buyers?	_____	_____
4. Conceal relevant factors about the buyer's financial difficulties from you?	_____	_____
5. Keep the buyer's earnest money deposit in the broker's business account?	_____	_____
6. Buy your property using a fictitious name?	_____	_____
7. Accept a bonus from a grateful buyer without your knowledge?	_____	_____
8. Keep confidential the fact that the buyers have said they'd pay more if they had to?	_____	_____
9. Refuse to take a ridiculously low offer to you?	_____	_____
10. Withdraw from your service—cancel the listing?	_____	_____

Answers:

1. No	6. No
2. No	7. No
3. Yes	8. No
4. No	9. No
5. No	10. Yes

IF YOU HAVE COMPLAINTS

Can you dismiss an unsatisfactory agent? Probably. Can you recover for damages suffered because of incompetence or breach of fiduciary duties? Possibly. For advice on either situation, talk with your lawyer.

Long before affairs reach such a state, however, you can take a number of different steps with your complaints. The first and simplest step is to *speak with the agent directly,* communicating your dissatisfaction as openly as possible.

If this brings no results, talk next with the *managing broker* in the office. Don't be afraid to make a pest of yourself. If telephone calls don't bring satisfaction, write a letter (keeping it as brief as possible) indicating the next steps you intend to take. Most brokers are highly sensitive to sellers' complaints and will intervene immediately to straighten things out.

Next, before going beyond the immediate office, it may be wise to speak with *your attorney*. If you want to cancel the listing, in many cases you have only to ask. Depending on the terms of your listing contract, type of agency granted and state law, you may be able to cancel at will, or you may be able to cancel with repayment to the broker for time and money expended. If you are told that the office does not cancel listings, a call from your attorney may break the deadlock. Multiple-listing systems may look with disfavor upon a broker who picks up a canceled listing and resubmits it, so check the procedure if you plan to transfer to another MLS office.

If you want to blow the whistle on a broker, a number of options are available. The local *Chamber of Commerce* and *Better Business Bureau* have no jurisdiction over agents. Neither does the *Action Line* or *Help Column* of the newspaper or television station. But a threat to complain to them touches a sensitive spot, for public opinion and reputation are of vital importance to the real estate brokerage business.

More serious is a complaint to the local *Board of REALTORS®*, if your broker is a member. The real estate industry is eager to retain as much self-regulation as possible, and has set up procedures for enforcing its Code of Ethics. Your broker's action will come under serious scrutiny by his or her peers, and your problem will receive prompt attention.

Finally, any serious violation can be reported to the *state licensing commission*. This is strong medicine, for this body, in addition to lesser punishments, can deprive brokers of their licenses, putting them out of business. The mere mention of a plan to contact this body usually brings prompt response from recalcitrant agents.

In the event of a serious offense that has damaged you materially, your attorney can advise whether a *lawsuit* is in order. If you should win a suit against a broker who cannot be reached for collection of damages, many states have a recovery fund, to which brokers contribute regularly. This money is available if you are awarded damages that cannot otherwise be collected.

YOUR RESPONSIBILITIES

Your primary duty is to compensate the agent as you originally promised. Unless otherwise provided, you owe a commission when a buyer is produced who is ready, willing and able to purchase on the terms and at the price you stipulated, and who was produced by the licensed broker involved. The obligation might exist even without your acceptance of the offer, or the property's actually changing hands. You could owe a commission even without a completed transaction, but many listing contracts and sales contracts provide that no commission will be paid until the sale is finally consummated.

You may be liable for a commission if you withdraw the listing to evade payment and then sell to someone first introduced to the property through the broker's efforts. You may be liable if you sell the property yourself after having given exclusive right-to-sell. Sellers have been ordered by the courts to pay a commission even though a spouse refused to cooperate and thus blocked the transfer, even though some time elapsed before the seller completed the deal directly with the buyer or even though the seller accepted the services of a broker without any written contract or promise to pay a commission. You may be liable if you simply change your mind and back out after a contract has been signed by both parties.

In practice, most brokers will not claim commissions in such situations if you have acted in good faith. Circumstances beyond your control can force a change of plans; the agent recognizes that fact and wants to maintain your goodwill.

Many sellers do not realize that they can be held legally responsible for certain real-estate-related activities of their agents. This responsibility could even extend to subagents, those other brokers who cooperate in multiple-listing arrangements. Problems of this sort are rare, but you should steer clear of any broker who seems shaky on ethics, fair housing laws, disclosure of defects or similar legal landmines.

THE BUYER'S BROKER

A few years ago, the Federal Trade Commission found that most buyers thought the selling broker represented them and put their best interests first. Many sellers thought so also and, most distressing, a large percentage of real estate brokers were under the same impression.

Since then, movements have been afoot in state after state to clarify the matter so that everyone understands who is working for whom. Growing in popularity, especially on the West Coast, is the employment of *buyer's brokers,* who owe fiduciary duties to the buyer. A buyer's broker is committed to obtaining not the highest, but the lowest, purchase price, and owes duties of confidentiality to the buyer, not to the seller.

Different arrangements are used to compensate the buyer's broker, who may be paid by the buyer on a flat fee, commission or hourly basis. In those cases, the buyer's broker should refuse to accept any share of commission originally promised by the seller. Sometimes the seller is asked to reduce the purchase price to compensate the buyer for this arrangement.

In some proposals, the seller is even asked to pay the buyer's broker, with the clear understanding that the agent is putting the buyer's interest first.

This new field—buyer representation—is still being worked out. One perplexing question is referred to as the problem of *subagency* (responsibility of the cooperating firm under a multiple-listing agreement). Some question whether a firm has a right to sell its own listings to someone who has retained that company as a buyer's broker.

Even without a buyer's broker agreement, problems arise when a broker sells a house for an owner, acting as fiduciary agent, and then finds another house for that seller to buy. It's easy to state the rule that the broker is usually the agent of the seller, but where does primary loyalty lie in the second transaction?

At any rate, more homeowners should be aware that a broker who violates fiduciary duty to the principal (seller) may have forfeited payment of commission, and may be liable for other damages.

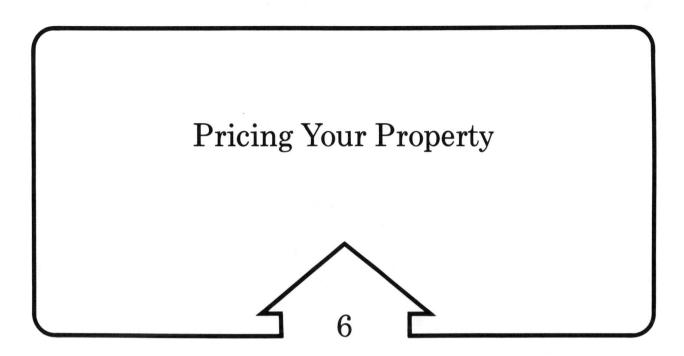

Pricing Your Property

6

If you offered your house for sale at $2 million, it would never sell (or it would remain on the market until inflation caught up with your price). If you asked $10 for it, you'd have a sale before your advertisement even hit the papers. (The supervisor of the newspaper's classified ad department would be at your door five minutes after you called.)

So you need only search for the figure, somewhere between $10 and $2 million, that will attract buyers *and* at the same time bring you the most money. One point is clear: If you can sell for $10 in five minutes, and for $2 million in 20 years, it is obvious that *time* and *money* are related in real estate sales.

If you are under no pressure to sell, you have the luxury of exploring the market, experimenting with price, and accepting an offer without pressure. This process is likely to yield the highest price.

If, on the other hand, you are working under a deadline, a no-nonsense price, slightly under true market value, will bring immediate action. When such a listing comes through the daily computer printout, one agent, idly reading, says to another, "Listen to this. A three-bedroom house in Suburban Heights for $170,000." And the other says, "Aren't they going around one-eighty over there? Won't last." Both reach for the phone to give the news to a penny-pincher they've been working with. The scene is repeated in any number of MLS offices, and that's one way houses are sold in a day.

A one-day sale, though, does not meet the standards set for fair market value of property. The concept of *fair market value* comes from the field of appraising.

Fair market value has been defined as the most probable price a property will bring if it has been widely exposed on the market, if sufficient time is allowed to find an informed buyer and if neither party is under undue duress. Fair market value may or may not be the same as the eventual sales price.

Pricing your property involves an attempt to estimate fair market value, depending on circumstances.

FACTORS TO IGNORE

Some sellers have misconceptions about where to start estimating value. Here are factors to ignore:

Your Cost.   Suppose you received your house as a gift; must you then give it away?

Your Investment in Improvements.   You put in that purple kitchen because you enjoyed it, but you are not likely to find a buyer who feels that the house is worth $15,000 more because of it. Certain viewers may even calculate the cost of tearing it out and replacing it with something in fuchsia.

Reproduction Cost.   The money it would take to duplicate your house, building it from scratch, is its reproduction cost. Reproduction cost is usually estimated for property insurance purposes, but it is of little value in setting a sales price except for a newly built house.

Assessed Value.   This figure, the result of a specific type of appraisal, is set by the taxing authorities as a basis for levying property taxes. No matter how often assessments are reviewed, and how sincere an effort is made to keep them in line with market value, assessed value is seldom a dependable guide.

Your Needs.   Also irrelevant to the proper asking price for your property is the amount of money you must take out of it. You may require $40,000 net in order to buy your next home. That fact may influence your decision to sell or not to sell: You cannot move unless you have the $40,000. But it is not the basis for pricing your present home.

Your problems are not the buyer's concern. The public is looking at various houses and comparing prices. *Supply and demand,* operating in the open market, will set the value for your house. Your home can be priced properly only if it is considered in competition with other property.

Emotion.   You cannot charge for sentiment, for the fact that your daughter took her first steps on the patio and your son had a clubhouse behind the garage. Your emotions can lead to serious mistakes in setting the asking price.

In the case of divorce, for example, emotions can play havoc with price. If one party is impatient to leave town, and the other isn't getting the money anyway, a buyer is likely to pick up a bargain.

Dramatic family changes may produce sellers who just want to turn their backs on the whole situation. Still, you must aim for a sale at fair market value, without letting emotions influence your listing price.

FACTORS THAT COUNT

These are the factors that you should consider:

Urgency of the Sale.   You will reduce your asking price in proportion to your need for a quick sale.

Competition.   If few homes are for sale in your desirable location, yours can be marked up a bit for scarcity. If, on the other hand, a local plant recently moved out of town, and the market is flooded with houses in your price range, you will have to discount to find a buyer. Your agent can tell you whether there is, at the moment, a buyer's or seller's market. If you are selling on your own, find out about local unemployment figures; they are a good quick guide.

Special Financing.   If your home has a large FHA or VA loan that can be assumed at a rate below today's levels, your mortgage is probably the most valuable part of the property. The house is likely to bring a premium from a buyer willing to exchange a higher total price for savings in interest payments in the years ahead. Much the same is true, in a difficult mortgage market, if you are willing to hold the loan yourself.

FINDING THOSE COMPS

Comparable sales are the key to proper pricing. Nothing matters as much as "comps," which are completed transactions as similar to yours as possible. The homes selected for comparison should be physically near, for no single factor determines value more surely than location. The sales should also be recent; two-year-old sales have almost no meaning in today's volatile market. And, they should be close in style, size and condition to your property—the closer the better.

Your agent can furnish figures on comparables; at least three are recommended, and if six close comps are available, so much the better. Pay little attention to neighborhood scuttlebutt; sellers exaggerate the amount received, and buyers minimize the price paid.

The agent will probably not offer you a *free appraisal*. Experts feel that if it's free, it isn't an appraisal. You will receive instead, a *comparative market analysis*. This computation lists several recent nearby sales, notes how long each was on the market, how close the asking price was to the eventual sales figure and then compares the houses with yours. The process is a simple version of the market approach, the technique most often employed for formal residential appraisals. A sample comparative analysis form is shown in Table 6-1.

Besides considering the comparative market analysis, you should study a complete list of homes currently on the market in your area. Buyers will be choosing homes to view from that group. Consider your property through their eyes and judge how your asking price compares—whether it would attract you before you knew the property.

You should also be studying classified ads for houses in your area to build a general background on the current market. A comparison of the average price of comparable sales with the average asking prices of similar homes not yet sold

TABLE 6-1: Comparative Market Analysis

Comparative Market Analysis

Date _____ Comparative Market Analysis for _____

Sugg. list price $ _____

Address	Style	Const	Age	No. of Rms	No. of Bdrms	No. of Baths	Gar	Fplc	Pool	C/A	Size Prop	Assess Value	Taxes	Comments & Extras	Fair Market Value

1. SIMILAR HOMES RECENTLY SOLD: These tell us what people are willing to pay . . . for this kind of home . . . in this area . . . at this time

Closed Price   Date   Adjustd Price

2. SIMILAR HOMES FOR SALE NOW: These tell us what we are competing against. Buyers will compare your home against these homes.

Askg Price   Days On Mkt.

3. EXPIRED LISTINGS – SIMILAR HOMES UNSOLD FOR 90 DAYS OR MORE: These illustrate the problems of over pricing.

PROBLEMS OF OVERPRICING:
A. HARD to get salespeople excited.
B. HARD to get people to make an offer.
C. HARD to get good buyers to look.
D. HARD to get financing.

SOURCE: John E. Cyr and Joan m. Sobeck, *Real Estate Brokerage: A Success Guide* (Chicago: Real Estate Education Company, 1992), p. 244.

can give you an idea of how much bargaining seems to be built-in. Community custom varies in this matter. Your agent may have a computer printout of past sales, with asking prices and sales prices listed for easy comparison.

Bargaining practices vary with individual preferences. Some sellers detest bargaining and list at a rock-bottom price that is firm. Others tack on a few thousand dollars just to see if they'll be lucky. Nevertheless, there is often a discernible trend, giving you a clue to what the average buyer might expect. You may find sales prices from five percent to ten percent under listing prices.

Remember that owning real estate means having control of it, and that includes setting your asking price. Your agent may be eager to persuade you to set a reasonable price or, on the other hand, may try to avoid making any recommendation. In the end, the decision is entirely yours.

EXPENSES OF SELLING

Know the definition of *equity:* the amount of money you will realize if you sell your home at fair market value and pay all the liens (claims) against it. Equity is often the sales price of the house minus the amount owed on the mortgage.

Although you cannot set your list price on the basis of the amount of money you need to receive, it is wise to estimate what you may net and what your selling expenses may be as you price the house.

Depending on your financing and the buyer's, state law and other factors, your costs of selling are likely to be these:

- Commission.
- Points (see Chapter 10). Your agent can orient you on points, taking into account the current mortgage market.
- Adjustments. You may owe the buyer for unpaid property taxes, or be owed money for fuel oil left in the tank. Items like these will be adjusted at time of closing.
- Legal fees. These may include your lawyer's fee or title insurance, escrow or title company charges. Your main responsibility is to prove clear and marketable title.
- Transfer taxes. In some states, this item must be paid by the seller, no matter how other costs are shared.

- Inspections. Depending on local custom, you may be expected to pay for code inspections, a termite check or a land survey.
- Special assessments. If, for example, your property is being assessed because of new sidewalks or similar neighborhood improvements, you might be asked to pay this lien in a lump sum at closing.
- Present liens. This includes your mortgage and other claims or judgments of record against the property.
- Required repairs. Your agent can help judge whether the FHA, DVA or a lending institution will require that you make specific repairs or bring your home up to code. The matter should be considered when you set your price.
- Prepayment penalty. Your present conventional mortgage, if paid before its due date, may involve a prepayment penalty.
- Unexpected credits. You may receive monies at closing that you don't anticipate. The fuel oil is an example. In some states, property taxes are paid in advance, and adjustments may result in a sizable refund to you. Prepaid insurance should also be refunded. You may have established an escrow account at your lending institution, with money collected in advance for tax and insurance expenses you will no longer owe. This sum is usually returned to you.

IF YOU PRICE TOO HIGH

At any given time, there is a large pool of buyers on the market, and these constitute your best prospects. It will take approximately three months to replace them with an equal number of newcomers to the market.

If your house is overpriced, you will lose the advantage of this ready group of buyers. They are accustomed to comparing properties and may refuse even to view yours. You and your agent may know that you will sell for $10,000 less, but the buyers may not know. Fiduciary duty prohibits your agent from telling them this or advertising the fact. So your overpriced property receives little attention.

Surveys show that the longer a house is on the market, the greater is the discount from listing price when it finally sells.

The buying public eventually sets an accurate price. The overpriced house lingers on the market, requiring a price adjustment before it attracts a buyer.

"We can always come down" is a phrase agents don't enjoy hearing. It implies a slow start, wasted advertisements, unpleasant discussions with the homeowner and, eventually, a shopworn property. Knowledgeable buyers ask how long a house has been on the market and why it hasn't sold. Even when the agent explains that only the price was wrong, buyers may remain suspicious.

If you have your heart set on trying a high price "just to see," first work out a written plan to drop the price at intervals: If the house hasn't attracted enough attention in two weeks, the price will be cut to a certain level. If you haven't had an offer within a month, you will lower it again. Make sure you will be down to real market value within six weeks. Such a commitment at the beginning assures a logical handling of the problem.

Even if lightning strikes and an out-of-town buyer, unfamiliar with the market, agrees to pay an inflated price, trouble lies ahead. You may then be faced with the question of whether "the house will appraise." The buyer's lending institution will send an appraiser to estimate the property's value. You and the buyer may have agreed that the house is worth $105,000. But if the bank appraiser doesn't agree, you have a problem. The mortgage loan will be offered on a lower figure, and the buyer may not be able (or willing) to complete the purchase.

IF YOUR HOUSE IS UNDERPRICED

The first serious consequence of underpricing, of course, is that you will lose money. Even the most experienced agent is fooled, occasionally, when a house that seemed properly priced suddenly turns out to be a "hot" listing.

What are the signs? One is an immediate rush of calls from other offices either to your agent asking how to show the property or directly to you requesting appointments. Another sure sign is a jam-packed open house. Prospects are piled up in the living room, waiting their turn to see the property, while your agent phones the office for reinforcements.

Whether using an agent or selling on your own, you may receive several purchase offers immediately if you have underpriced. Experienced agents may advise prospective buyers to offer more than the asking price, so that if their proposal is presented at the same time as several others, it stands a good chance of acceptance.

If such a situation develops, consult your attorney immediately. It appears that a mistake has been made in the asking price; can you now refuse a full-price offer? Can you raise your list price? Obtain legal advice as quickly as you can.

In the absence of any offers, it is possible to raise your asking price immediately. Your agent or your lawyer will know the procedure, although it is seldom used.

The $10,000 Barrier

One final point to be considered in pricing your property is the $10,000 barrier. There is very little difference in market reaction between a house priced at $97,000 and one priced at $99,000, and a great deal of difference between houses priced at $99,000 and $101,000. If you are wavering over a few extra thousand and the higher figure will take you just above $150,000, remember that you are automatically cutting out of your buying public all those who told their agents, "Don't show us anything over $150,000." You could be eliminating the best prospects for your home. Consider $149,999.99 instead. It is just as useful in attracting buyers as $149,000 would be.

PROFESSIONAL APPRAISALS

Although most sellers rely on their agents' comparative market analysis figures, watch out for the few who will quote almost any price to secure your listing. Others may recommend a low price, hoping for a quick and easy sale. A few feel that they have no right to recommend any price on a property for which they may earn a commission.

The money invested in a professional appraisal may be worth spending in the beginning, or later if you and the agent are stymied as to the proper price.

An appraisal can be a valuable bargaining tool during contract negotiations with your buyer. Although it is simply an estimate—albeit an informed, skilled one—the buyer usually accepts it as an impartial, almost scientific proof of value, as indeed the courts do.

SELLING ON YOUR OWN

Those who don't use a broker are usually advised to pay a few hundred dollars for a complete written appraisal done by a professional appraiser with a designation, appraiser's license or certification—someone with special study and qualification. (Make it clear that you need only a simple written report; you don't want to pay for a 30-page dissertation with floor plans and photographs of the neighborhood.) You have little to gain from selling your house in one day because you've priced it too low.

Can you ask real estate brokers for free advice on the matter? Yes and no.

It's manifestly unfair to mislead an agent by asking for a market analysis on the pretense that you plan to list the property. But what if you were upfront about it? You might call several firms, explain that you intend to try marketing the house yourself and ask whether they are willing to confer with you on that understanding.

Even an oral off-hand opinion will require an hour's preparation time on the agent's part, and another hour traveling to your home and inspecting it. Understandably, some brokers will refuse to donate their time and expertise to your project.

Others, though, may be perfectly willing to provide the service, hoping to make a friend in the process. Some brokers believe that nine out of ten FSBOs eventually do list, and they're glad for a chance to meet them and try to sell their services.

Preparing Your House for the Market

Consider the marketing of a used car. Is there anything more delightful than a standard doll-up? The buyer knows that the car has been polished to a fare-thee-well, but can't help being influenced. Somehow, the buyer ends up believing that the spotless interior means the car has been beautifully maintained for all of its 93,999 miles.

Your home deserves a doll-up for the market also.

What can you do to show it to best advantage? Start by asking your agent for suggestions. You have learned to compensate for the broken front step and no longer even notice it. The salesperson's practiced eye, on the other hand, can pinpoint spots that need attention.

If you are selling on your own, call in a blunt friend. You want someone who will view your house with a fresh eye. And you can go over house and grounds yourself with the checklist in this chapter (see Table 7-1).

What you are looking for is advice on which features can be inexpensively improved and which may be left alone. You can spend little or no money and enhance your property markedly. Attend to all those items that require no outlay.

TABLE 7-1:   House and Grounds Preparation Checklist

	Needs Work	When To Do
Exterior		
Cut grass (shovel snow)	_____	_____
Mend fence, gate, steps	_____	_____
Install house numbers	_____	_____
Plant annual flowers	_____	_____
Pick up toys, tools, etc.	_____	_____
Move camper, old car	_____	_____
Trim shrubs	_____	_____
Edge lawns	_____	_____
Seal blacktop driveway	_____	_____
Close garage door	_____	_____
Store trash cans	_____	_____
Wash windows	_____	_____
Entrance		
Tighten handrail	_____	_____
Replace light bulbs	_____	_____
Mend doorbell	_____	_____
Buy new doormat	_____	_____
Mend screen	_____	_____
Remove pawprints and fingerprints	_____	_____
Paint threshold	_____	_____
Polish brass	_____	_____
Front hall		
Clean out closet	_____	_____
Remove clutter	_____	_____
Add plant, fresh flowers	_____	_____
Living room		
Remove crowded pieces	_____	_____
Pack away distracting items	_____	_____
Clean out fireplace ashes, lay fire	_____	_____
Shampoo carpet	_____	_____
Repaint stained ceiling	_____	_____
Kitchen		
Clean stove and oven	_____	_____
Clear counters	_____	_____
Scrub sink	_____	_____
Remove fingerprints	_____	_____
Replace faucet washers	_____	_____
Starch curtains	_____	_____
Add a plant	_____	_____
Bathroom		
Replace shower curtain	_____	_____
Freshen grout around tub	_____	_____
Change toilet seat	_____	_____
Remove personal items	_____	_____
Bring in a plant	_____	_____

TABLE 7-1: (Continued)

	Needs Work	When To Do
Clean (repaint) medicine cabinet	_____	_____
Buy new towels	_____	_____
Remove tub mat	_____	_____
Bedrooms		
Store personal items	_____	_____
Remove valuables	_____	_____
Clear dressers	_____	_____
Clean out closet	_____	_____
Add live plant	_____	_____
Remove excess furniture	_____	_____
Attic, basement		
Clear stairs	_____	_____
Check light bulbs	_____	_____
Vacuum floors	_____	_____
Dust away cobwebs	_____	_____
Straighten stored items	_____	_____
Garage		
Hose down floor	_____	_____
Tidy stored items	_____	_____
Keep doors closed	_____	_____
Replace light bulbs	_____	_____

EXTERIOR WORK

Prospective buyers will probably park across the street—that's where the agent will guide them. Sit there in your own car and see how the house strikes you. Remember, your property will never get a second chance to make a first impression. Is the lawn as near perfect as possible, or could it benefit from a little fertilizer? Are the bushes trimmed? Is your garage door closed? One detail can make a great difference. Of course it's too late to landscape but, in season, a few showy annuals can add sparkle to your front lawn at small expense.

Your fences and gates should be in good repair, possibly repainted. Rusty toys and moldering shopping guides must be picked up. Downspouts and gutters should be firmly attached; house numbers need checking also. Don't forget your driveway; remove unsightly oil stains and fill in small cracks. Old cars or a camper that lives in your driveway may need another home for the interim.

No matter how attached you may be to flamingos, wooden whirligigs, decorative eagles and artificial flowers, all such items are a matter of personal taste. Your exterior will look more spacious and serene without them; store them neatly in your garage for the duration.

Trash cans should come in for consideration here; put in extra effort to keep them neatly concealed at all times.

You already have enough assignments for a full Saturday's work, and you haven't reached the front door yet!

THE MAIN ENTRANCE

Stand at your front door where the buyer will stand, and look around. Are the light and the doorbell in working order? It goes without saying that your screen door is in good condition and the muddy pawprints beside the door have been scrubbed. The glass panels in the door sparkle, as does every window in the house. Even if you don't paint any other part of the house, consider freshening the front entrance. A bit of black paint can do wonders for a worn threshold.

Your front hall should be free of clutter, and you may add a vase of (fresh) flowers or another welcoming touch—just one. In the front-hall closet, remove out-of-season clothing and dead storage. All your closets will look larger if they are orderly and uncrowded.

THE LIVING ROOM

Lay a fire in the fireplace, consider whether the carpets could benefit from a shampoo, remove unnecessary pieces of large furniture. Even though you cherish them, consider removing personal possessions such as trophies, artificial flowers, family pictures, political and religious items. Most living rooms can be improved if two-thirds of their distracting accessories are taken out. You want a room that the buyers can try on for size, with plenty of space for *their* personal items. Excess belongings can be packed away; after all, you will be doing that when you move, anyway. Pack-rat homeowners have been known to strip a crowded house of half their possessions and rent a self-storage commercial locker.

Although there is no hard-and-fast rule about repainting your home's interior, you must attend to cracks and water stains in the ceilings. The stain may go back five years to the time when Uncle Erwin let the tub overflow. Even if you try to explain it, the buyer will remain nervous about your plumbing system. Simply repaint the ceiling. You must not cover your problems in an attempt to hide them, but neither do you owe the buyer a complete history of your troubles with Uncle Erwin.

As for small cracks in walls or ceilings, they may have been there for decades, but some buyers will be sure they indicate danger of imminent collapse. And cracked window panes leave an impression that the house has been neglected; attend to them before anyone views the property.

THE KITCHEN

The kitchen and bath are the rooms that traditionally sell houses. It seldom pays to remodel in anticipation of selling, so the kitchen will have to remain basically as it is. You can, however, check a number of items. Leaky faucets must be repaired and stains bleached out of the sink. To show off your expanse of kitchen counters, remove most items, leaving only one or two decorative pieces or basic appliances.

Even if your stove is not included in the sale, someone will be sure to open the oven; have it spotless. A greasy oven is a real turn-off and the impression it conveys will extend to the rest of the house. Glass doors on oven, toaster oven or microwave should be polished.

In insect-prone areas, keep extermination up to date. Remove sticky fingerprints everywhere. If you want to invest a small amount of money, try bright, inexpensive curtains, or dress up your cupboards with modern knobs.

THE BATHS

Looking at other people's bathrooms can be an unappealing process; make it as easy as possible. Take a good look at your shower curtain; a stained one can be replaced with a sparkling, inexpensive new one in a solid neutral color. White is always a good choice. Consider replacing a chipped toilet seat as well. Bring in a potted plant. Check grout around your tub and shower. Remove tub mats. Buy a set of solid-colored towels and washcloths to be set out at the last minute before the house is shown.

This is a good time to clean out the medicine chest; the inside can be painted with a few minutes' effort.

THE BEDROOMS

In bedrooms, straighten out closet clutter, remove large or crowded pieces of furniture if possible, put out your best bedspreads; make sure, again, that the windows are spotless.

THROUGHOUT THE HOUSE

Throughout the entire house, replace burnt-out light bulbs. Wash doorknobs and light switches. Check staircase treads and tighten railings. Make it easy for house hunters to use your attic and basement stairs, which should be free of clutter.

If you are not a plant person, consider borrowing some particularly full and healthy ones from friends. Just a few plants or trees, judiciously spotted around the house, add warmth.

This is a good time to hose down your basement floor and garage. Your electric box will be inspected, so clean off cobwebs and dust.

SPENDING MONEY

Except in rare instances, it is unwise to invest much cash in improving a house that is going on the market. It is usually impossible to recoup the outlay by raising your price. Eliminate major improvements from your plans.

If you are prepared, though, to spend some money on a fixup, your best investment—after soap—is probably paint. Take a tip from the merchandisers of new model homes: Paint every room the same color to make the house look larger. A light neutral shade is the best choice. This is not the time to strive for spectacular results, for you want to harmonize with almost anyone's furniture. Don't forget, when painting, to do the insides of closets also.

One most-for-your-money item is resealing a blacktop driveway to give the outside of the house a crisp clean appearance. Ambitious homeowners may go on from there to sand and refinish floors.

If your house features what appraisers tactfully call casual housekeeping, your agent is in a delicate situation. The broker knows that time and again such a house remains on the market for months, and eventually sells for thousands of dollars under its real value. But suggestions that a house needs cleaning and tidying are difficult to put politely.

Take seriously, therefore, any suggestion by your broker that you consider a professional cleaning service. If you have doubts about your housekeeping, ask your agent, or that blunt friend, whether a professional job is indicated.

FINAL PREPARATIONS

As you look forward to the first showing of your home, gather your fact sheets, copies of the listing material and past fuel and utility bills. If you have pictures of the back lawn when it was blanketed with snow, or the front lawn with the cherry trees in blossom, display them prominently so that prospects can appreciate the beauty of your home in every season.

ADVERTISING

One of the agent's first tasks is to write *advertising* for your property. You may be asked to help, or to suggest phrases, if you like that kind of challenge. It can be useful to mention your own reasons for buying the house.

If you are placing your own advertisements, you may be shocked when the first bills come in. Remember that long ads are not necessarily better than short ones. Buyers do not catch fire from lists that simply catalog the house's features, and they may even skip over long ads. Buyers read the bewildering variety of offerings not to select, but to reject houses.

Too much information may include the one fact that eliminates your home from the list. Leave them something to call up about.

Your ad should include location, number of bedrooms and baths, price level and one or two picture-making phrases. "For Sale by Owner" is always an attention-getter, and so, for your initial ad, is "First Offering Today."

If you do sell through an agent, the chances of the right buyer calling on your particular ad are remote. In the end, your buyer will probably have first contacted the broker about another property. Although advertising represents the largest item in the broker's budget, it accounts for only one-third of the sales. Most sales come from referrals or other contacts, For Sale signs and the firm's backlog of purchasers.

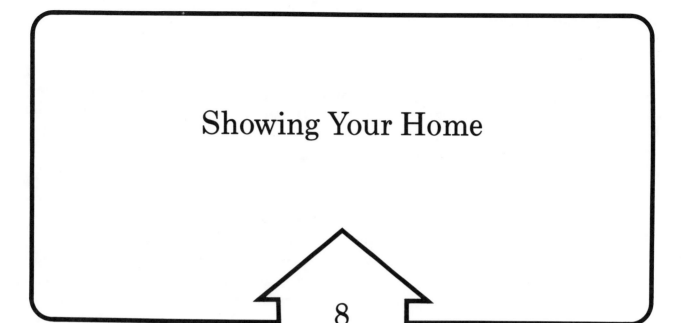

Showing Your Home

8

Put a gingerbread mix in the oven, throw out the kids and gather last year's utility bills. The buyers are coming, the buyers are coming!

SELLING ON YOUR OWN

Put the words, "By Appointment Only," and a phone number on your For Sale sign. You don't want to invite in anyone who knocks on your door; if people do this, ask them to phone for an appointment. When you receive the call, ask for the caller's own phone number "so I can call you back and confirm." This provides a certain amount of identification ahead of time, for safety's sake.

The advance appointment gives you time to prepare your home and to arrange for another adult to be in the house with you if you wish.

When you give prospects directions to your house, consider the most attractive approach. There's no law that says you must direct them past the town dump if the route through the park works as well.

Right after your house goes on the market, watch out for bargain hunters on the prowl for unsophisticated FSBOs. They will be less interested in the house itself than in finding out whether you will sell with no down payment and whether you will take back financing (discussed in Chapter 10). Such buyers often cannot qualify for bank loans because they have poor credit or insufficient income.

Before you place your first advertisement, you will have calculated the amount of cash and income a buyer would need to qualify for a mortgage loan on your property (again, see Chapter 10). You will not, therefore, invite in everyone who inquires. Apply the same standards to every caller to make sure you observe human rights law. You have a right to ask name, phone number and present address and whether they rent or have another house to sell. You may also ask about employment and income. They may, of course, refuse to answer. Then you'll have to play it by ear.

See Table 8-1 for a handy list of "things to do" when selling on your own.

TABLE 8-1: Checklist for Selling on Your Own

____ Retain a lawyer who specializes in real estate.

____ Visit open houses in your neighborhood for three weeks.

____ Clip classified ads for houses in your neighborhood.

____ Phone agents for information on ads you clipped.

____ Interview at least three local brokers (see Chapter 3). Be frank about "not wanting to list yet."

____ Polish your home to show it at its best (see Chapter 7).

____ Ask your lawyer for a blank copy of a typical purchase offer.

____ Prepare fact sheets on your property.

____ Prepare a lawn sign.

____ Place your classified ad. Buyers need to know neighborhood, style of house, number of rooms and bedrooms and price or price range (and baths and garages, if more than one). Keep the ad short.

____ Never answer "How much would you take?" directly.

____ Ask serious prospects to bring you a credit report.

____ When you receive an oral offer you like, ask your lawyer to prepare a contract acceptable to both parties.

____ Follow the buyer's mortgage application process, and check at least once a week—or have your lawyer do so—to see how it's going.

IF YOU'RE USING AN AGENT

If the broker has a prospect waiting in the wings for property like yours, arrangements for the first showing may be made as soon as you sign the listing. In areas where there is a strong multiple-listing service, you can expect to hear from other brokers soon after your properly priced house goes on the market.

Advance Notice

Agents always try to arrange appointments by phone. If they are setting up several houses for the buyer, they might say, "We'll be over between two and three o'clock," rather than promising to ring the bell at 2:30 P.M.

Don't hold out for too much advance notice. This requirement eliminates one of the most promising prospects, the transferred employee who is in town for a few hours, determined to find a place today and wants to come right over. Try to say yes. After all, it will take the salesperson half an hour to drive over, and you can accomplish a great deal of last-minute polishing in the interim. Make the house as freely available as possible.

Even if you have left a key with the lister, so that the house can be shown while you are at work, most agents will still phone ahead to see if anyone is at home. Since they may come in while you are absent, you'll have to see that the place is tidy before you leave each day. In the event someone does enter, you should find a business card left behind, ideally with the time of the visit noted on it.

No Advance Notice

Even with a broker's sign out front, people may simply knock on your door asking if they may see the house. Tell them pleasantly that it is being shown only by the office whose telephone number is on the sign outside. Do not admit any strangers; you retained an agent to avoid just such situations. Chances are slim that random inquirers are really qualified to buy. If, on the other hand, they are good prospects, they should receive professional treatment from the first. A slight difficulty in getting into the house will only make it more desirable.

Once in a while, an agent may ring your doorbell without phoning in advance: "I was just driving by with some folks who noticed the sign and like the looks of the house. They won't be here tomorrow; they're waiting in the car to hear if they can come in."

If possible, welcome them. The broker knows what they can afford and what they seek; if the agent thinks it's worth the trouble, it probably is. You can gain a few minutes to tidy up by suggesting that they inspect the exterior first.

Prospects who enter a house this way are already half sold. They are grateful for your cooperation, and the sense of discovery and unplanned adventure in such a showing often results in a sale.

PREPARING FOR AN OPEN HOUSE

Your home may also be marketed through an open house. The first weekend after listing is probably the most productive time to tap the existing pool of buyers and to allow buyers and brokers to view the house without the bother of an appointment.

You—or your agent—advertise the open house and put out signs inviting all comers to visit during specified hours. It's helpful if the open house takes place when there are others in the neighborhood, usually on Saturdays or Sundays. Some localities restrict signs; in other areas balloons, flags and streamers lend a festive atmosphere.

After all the work of preparation, you will be longing to see the fun. If you have an agent, though, you'll probably be asked to leave before the open house starts. If you can't bear to go away, visit a neighbor so you can see what happens.

Unless your house is strikingly underpriced, don't expect hordes of visitors. And remember that fewer than one house in 20 is sold through an open house. The agent is experienced in handling visitors and will probably insist that they identify themselves and sign in. For the agent, it's an opportunity to meet buyers.

If you run the open house yourself, always ask people to sign in, and ask for identification. If you have several prospects at once, ask them to wait in the living room or, in good weather, outside, while you escort one couple at a time through the house.

Your neighbors, who have always been curious about what's in your cupboards and attic, will probably show up somewhat shamefacedly at the first open house. It is wise to welcome them, and even to have invited them. Neighbors may have friends or relatives who have always wanted to live nearby. An agent, of course, has an extra motive for being cordial, hoping to produce a successful sale and to be remembered when it's time to list the next house on the street.

Set for Seduction

After all the preparation you've put in during the past few weeks, what more can be done to show your house at its best?

Plenty—whether for an open house or a private showing. Go through the house and raise every window shade. Draw the drapes back from those spotless windows. A bright house looks larger and more cheerful.

Turn on lights from top to bottom, even in the daytime. If you've ever gone through a builder's model home, you know how much extra charm a living room gains from shaded lamps, and how a chandelier adds sparkle. Buyers shouldn't have to grope for the pullcord in the gloomy corner of the basement, and they should find your attic stairs well-lighted.

Your house can appeal to all five senses as much as it can to rational inspection. Consider the sound level. Stop your dishwasher or clothes dryer in midcycle and check for other noisy appliances. If you want to leave your stereo set on, play neutral easy-listening music, very softly. You are trying, after all, to set up a seduction scene.

The beds are made, of course, with your best spreads, and every room is as tidy as possible. Toilet seats are down, and those new towels have replaced the family ones. This doesn't mean there should be no signs of life—if you have fine linen and china, a beautifully set table adds appeal.

The subtle fragrance of onion and bay leaf from a pot roast simmering on the back burner won't hurt at all. Homeowners have been known to put a cake in the oven every time a prospect was on the way, or to simmer a cinnamon stick for a few minutes. If, on the other hand, you have a heavy smoker in your home, empty ashtrays and spray air freshener at the last moment.

On any day that isn't sweltering, start a fire to dramatize your open hearth. If you regard a wood fire as a nuisance, buy pressed logs. One will burn alone and add a cozy glow throughout an afternoon's open house, leaving very little ash. And the viewers won't have to wonder if the fireplace works.

Time to Clear Out

No matter how charming your children and pets, getting them out of the house during viewings is an absolute must. Set up an emergency routine. On two minutes' notice, your kids should be able to corral Rover, put him on a leash, turn off the television, and dash out the back door for sanctuary in a neighbor's kitchen.

It's important that the house be as empty as possible and free from distractions. House hunting is confusing and tiring work. The buyers are probably looking at several places within a few hours, trying to fix each in their minds. Ideally, they like to wander and explore, trying the place on for size, perhaps pretending it's already theirs.

SELLING TECHNIQUES

If you are showing the house yourself, learn to do it professionally. Study the description below of the broker's standard techniques. You may wish to use a last-minute checklist before your buyers arrive, whether selling on your own or using a broker (see Table 8-2).

IF YOU HAVE AN AGENT

Falling in love with a house is like falling in love with a person, and three's a crowd. Your role is to be pleasant and unobtrusive, if not downright unavailable. This spares your feelings and the buyers'.

It's difficult to watch strangers go through your house. You might be surprised by the strength of your emotional reaction to a random word of criticism. You would probably be upset by the buyers who never get farther than your front

TABLE 8-2: Last-Minute Checklist

___	Kids out
___	Pets out
___	Dishwasher, television off
___	Window shades up (daytime)
___	Drapes pulled back (daytime)
___	Fire started
___	Cinnamon simmered or gingerbread in the oven
___	Lights on throughout
___	Clean towels
___	Empty, scoured sink
___	Fact sheets available
___	Guest book for sign-in
___	Garage door closed
___	Beds made
___	Soft music
___	Utility bills handy

hall, or who whiz through in one minute flat. The agent is used to it and knows that if buyers are searching for an eat-in kitchen or dead-end living room, they look for that first, cross your house off the list if it isn't there, and save their energy for the next house.

With you watching, prospects are inhibited about opening closets, trying out windows, stroking the banister and performing all those get-acquainted gestures that are the house-hunting equivalent of kicking the tires and slamming the doors of a new car.

Of course, if you are showing the house yourself, you need to monitor prospects unobtrusively just for security reasons.

Here They Come

And so, buyers are on their way over, you've given the house its last-minute sparkle, and you peek out the windows as they pull up.

They're probably traveling in one car; this gives the broker more control and opportunity for conversation. It's customary to park across the street for a good view of your property. You may think they are taking an unreasonably long time to reach the front door. Remember that in good weather, many brokers make it a practice to show the outside first, building suspense for the house itself.

When the doorbell rings (aren't you glad you fixed it?), greet the buyers with a smile, wait to be introduced and then excuse yourself. "Don't bother with the lights; I'll take care of them later. If you need me, I'll be next door." There is a proper time for you to reappear, but consider first the reasons why you shouldn't hang around.

Let the Broker Show the House

Potential buyers are reluctant to voice objections with you standing by. They can speak frankly to the broker, who knows whether the house might fit their needs and how to respond.

"That den is so tiny."

"Yes," agrees the broker, who would never contradict a valid observation. "You did say you were looking for a sewing room, though. I suppose it could be down on this floor. . . ."

"You know, it might just do. Ben, come and look at this little room." When they start showing the house to each other, the wise broker fades into the background.

Although you know your home, the agent knows these buyers. They've already looked at several properties today, they are remarkably suspicious about plumbing problems, they want a neighborhood full of kids and they need a long dining-room wall for an heirloom breakfront.

An eager home seller, full of nervous chatter, can blunder in several ways with these people. Proud of the new paint job, you might point out that the living-room ceiling was just re-done to get rid of an old stain from the time when crazy Uncle Erwin. . .you'd never realize the needless anxiety this stirs up in some buyers.

If they ask about children in the neighborhood, you might voice your own attitude and reply, "They never bother us; you wouldn't know there were any around." And the buyers conclude that your street lacks just the playmates they had hoped to find for their children.

As for that dining room, the broker won't say a single word while the buyers stand spellbound in the doorway, mentally placing their furniture against the long wall. If you stick around while a skilled broker shows your house, you may become nervous listening to the silence. But although the broker may not say much, he or she is listening very hard. Don't expect a stream of patter and salesmanship. A good broker uses skill and expertise to match buyer and house, and then lets the place sell itself, putting in a few deft words where they will do the most good.

The agent tries never to argue, and fades away discreetly when it becomes obvious that husband and wife need to confer in private. Such moments come as they begin to feel they may have found the right house, but neither can voice that conviction until they have compared notes. Your house showing is likely to involve a great deal of silence, which can be unnerving to a homeowner.

Another problem, if you join the group, is the simple matter of space. It's easy for stairways and halls to become crowded. The broker knows better than to enter small bedrooms with prospects.

If it's obvious that they might be really interested in your home, the broker may suggest that they go back through it once more, on their own. If they say "yes, we'd like to," you're close to a sale.

When You Reappear

If you've been over at the neighbor's house and now realize that these prospects have been in the house a long time (20 minutes or more), it may be helpful for you to put in an appearance.

The broker wants to begin and end the viewing in the most pleasant room: the living room (with the log burning on the hearth), the kitchen (with the cookies cooling on the counter) or the family room (with the bowl of polished apples on the television set). This is a good place for you to be discovered, sitting at your ease and prepared to answer questions. If the buyers are serious, they'll accept your invitation to sit down and chat.

You have valuable information for them: the age of neighbors' children, the time the school bus comes, how far it is to the library or the tennis club. Have your past utility bills available at this point, with exact costs detailed.

Remember that you must tell the truth about your property. Don't vouch for facts you're not sure of. They could come back to haunt you later. Refer troublesome questions back to the listing agent, who has probably heard them all before.

It will help in future negotiations if you and the buyers like one another, but you may notice some nervousness on the part of the broker if you become too informative at this point. The broker expects to act as a buffer between buyers and sellers.

Topics to Avoid

Don't answer any questions about price. The correct answer to "Would you take $162,000?" is "We'll consider any written offers that come through our agent" (or, with no agent, "through our lawyer"). You should have asked your lawyer for a blank contract, which you can offer to a buyer who doesn't seem to know what to do next.

If you hear, "We need to move in by September; are you going to be out by then?" you might reply, "I'm sure we could work out the details."

This is also a poor time to discuss the sale of furniture or appliances. It's destructive to get hung up on small matters before the main event. If you've listed your stove and refrigerator as "negotiable" and are now asked if you'd leave them, say "that depends." The unspoken words here are "that depends on how close you come to our list price." To a question about whether you'd sell the pool table or the portable bar, a good response is "We thought we'd decide after the sale of the house is settled."

GET A REPORT

If you were away from home while the house was being shown, you can request that the broker call back later to report. Remember that the prospects have looked at several houses. If they decide to put in a purchase offer on one of the others, the agent will have a busy day or two, handling paperwork, negotiations, lenders and lawyers.

You can still ask for a call when the broker is free, to learn what the reaction was to your home. Request a frank report and you'll have valuable information on how your asking price strikes the buying public, or suggestions on ways your home's appeal can be further enhanced.

Or, perhaps you'll hear the real estate broker's ultimate compliment, "Your place shows well." And then, "They want to think it over. I may be getting in touch with your listing agent in a day or two with an offer."

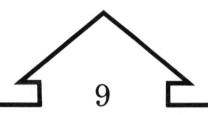

Negotiating Your Sales Contract

9

The word "broker" derives from an old Middle English word for "go-between," and nowhere is this more evident than when the agent brings you and your buyer to what is legally known as a meeting of the minds. A successful agent develops valuable skills in negotiation, and a new salesperson will call upon the broker's experience in this matter. With both parties under stress, tact and diplomacy are called into action. The broker knows enough of law and finance to make suggestions for dealing with difficulties. In the end, your salesperson derives the most satisfaction from a "win/win" situation, in which both parties feel they have achieved their goals and made a good deal.

With no broker involved, you must deal face-to-face with the would-be buyer. Always remember that oral agreements for the sale of real estate are not binding. The buyer could offer you $140,000 cash in front of five witnesses; you could shake hands on the deal and even accept a $10,000 deposit. And the buyer could still back out of the deal the next day and demand return of the deposit. As far as the law is concerned, there was no contract.

The Statute of Frauds demands that certain contracts be in writing to be legally enforceable, and one of those is any contract for the sale of real property.

This makes negotiation particularly delicate, for you will only give yourself away if you engage in too much oral dickering.

YOUR PREPARATIONS

Study the sample contract to purchase shown in Table 9-1 to familiarize yourself with typical provisions—don't try to use it. Obtain a contract suitable to your area from your broker or lawyer. If your agency uses one specially designed form for its transactions, try to obtain samples of other standard contracts used in your area.

Local custom dictates the manner in which the offer to purchase will be made. The form may be called an agreement to buy and sell, a binder receipt and option, an agreement to purchase, a sales contract, or an offer and acceptance. Study it ahead of time, so that when an offer comes in, you will be familiar with the standard provisions and can concentrate on the specific terms being offered.

It is helpful, also, if you familiarize yourself with the financing options open to potential buyers of your home. Chapter 10 discusses some alternatives. Since you will be asked to make decisions based upon the buyers' plans for financing, be conversant with their choices. Your salesperson or attorney will have information on current financing opportunities.

Before any purchase offers come in, ask your lawyer for preliminary advice.

PRESENTATION OF THE OFFER

If you are selling on your own, it's best to ask for time to consider a written offer in privacy. A day or two is not unreasonable, and will give you time to consult your attorney and to formulate a response.

If you are using an agent, you will probably hear first by telephone that a written offer has come in on your property. Because offers must be presented immediately, you might even be notified while you are out of town.

TABLE 9-1: Real Estate Sales Contract

DUPAGE ASSOCIATION OF REALTORS®
STANDARD RESIDENTIAL SALES CONTRACT

1. **BUYER(S),** _____

Address _____ ; City _____ ; State _____ ; Zip _____

agrees to purchase, and SELLER(S), _____

Address _____ ; City _____ ; State _____ ; Zip _____

agrees to sell to Buyer(s) at the PRICE of _____ **Dollars**

($ _____)

PROPERTY commonly known as _____

(City of _____ County of _____ Illinois.)
a complete legal description may be attached as an exhibit by either party, (hereinafter referred to as "the premises") with approximate lot dimensions of _____ together with all existing improvements and fixtures, if any, which shall be left on the premises, are included in the sale price, and shall be transferred to the Buyer (s) by a Bill of Sale at the time of closing; including, but not limited to: hot water heater; plumbing and electrical fixtures; sump pumps; central heating and cooling; humidifying and filtering equipment; fixed carpeting; built-in kitchen appliances; equipment and cabinets; water softener (except rental units); storm and screen windows and doors; attached shutters, window treatment hardware, blinds and shades, shelving systems, fireplace screen; roof or attic T.V. antenna; all planted vegetation; garage door openers and car units; and the following items of personal property:

2. **THE EARNEST MONEY:** Buyer(s) has paid $ _____ by check/note due date _____
(and will pay within_____ days the additional sum of $ _____) as earnest money to be applied on the purchase price. The earnest money shall be held by the Listing Broker for the mutual benefit of the parties concerned and upon the closing of the sale, shall be applied first to the payment of any expenses incurred by Listing Broker for the Seller(s) in respect to this transaction, and second to payment of the broker's sales commission, rendering the overplus, if any, to the Seller(s). The balance of the purchase price shall be paid at closing.

3. **THE CLOSING DATE:** The closing date shall be_____, 19_____ (or on the date, if any, to which said date is extended by reason of paragraphs 6 and 11) at _____, or at Buyer's lending institution, if any.

4. **POSSESSION: POSSESSION SHALL BE GRANTED TO BUYER(S) AT THE TIME OF CLOSING, UNLESS OTHERWISE AGREED IN WRITING BY THE PARTIES.**

5. **THE DEED:** Seller(s) shall convey or cause to be conveyed to Buyer(s) (in joint tenancy) or Buyer's nominee, by a recordable, stamped general warranty deed with release of homestead rights, or Trustee's Deed if applicable, good title to the premises subject only to the following "permitted exceptions" if any, none of which shall impair the use of the property as a residence: (a) General real estate taxes not due and payable at time of closing; (b) Special Assessments confirmed after this Contract date; (c) Building, building line and use or occupancy restrictions, conditions and covenants of record; (d) Zoning laws and Ordinances; (e) Easements for public utilities; (f) Drainage ditches, feeders, laterals and drain tile, pipe or other conduit; (g) If the property is other than a detached, single-family home, party walls, party wall rights and agreements; terms, provisions, covenants, and conditions of the declaration of condominium, if any, and all amendments thereto; any easements established by or implied from the said declaration of condominium or amendments thereto, if any; limitations and conditions imposed by the Illinois Condominium Property Act, and if applicable; installments of assessments due after the date of closing.

6. **FINANCING CONDITION:** (a) This Contract is subject to the condition that on or before_____, Buyer(s) shall secure, or there shall be made available to Buyer(s), a written commitment for a loan to be secured by a mortgage or trust deed on the premises in the amount of $ _____, or such lesser sum as Buyer(s) accepts; (b) If after the Buyer(s) has submitted a true loan application and otherwise made every reasonable effort to procure a loan commitment from any source made available to Buyer(s) and has been unable to do so, and after serving written notice thereof upon Seller(s) or Seller's attorney within 1 day of the time specified herein for securing such commitment, then this Contract shall become null and void, and all monies paid by Buyer(s) hereunder shall be refunded; however, if Seller(s), at Seller's option, notifies Buyer(s) within 10 days of Buyer's notice, that Seller(s) intends to procure for Buyer(s) such a commitment within 45 days, then this Contract shall remain in full force and effect. **IN THE EVENT BUYER(S) DOES NOT SERVE NOTICE OF FAILURE TO PROCURE SAID LOAN COMMITMENT UPON SELLER(S) AS HEREIN PROVIDED, THEN THIS CONTRACT SHALL CONTINUE IN FULL FORCE AND EFFECT WITHOUT ANY LOAN CONTINGENCIES;** (c) Buyer(s) shall, at Buyer's expense, execute all documents necessary to procure a mortgage loan from any source. Buyer(s) shall be allowed a reasonable time prior to closing to have a mortgage or trust deed placed of record and to arrange for access to the proceeds thereof, and any delays caused by Buyer's Lender shall not constitute a default by Seller(s). Seller(s) shall allow reasonable inspection of the premises by Buyer's Lender and furnish any pertinent information requested by lender's representative; (d) The type of loan Buyer(s) shall secure is as follows:
(DELETE THOSE ITEMS WHICH DO NOT APPLY)

    (1) **Conventional** (Fixed or Adjustable Rate) Mortgage. Rider 401 shall be completed, executed by the parties and shall become a part of this Contract.
    (2) **F.H.A. Mortgage.** Rider 402 shall be completed, executed by the parties and shall become a part of this Contract.
    (3) **V.A. Mortgage.** Rider 403 shall be completed, executed by the parties and shall become a part of this Contract.
    (4) **Assumption of existing mortgage.** Rider 404 shall be completed, executed by the parties and shall become a part of this Contract.
    (5) **Financing by Seller(s).** Rider 405 shall be completed, executed by the parties and shall become a part of this Contract.

7. **SELLER'S REPRESENTATIONS:** Seller(s) represents: (a) that Seller(s) has not received any notice from any governmental body of any ordinance or building code violation or pending rezoning, reassessment, or special assessment proceedings affecting the premises; (b) that all equipment and appliances to be conveyed, including, but not limited to, the following are in operating condition on the date of closing: all mechanical equipment, heating and cooling equipment, water heaters and softeners, septic and plumbing systems, electrical systems, kitchen equipment remaining with the premises, and any miscellaneous mechanical personal property to be transferred to the Buyer(s); (c) if the property is being sold in an "AS IS" condition, Rider 406 shall be attached and made a part of this Contract, and representations contained in paragraph 7(b) of this Contract shall not apply.

8. **COMMISSION:** Seller(s) agrees that _____, Listing Broker, brought about this sale and agrees to pay a Broker's commission as agreed. COOPERATING BROKER: _____

9. **OTHER TERMS AND CONDITIONS:** This contract incorporates the Terms and Conditions set forth above, on the reverse side and the Riders signed by the parties and attached hereto numbered:_____. THE PRINTED MATTER OF THIS CONTRACT HAS BEEN PREPARED UNDER THE SUPERVISION OF THE DUPAGE ASSOCIATION OF REALTORS® AND THE DUPAGE COUNTY BAR ASSOCIATION. THE PARTIES ARE CAUTIONED THAT THIS IS A LEGALLY BINDING CONTRACT AND TO SEEK LEGAL COUNSEL. ALL BROKERS INVOLVED IN THIS TRANSACTION HAVE AN AGENCY RELATIONSHIP WITH THE SELLER(S).

Date of Acceptance _____
(The date shall be inserted only after the parties have agreed to all the terms and conditions of this Contract)

BUYER(S) _____   SELLER(S) _____
Tax I.D./S.S. # _____   Tax I.D./S.S. # _____
BUYER(S) _____   SELLER(S) _____
Tax I.D./S.S. # _____   Tax I.D./S.S. # _____
Form # 100 Copyright 1959 rev. 8/87

TABLE 9-1: (continued)

10 ATTORNEYS MODIFICATION: The terms of this Contract, (and all riders attached) except purchase price are subject to modification by the parties' attorneys within 5 business days from the date of acceptance Notice of modification, if any, shall be in writing and shall state the specific terms being modified and the suggested revisions. If within 10 business days of the date of acceptance, agreement is not reached, this Contract shall be null and void, and all earnest money shall be returned to Buyer(s).

11. TITLE: (a) At least 1 business day prior to the closing date, Seller(s) shall furnish or cause to be furnished to Buyer(s) at Seller's expense, an Owner's Duplicate Certificate of Title issued by the Registrar of Titles and a Special Tax and Lien Search and a commitment issued by a title insurance company licensed to do business in the State of Illinois, to issue an owner's title insurance policy on the current form of American Land Title Association Owner's Policy (or equivalent policy) including coverage over General Schedule B exceptions in the amount of the purchase price covering the date hereof, subject only to: (1) the "permitted exceptions" as set forth in paragraph 5, (2) title exceptions pertaining to liens or encumbrances of a definite or ascertainable amount, which may be removed by the payment of money at the time of closing (an amount sufficient to secure the release of such title exceptions shall be deducted from the proceeds of sale due Seller(s) at closing), and (3) acts done or suffered by, or judgments against Buyer(s), or those claiming by, through or under Buyer(s). (b) If the title commitment discloses unpermitted exceptions, Seller(s) shall have 30 days from the date of delivery thereof to have the said exceptions waived, or to have the title insurer commit to insure against loss or damage that may be caused by such exceptions and the closing date shall be delayed, if necessary, during said 30-day period to allow Seller(s) time to have said exceptions waived. If Seller(s) fails to have unpermitted exceptions waived, or, in the alternative, to obtain a commitment for title insurance specified above as to such exceptions, within the specified time, Buyer(s) may terminate the Contract between the parties, or may elect, upon notice to Seller(s) within 10 days after the expiration of the 30-day period, to take the title as it then is, with the right to deduct from the purchase price, liens or encumbrances of a definite or ascertainable amount. If Buyer(s) does not so elect, this Contract between the parties shall become null and void, without further action of the parties, and all monies paid by Buyer(s) hereunder shall be refunded. (c) Every title commitment which conforms with subparagraph "a" shall be conclusive evidence of good title as therein shown, as to all matters insured by the policy, subject only to special exceptions therein stated.

12. AFFIDAVIT OF TITLE: Seller(s) shall furnish Buyer(s) at closing with an Affidavit of Title, covering the date of closing, subject only to those permitted special exceptions set forth in paragraph 5, and unpermitted exceptions, if any, as to which the title insurer commits to extend insurance in the manner specified in paragraph 11. In the event that this Contract between the parties calls for title to be conveyed by a Trustee's Deed, the Affidavit of Title required to be furnished by Seller(s) shall be signed by the beneficiaries of said Trust.

13. INSPECTIONS AND WARRANTIES: Buyer(s) shall be permitted reasonable inspection of the premises prior to closing. Buyer(s) is requested to make a preliminary inspection at least 10 days prior to closing and thereafter promptly to serve written notice to Seller(s) of any non-compliance with paragraph 7(b), which Seller(s) shall promptly remedy, at Seller's expense. A final inspection of the premises including all equipment, appliances and systems shall be made, if requested, within 5 days prior to the closing date. The covenants, warranties and other provisions of this Contract shall survive the closing of this transaction; however, nothing contained in paragraph 7(b) shall be construed as a warranty that the items therein mentioned will remain in good repair beyond the closing. IN THE ABSENCE OF WRITTEN NOTICE OF ANY DEFICIENCY FROM BUYER(S) PRIOR TO CLOSING, IT SHALL BE CONCLUDED THAT THE CONDITION OF THE PREMISES AND THE ABOVE EQUIPMENT IS SATISFACTORY TO BUYER(S), AND SELLER(S) SHALL HAVE NO FURTHER RESPONSIBILITY WITH REFERENCE THERETO.

14. PRORATIONS: (a) General real estate taxes shall be prorated as of the closing date on the basis of the tax assessor's latest assessed valuation, the latest known equalization factors, and the latest known tax rate. (b) Premiums on any insurance policies assigned to Buyer(s); rents, if the subject real estate is not owner-occupied; accrued interest on any assumed mortgage, water and sewer charges, fuels, and private service contracts; homeowners and/or condominium association dues and assessments, if any, shall be prorated as of the closing date.

15. CLEAN CONDITION: Seller(s) agrees to leave the premises in broom clean condition. All refuse and personal property not to be conveyed to Buyer(s) shall be removed from the premises at Seller's expense before the date of possession.

16. ESCROW CLOSING: At the election of Seller(s) or Buyer(s), upon notice to the other party not less than 5 days prior to the closing date, the sale shall be closed through an Escrow with a title company licensed to do business in the State of Illinois, in accordance with the general provisions of a deed and money escrow agreement consistent with the terms of this Contract. Upon creation of such an Escrow, anything in this Contract between the parties to the contrary notwithstanding, payment of the purchase price and delivery of the Deed shall be made through the Escrow. The cost of the Escrow shall be divided equally between Seller(s) and Buyer(s), except that Buyer(s) shall pay the money lender's escrow charges.

17. PERFORMANCE: Time is of the essence of this Contract. Should Buyer(s) fail to perform this Contract, then at the option of Seller(s) and upon written notice to Buyer(s), the earnest money shall be forfeited by Buyer(s) as liquidated damages and this Contract shall thereupon become null and void and Seller(s) shall have the right, if necessary and applicable, to re-enter and take possession of the premises aforesaid, and all right in and title to the premises and any and all improvements made upon said premises by Buyer(s) shall vest in Seller(s). Buyer(s) or Seller(s) shall pay all reasonable attorneys' fees and costs incurred by the prevailing party in enforcing the terms and provisions of this Contract, including forfeiture or specific performance, or in defending any proceeding to which Buyer(s) or Seller(s) is made a party as a result of the acts or omissions of the other party.

18. NOTICES: All notices required to be given under this Contract shall be construed to mean notice in writing signed by or on behalf of the party giving same, and served upon the other party or their attorney personally or deposited properly addressed to such party at the address herein set forth in the U.S. mail postage paid, certified or registered mail, return receipt requested.

19. SURVEY: Prior to closing date, Seller(s) shall at Seller's expense deliver to Buyer(s) or Buyer's attorney a spotted survey of the premises, dated not more than 6 months prior to the closing date, certified by a licensed surveyor, having all corners staked and showing all improvements, easements, and building lines existing as of this contract date. (In the event the premises is a condominium, only a copy of the pages showing said premises on the recorded survey attached to the Declaration of Condominium shall be required.) If requested, Seller(s) shall provide an affidavit verifying that no changes in improvements have been made since the date of said survey.

20. RISK OF LOSS: In the event that, prior to closing, the subject premises shall be destroyed by fire or other casualty to an extent that the cost of repair thereof exceeds 10% of the purchase price set forth herein; or in the event any portion of the subject premises shall be taken by condemnation, then, at the option of either party hereto, this Contract shall be declared null and void, and Buyer(s) shall be entitled to a return of all monies paid hereunder.

21. FLOOD PLAIN: Buyer(s) will obtain flood insurance if the premises is located within a designated flood plain as determined by the Flood Plain Maps or the Department of Housing and Urban Development, and if said insurance is required by Buyer's lender.

22. TRANSFER TAX STAMPS: (a) Seller(s) shall pay for the State of Illinois and County Real Estate Transfer Tax Stamps. (b) Any applicable City or Village transfer tax shall be paid by the party designated in the Ordinance of the Municipality imposing the tax except if no party is so designated, then the City or Village transfer tax shall be paid by Buyer(s)

23. WELL AND SEPTIC TEST: In the event the premises has either a well or a septic system, Seller(s) shall provide to Buyer(s) at Seller's expense, prior to closing, test results indicating such system to be in compliance with the applicable state statutes and county health department regulations.

24. STATEMENT OF ASSESSMENTS: In the event the premises is a townhouse, condominium, or otherwise subject to a homeowner's association, Seller(s) shall prior to closing furnish Buyer(s) a statement from the Board of Managers, Treasurer, or Managing Agent of the owner's association certifying payment of assessments for common expenses through the date of closing, and, if applicable, proof of waiver or termination of any right of first refusal or general option contained in the Declaration of Condominium or Declaration of Covenants, Conditions and Restrictions, and any other documents as required by Statute, Declaration, Bylaws, or Covenants as a precondition to transfer of ownership.

25. 1445 COMPLIANCE: Buyer(s) and Seller(s) agree that if Seller(s) is a "foreign person" within the meaning of Section 1445 of Internal Revenue Code, then Buyer(s) shall withhold and deduct from sale proceeds a tax equal to 10% of the amount realized. This provision shall not apply if: (a) Seller(s) furnishes to Buyer(s) an affidavit stating under penalty of perjury, Seller's U.S. Taxpayer I.D. number, and that Seller(s) is not a foreign person as defined by the Internal Revenue Code, or (b) the premises is herein acquired by Buyer(s) for use by Buyer(s) as a primary residence, as defined by the Code, and the amount realized on the sale does not exceed $300,000.00, or (c) such other exceptions as are permitted in Section 1445 of the Internal Revenue Code.

26. MERGER OF AGREEMENTS: This Agreement contains the entire agreement between the parties hereto. All negotiations between the parties are merged in this Agreement, and there are no understandings or agreements other than those incorporated in this Agreement.

This form was developed for use by, and is reproduced with the permission of, the DuPage Association of REALTORS® and the DuPage County Bar Association.

Most homeowners react by asking immediately how much the buyers are prepared to pay. The agent, however, has learned to parry such questions. Revealing the purchase price over the telephone, without discussing accompanying matters, is considered a poor practice. You will probably be asked to set a time for face-to-face presentation of the offer. Some brokers ask a secretary to set up the appointment, heading off your direct request for information. You will be asked to name a time when all owners of the property can be present.

When you have listed your house with one member of a multiple-listing system and the offer is secured by another office, local custom governs the procedure. The offer may be turned over to your listing agent for presentation. In other areas, the selling office may contact you directly. Or, your lister may be notified and asked to set up the appointment for the selling broker. In any event, you may request that your original agent attend the meeting for presentation of the offer. The buyers will probably not be present.

Bear in mind that your agent, although duty-bound to find you the best deal, is naturally eager to sell the house through his or her own office and thus retain the whole commission. When an offer comes in, ask whether any other offers are in preparation elsewhere, or rumored to be in the offing.

If several offers come in, it is best to consider all of them at the same time. The one first signed by would-be buyers does not have precedence. As long as you have not acted on any offer, you are free to consider all of them and to respond to whichever one you choose.

In some areas, notably around New York City, the broker brings you a simple memorandum of price and terms for the proposed purchase. In other areas, the purchase offer is a detailed proposal. If you sign an acceptance, it becomes a full-fledged, binding purchase contract.

Price

You may have done some research on the probability of receiving your full asking price. Throughout the country, brokers believe one transaction in ten goes through at the list price; the proportion may well be different in your area. Among factors that may limit the price offered are the cost of comparable properties now on the market, the buyers' knowledge of recent similar sales, and—often most important—the buyers' ability to pay. Bear in mind that although you and the buyers can agree on any price, there may be hazards ahead if they cannot carry a proposed mortgage loan, or if the lender makes an unfavorable appraisal of your home's value.

Terms

The buyers will detail the terms on which they plan to buy the property. Before you take your house off the market on their behalf, you want some assurance that the transaction is likely to conclude successfully.

If you receive an all-cash offer, ask the broker, attorney or buyers themselves about their ability to come up with that amount of money, and the source of the funds. Although this might appear to be none of your business, you will be making a decision based upon their ability to fulfill their obligations.

If the buyers want to take over your present mortgage, your lawyer can advise you of any legal complications. Ask for an explanation of contingent liability.

If the buyers plan to place a new loan on the property, you may be asked to pay points to a lending institution. This subject is discussed at length in Chapter 10.

You may be asked to take back the financing: hold the mortgage yourselves. Before agreeing to such an arrangement, read carefully the section on purchase money mortgages in Chapter 10. You can make your response conditional: "We accept the offer, subject to verification of employment and income and a satisfactory credit report...."

Contingencies

Often the buyers will make their offer subject to certain happenings or contingencies. This means they promise to buy the property, but:

- only if they are able to secure an FHA mortgage loan in the amount of $92,000 with interest at a certain percent,
- only if their present home is sold,
- only if a spouse approves the house, or
- only if there is a satisfactory engineering report.

Other contingencies are possible. To protect yourself, each contingency should be accompanied by a time limit. The engineer's report can usually be obtained within three days; so might the spouse's approval. You will not run much of a risk if you accept and take your house off the market for a few days.

The stipulation that financing must be obtained is understandable. You can request that the buyers promise prompt application to a lending institution. The contract may even stipulate that they will apply to three lending institutions, if necessary, and under the guidance of your agent. Again, a time limit can be set for application and, as with all the provisions of the agreement, everything must be in writing within the contract itself.

When the contingency is for the sale of the buyers' present property, judgment is called for on your part. Some sellers simply refuse all contingent offers. Others find them reasonable, since the buyers will need the money from their sale to buy your house.

When you accept a contingent offer, you are trading worry about the sale of your own property for worry about the sale of someone else's, over which you have no control. You have a right to investigate how likely the other house is to sell, and whether it is being listed at a reasonable price. You can even insert into your contract provisions about this matter.

The terms of an offer—whether it is a clean, all-cash deal or one that involves accepting a contingency—often affect the sales price eventually agreed upon. If you are going to wait for the sale of the buyers' house, you have some justification for sticking to a higher price in return for the uncertainty.

In any event, make sure that any offer contingent upon the sale of the buyers' present property includes an escape clause, sometimes called a *kick-out*. This provision allows you to continue showing your home. If you receive another offer that you want to accept, you notify the first buyers that they must remove their contingency or withdraw. Either they agree to buy your home by the specified date, come what may, or they must void the contract and drop out of the picture, allowing you to negotiate with your new purchaser.

Local custom suggests the exact terms of the escape clause. You might allow a period of one month in which the buyers can be secure in their contract; after that, if their own home hasn't sold, they could be bumped by another offer. Usually you promise the first buyers a period of three to five business days in which to make their decision, should an escape clause be invoked.

Personal Property

The purchase contract should detail all of the gray-area items mentioned at the time of listing: swing sets, carpeting, mirrors, chandeliers and, in general, all fixtures that you will leave with the property. In addition, you may agree to include items of personal property such as kitchen appliances, washer and dryer or drapes.

The contract should also mention those items you will remove. Oral agreement is not a sufficient guarantee against misunderstandings later.

Earnest Money

Your buyers will be asked to put a deposit into the hands of the broker to prove that their intentions are serious and to serve as a source of damages should they back out for no good reason. You can expect to see their safeguards written into the contract: that their deposit will be returned if the lender's appraisal comes in below the purchase price, if you renege for no good reason or if they fail to receive their mortgage commitment, for example. You can request a similar provision: that their deposit is in jeopardy if they do not act in good faith.

The deposit is not a legal requirement for the contract. If the cash for their purchase is coming from the sale of their present home, the buyers may be unable to deposit earnest money, or may be reluctant to do so. You should not accept an offer, however, unless it is accompanied by some sort of deposit. The money signifies that the buyers mean business.

Local custom varies, and the buyers may have been told that six percent or even ten percent is standard. They may well come up with less. One thousand dollars is a respectable deposit, and even a smaller sum may suffice to make the buyers feel a commitment to going through with the transaction.

Pay attention to the form of the deposit. The buyers may be out-of-towners who do not keep large sums in a checking account; have they promised to make the check good as soon as they get back home? A promissory note is of little value in this matter, and a cash deposit of $500 is often more useful than a note for $5,000. The broker is legally liable to you for any representation about the earnest money, since you are basing your decisions upon what you are told.

Buyers may be understandably reluctant to hand a deposit directly to a seller. Where agents are involved, the money is usually kept in the broker's escrow account. If there is no agent, suggest that the money be held by your attorney, or failing that, by the buyers' attorney or an escrow company.

Other Provisions

The purchase contract will contain details on those items that must be apportioned between you and the buyer at closing: water bills, property taxes and the like. It stipulates the type of deed you must deliver, which party bears responsibility for loss resulting from fire before the time of closing, the procedure if a cloud on the title is found and many other matters intended to head off disagreements as the transaction progresses. Table 9-2 lists these and other costs for which the contract should specify responsibility.

TABLE 9-2: Responsibility for Costs

	Buyer	Seller
Survey	_____	_____
Points	_____	_____
Title insurance	_____	_____
Pest inspection	_____	_____
Recording fees	_____	_____
Transfer fees	_____	_____
Escrow or closing fees	_____	_____
Title search	_____	_____
Bank's attorney	_____	_____
Broker's commission	_____	_____

A closing date will be specified. Unless the powerful legal clause "time being of the essence" is included, the closing date mentioned is merely a target and might come and go with the contract still continuing in effect. If a certain date is essential to you, be sure to consult your lawyer before declaring time of the essence.

Possession of the property is usually given on the date of settlement. It rarely becomes necessary to let the buyers move in ahead of time, or for you to remain after closing. If the buyer moves in as a tenant you should take certain precautions, which are discussed in Chapter 11; try to avoid such an arrangement. If you plan to stay on after closing, you may be asked to pay rent and even to deposit a large sum in escrow to ensure that you will eventually move out as agreed. Like all other arrangements, these should be written into the original sales contract.

To safeguard yourself, you may wish to include certain limitations in the contract. Perhaps you will make repairs, if they are required by the lending institution, only up to a certain dollar amount. You may want to limit the number of points you pay. If appliances are included in the sale, you will want to transfer them "as is" where state law permits.

The offer you receive will probably contain a time limit, "This offer is good until Saturday noon...". In most states, the buyers are free to withdraw their offer before you have accepted it. If they do not, and if you accept before Saturday noon, then you have a firm purchase contract, binding upon both parties.

Some, but not all, of the protections you need from a written contract are listed in Table 9-3.

TABLE 9-3:   Contract Provisions

	YES	NO
Approval by your attorney before contract becomes firm?	___	___
Items you want to remove from the property (lighting fixtures, etc.)?	___	___
Escape clause (kick-out) if the offer is contingent upon the sale of buyer's present home?	___	___
Assurance the buyer will apply for mortgage loan in timely fashion?	___	___
Time limit for buyer to obtain mortgage commitment?	___	___
Dollar limit on repairs you may be required to make?	___	___
Reimbursement for property taxes you may have prepaid, heating oil in your tank and the like?	___	___
Return of money in your escrow account with your lender?	___	___
"Assumption of," not "taking title subject to" your present mortgage, if it is to be turned over to the buyer?	___	___
Substantial "good faith" earnest money deposit?	___	___
Forfeiture of earnest money if buyer withdraws for no good reason?	___	___
Specific target date for closing?	___	___

You have three possible responses to the offer: yes, no and maybe.

YOUR RESPONSE

...Yes

Yes is an acceptance of the offer as it stands, without any alteration. You can write above your signature the words, "subject to the approval of my attorney." In this case, your lawyer must later approve the wording and provisions of the contract. If he or she does not, you may void the contract, or both parties may agree to amend it.

You may have arranged beforehand to telephone your lawyer while you are considering the purchase offer. Some attorneys do not mind holding themselves available during the out-of-office hours that may be involved. If the offer is on a standard form with which the lawyer is familiar, a few minutes may suffice to go over the specific terms detailed, so that you can receive legal counsel by phone.

Alternatively, you can take the contract to your lawyer before you accept it. Two precautions must be kept in mind. First, many attorneys will not counsel you on price, a matter that they consider out of their field of expertise. And second, there is always the possibility that you have a nit-picking lawyer, unaccustomed to real estate transactions, who may delay and fuss around until you lose a favorable offer. In the end, you must make your own decision, taking into account the advice of both agent and attorney.

...No

You can always refuse an offer completely. Once you have rejected it, you cannot change your mind, even five minutes later, and get it back. Suppose, for example, that the offer is good until Saturday at noon. On Friday night you reject it. You cannot then change your mind on Saturday morning and accept it. If you did you would have to ask the buyers whether they would like to reinstate their offer.

Because you know that an underpriced house sells quickly, you may be skeptical of a good offer that comes in promptly. It is only human to argue that, "If I received an offer for $120,000 after only one week, what might I get by waiting a while longer?" The true bargain, however, is usually snapped up within a day or two. After a week, you can assume the market is operating normally. Experience has shown that the first offer is often the best one. This is because a new home on the market is exposed to a large group of potential buyers. Your best offer is likely to come from that group. Be cautious, then, about rejecting a first offer out of hand. Agents find little comfort in saying "I told you so," if you are waiting vainly three months later to equal that first proposal.

. . .Maybe

Better than a simple refusal is a counteroffer. With a counteroffer, you agree to accept the buyers' proposal if a few changes are made.

Again, you run the risk of losing your buyers. You have not accepted their proposal, and they are now free to accept or reject yours. A counteroffer, with its possibility for reaching eventual agreement, is much better than an outright rejection.

While a counteroffer is pending, your house is more or less tied up. Make the counteroffer good for only a short period of time only, perhaps a day or two.

If your house has turned out to be a hot property and you anticipate other offers within the next few days, you may prefer not to be bound by a written counteroffer. "Tell them to come back five thousand dollars higher and I'll consider it," you might say informally, without committing yourself.

Inexperienced negotiators sometimes assume that the proper procedure is for the buyer to start with a low offer and for the seller to counter somewhat under the asking price, depending on a series of counter-counteroffers to bring them eventually to a price halfway between. In practice, too many counters usually kill a transaction. The parties lose sight of the main goal—reaching an agreement—as emotions rise and the process becomes a test of wills.

Your buyers are well advised to make their first offer as high as they are prepared to go, and you to make any counteroffer close to the price you would take. If you are determined to stand pat on your list price, consider the buyers' pride and offer a token reduction—perhaps a few hundred dollars—to signal your goodwill. Offer to throw in the refrigerator or the drapes. These could be items that the buyers do not particularly want, but they provide a way for the buyers to save face while accepting your price. At least, they may reason, their low offer was not wasted, for it won some concessions.

During price negotiations, it is essential to remember your objective. You may insist upon the last few dollars as a matter of principle, completely overlooking the fact that when you set your original asking price, that extra thousand was tacked on "just to see." Resolve before you start that you will not lose a deal over a mere thousand dollars.

A counteroffer may concern itself with matters other than price. You might "accept all terms and conditions except that purchase price shall be $132,000," or "accept all terms and conditions except that date of closing shall be June 30" or request that an escape clause be added to the contingency regarding the sale of the buyers' present property. Any of the terms discussed earlier in this chapter can be added to your counteroffer. Special circumstances may suggest other provisions. As long as both parties agree and the matter is not illegal, almost anything can be written into your contract. For unusual provisions, wording should be supplied by your attorney or the buyers'.

SIGNATURES

Do not be surprised if the agent prefers not to leave an offer with you overnight or drop it at your attorney's office. The agent's experience is that the transaction proceeds best when he or she retains possession of the original contract. Duplicates can, of course, be left with you or taken to the lawyer. As soon as you and the buyers have signed a final acceptance, all parties will receive duplicate originals.

It is not essential for all buyers to sign the offer, but all sellers must. In some states, various provisions dictate that a spouse sign, even if not an owner of record.

When you and the buyers have signed an exact acceptance of all terms, the contract is binding and the commission has theoretically been earned.

ROLE OF THE BACKUP

In rare situations, it is possible to accept a backup offer on your property. Perhaps you sign a firm contract with Buyer A, only to find Buyer B beating down your door on the next day. Buyer B is willing to do anything to own your house, and to wait around in hopes that A's transaction somehow falls through. You can then accept an offer from B "subject to the nonperformance of existing contract with A." Buyer A, of course, has a firm contract with you, and will probably be the next owner. But if anything goes wrong with that transaction, you can then obtain a release from A and sell to B, with the price and the terms already agreed upon in your backup contract. You are in the enviable position of a man with both a belt and suspenders.

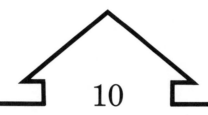

Your Buyer's Financing

You may think financing is the buyer's concern, but it is of vital importance to you. How will you respond to these questions?

"Are you willing to consider an FHA offer?"

"Will you hold the mortgage yourself for high interest and a five-year balloon?"

"Can I take over your VA loan if I'm not a veteran?"

"Would you drop your price $15,000 for all cash?"

Preparing to judge the buyer's financing proposal requires homework on your part. Become familiar with the possibilities. Ask an agent for a briefing on the current alternatives. Find out about new and innovative programs as they become available locally.

There is no single best financing plan out there. More than a hundred different mortgage plans are available from lending institutions in almost any locality. Each of these plans is there because it fits a certain situation best—buyer's need, seller's convenience, type of property.

To ask, "What's the best mortgage around right now?" is like walking into a drugstore and asking, "What's the best medicine you have?"

A broker, working with a customer, develops a financing strategy for that buyer within the first few minutes of conversation. Recent bankrupt? Better search for an assumable mortgage. Two young professionals? Suggest an ARM. Ambitious young carpenter? Find an older seller with a run-down house that can't be financed through a regular lender.

IS THE BUYER CAPABLE?

If you are using a real estate broker, your agent will "qualify" the buyer. The process involves an analysis of income, debts, assets, credit rating and available cash, to determine whether the buyer is financially capable of purchasing your home.

You need the same assurance, if you are selling on your own, before you accept an offer and take your home off the market. The buyer who is serious should not mind filling out a financial statement that you can take to your lawyer or accountant for analysis, before you make a firm commitment to sell. One of the seller's worst mistakes is tying up the house for months, only to find that the prospective buyer is financially unable to complete the purchase.

The questions a bank will ask of a mortgage applicant are shown in Table 10-1. The more you know about prospective buyers, the more likely you are to have a problem-free sale.

ALL-CASH BUYERS

Most agents can count on one hand the number of contracts they have written involving all-cash purchases. Such buyers are so few that the subject is easily disposed of. The advantages to you in an all-cash sale are these:

- You will not be asked to pay points to a lender.
- You will receive your money immediately.
- The closing date may be set for your convenience, since no mortgage commitment need be obtained.
- With no contingencies for obtaining financing, you can count on a firm sale and make your plans with confidence.

Possible negatives are these:

- You may prefer not to receive all proceeds immediately, for income tax or personal reasons.

- The buyer, aware of the value of an all-cash sale, may expect a price concession in return. (Consider giving it!)

Before accepting an all-cash offer, though, insist upon proof that the money is available (a "gift letter" from a grandmother isn't really proof—are you sure she has the money?). Insist upon a substantial deposit, with a written provision that it will be forfeited if the buyer is unable to perform.

TABLE 10-1: Buyer's Qualifying Interview Form

Names: _____ / _____

Social security numbers: _____   _____

Current address: _____ Zip code: _____

Business telephone: ( ) _____ Home telephone: ( ) _____

Own or rent: _____ Monthly payment: _____ Lease expires: _____ sublet? _____

Mortgage balance: _____ Mortgage type: _____ Do you intend to sell: _____

No. children: _____ Eligible for VA: _____

Employment (last two years)

Employer: _____ Title: _____ Salary: _____ Dates: ___/___

Employer: _____ Title: _____ Salary: _____ Dates: ___/___

Employer: _____ Title: _____ Salary: _____ Dates: ___/___

Employer: _____ Title: _____ Salary: _____ Dates: ___/___

Monthly income (all sources):   Monthly debts (including alimony, child support and day care):

_____   _____

_____   _____

Total: _____   Total: _____

Assets available: _____   Credit problems: _____

_____   _____

_____   _____

ASSUMING YOUR LOAN

Your mortgage may or may not be assumable by the next owner of the house. If it is, it will fall into one of two categories: freely assumable or assumable with lender's approval.

Freely Assumable Mortgages

These include all FHA loans placed before December 1, 1986, and all VA loans placed before March 1, 1988. (More about new rules for FHAs and VAs placed after those dates in a moment.) If your mortgage is presently one of these types, any buyer may take it, along with the house, with no change in interest rate or term. The buyers need not prove that they can qualify to carry the loan. The lending institution has no say in the matter. All that is necessary is your assent. The buyers pay the difference in cash at time of closing, or they may request that you hold a second mortgage—more on that later. Suppose, for example, that you own a $100,000 house with a VA loan on which you presently owe $85,000. The buyers (who need not be veterans) can take the loan along with the house, paying you the remaining $15,000 in cash.

Your advantages are these:

- As with an all-cash sale, no points are due, you receive your money immediately, the sale is firm and the closing date need not be subject to a lender's convenience.
- Your house is easily sold, for a large number of buyers are looking for such mortgages and can afford the down payment. Your VA or FHA loan, which may have a lower interest rate than is currently available, may be the most valuable thing about your house.
- You may command a premium for your property. The fortunate buyers have few closing costs to pay, save on mortgage or appraisal fees and need not pass bank inspection. The buyers may be willing to pay something extra for the savings anticipated over the years from a low interest rate.

The main drawback to allowing a mortgage assumption is that you may retain contingent liability. If the mortgage were foreclosed and the property could not be sold for sufficient money to clear the debt, the lender, FHA or VA, could eventually require you to make up the deficiency. This possibility becomes more remote with every passing day, however, as the debt is reduced and if the dollar value of the house increases. Caution is indicated, though, in a neighborhood that is deteriorating or an area that is economically depressed.

There is, however, a procedure under which the new borrower, if willing, can prove qualifications and release the seller from futher liability. The buyer who assumes an older VA loan, if the seller is to be released, must be a veteran with an entitlement.

FHA and VA Mortgages Assumable with Approval

For FHA loans made after December 15, 1989, and VA mortgages placed after March 1, 1988, the buyer assuming the loan must prove financial qualification to the satisfaction of the lending institution. The original borrower would have no further liability.

If the buyer assuming this newer FHA loan is not able or willing to prove qualification, a simple credit check and appraisal of the property may be substituted, and the seller retains liability for five years. After that time, if mortgage payments are current, the original borrower is no longer liable.

Mortgages Assumable with Approval

Conventional loans, those not backed by the FHA or VA, are usually not assumable. The majority must be paid off when the property is sold.

But a third category of loans exists—those assumable with the lender's approval. Many adjustable rate mortgages (ARMs) fall into this group; so do new FHA and VA loans.

If your present mortgage is of this type, your buyer can apply to the lender to assume your loan. The new borrower must prove qualifications to carry the debt and, in the case of an ARM, the interest rate may be adjusted. Closing costs are less than those required for placing a new loan.

Conventional mortgages vary in this matter and in other provisions. If yours is being assumed, your attorney can tell you whether you run any risks.

SECONDARY MORTGAGE MARKET

When every bank in town sets the same limits on some of their loans, chances are the regulations are set by the secondary mortgage market. Many lenders make loans and then turn around and sell them (packaged with many other mortgages) to big investors in the secondary mortgage market. The largest buyer in this field is Fannie Mae, the Federal National Mortgage Association. When Fannie Mae announces that it will buy a certain type of mortgage, lending institutions listen.

PORTFOLIO LOANS

If you and the buyer have a situation that doesn't meet the standards of the secondary market, search for a local lender making *portfolio loans*. These are old-fashioned mortgages, in which the bank (or savings and loan institution) lends its own money, collects and keeps the payments and retains the mortgage in its own portfolio.

POINTS

The payment of points when a new mortgage loan is made compensates the lender for an interest rate that does not reflect the true cost of the money. Each point is one percent of the loan being placed. It is due as a one-time, lump-sum payment, usually at the time of transfer of title.

If your buyer is looking for a $100,000 mortgage, and the lending institution demands four points, $4,000 will be due.

When interest rates fluctuate daily, lending institutions prefer to change the number of points charged rather than constantly alter the interest rates on mortgages. On VA loans, indeed, they cannot change interest rates at will (VA rates are set by the federal government). The number of points charged, thus, may vary from one lender to another and from one week to another. Keeping track of the local situation is one of a broker's major concerns.

If $4,000 is due in points before your buyer can place a $100,000 mortgage, who pays this sum? On VA loans, federal regulations forbid the buyer from paying more than one point; other points are usually paid by the seller. On conventional loans, the matter is usually negotiable between you and your buyers.

If you are committed to paying points, make sure the buyers consider your interests when they choose their lender.

In times of high interest rates, which might make it impossible for your buyers to qualify for the proposed mortgage loan, you may be asked to participate in a *buydown*—a relatively new idea. A lending institution offers you the opportunity of paying extra points; in return, your buyers can place their loan at a lower interest rate. Although this process reduces your proceeds from the house, it does enable the buyers to purchase.

Although points represent upfront interest payments, they are subject to varying treatment by the Internal Revenue Service. Your buyer can deduct immediately, in the year they are paid, all points on a mortgage to buy a residence. If you are selling income (rental) property, the buyer will have to amortize the points, deducting them bit by bit over the years.

Most important to you: *Points paid by the seller are not income-tax-deductible at all.* One may deduct only interest paid on one's own debts.

This factor may be significant when you are working out a sales contract; points (if the buyer has the extra money to pay them) don't cost the buyer as much as they cost you, because the points represent an income tax deduction for the buyer.

CONVENTIONAL MORTGAGES

Conventional loans are those transactions negotiated between borrower and lender with no government backing—"regular bank mortgages." If the buyer puts less than 10 or 20 percent down, a conventional loan may require the borrower to purchase private mortgage insurance (PMI) to protect the lender in case of default.

Your advantages, if the buyer secures a conventional loan, include the following:

- The application process is less complicated than it is with FHA or VA, and the time between application and mortgage commitment may be shorter.
- If points must be paid to the lender, the question of which party pays them is completely negotiable between you and the buyer.
- The lender is more concerned with the security of the loan than with the condition of the house, so you are less likely to be asked to make repairs than with FHA- or VA-backed mortgages.

Drawbacks to conventional loans, from your point of view, are these:

- They usually involve large down payments, unless PMI is purchased. In a difficult mortgage market, down payment requirements and interest rates may rise to impractically high levels, effectively shutting out many of your potential buyers.
- The bank will base its loan on the value reported by its own appraiser.

ADJUSTABLE RATE MORTGAGES

As interest rates rise, more buyers opt for adjustable rate mortgages (ARMs); when rates fall, buyers jump for fixed rate loans. Adjustables involve a vocabulary that may be entirely new to you if you haven't shopped for a loan lately.

Adjustment period. Most buyers choose loans that are adjusted yearly; six-month, three-year and five-year periods are also common.

Index. Rates will be adjusted up or down according to a nationwide index, most commonly based on recent yields for Treasury securities.

Margin. To the index, the lender will add an agreed-upon margin, perhaps two or three percent. If T-bills were selling at nine percent, the loan with a two-percent margin would be repaid at 11 percent.

Cap. Most ARMS contain limitations on how far the rate can rise or fall at each adjustment.

Lifetime cap (ceiling). Most ARMs contain a certain limit beyond which the interest rate cannot rise. A five-percent cap is commonly offered; the ARM that started at an eight-percent rate could never go beyond 13 percent.

Convertibility. The provision allows the borrower to choose, at some time or times during the life of the loan, to change to a fixed-rate loan. Convertible loans may start at slightly higher rates in return for this privilege, or—of concern to you as seller if you were paying the points—an extra point may be charged.

FHA AND VA MORTGAGES

These loans, government insured or guaranteed, are oriented to the borrower's benefit. Since the money comes from local lenders, they may not be available in all localities, and the top loan amount, particularly in the case of FHA, is limited and of little use in high-cost areas.

A number of special FHA programs are available with little or no down payment. VA loans can be made with no down payment.

If your house falls within the price limits for these loans, you will have a wide pool of buyers. The low down-payment provisions and fixed interest rate, as well as the fact that all of these mortgages are assumable if the house is later resold, make FHA and VA loans attractive to buyers.

Your disadvantages as a seller are these:

- More paperwork and a longer wait for mortgage commitment are involved. The house and the buyers must be approved by both the local lender and by a government agency.
- A stringent inspection of the property is conducted, and specific repairs may be requested before the mortgage is granted. In most cases, repairs must be paid for by the seller. You always have the option, though, of refusing to

make repairs and voiding the contract. Your contract can state that you will make repairs only up to a given dollar amount.

FmHA LOANS

In some rural areas, the Farmers Home Administration, a division of the U.S. Department of Agriculture, makes direct loans to buyers. Strict income limits are set, usually in low- to middle-income brackets, and monthly payments are tailored to the borrower's income. You might find a buyer who plans to use FmHA if you are located in an area with fewer than 10,000 residents and your home is of modest size and price. One drawback is that the source of loans can be cut off when available funds are depleted for the fiscal quarter-year.

PURCHASE-MONEY MORTGAGES

Although any loan used for buying real estate is strictly called a purchase-money mortgage, the term is often employed for seller financing, those transactions in which you are asked to "take back" the loan yourself. These arrangements are possible, of course, only when you do not need your proceeds immediately for the purchase of another home.

You may lend money on a first mortgage, the buyers' primary loan on the property. Or you may take back a second mortgage, lending the buyers some of the down payment needed to assume your first mortgage.

When times get rough in the mortgage market, you may receive proposals for "creative financing," a term that denotes all sorts of ingenious devices for making a detour around regular mortgage arrangements.

One possibility is a *land contract,* or contract for deed. With this arrangement, you retain title to the property until the buyers have made all their mortgage payments to you. Or, a land contract may be in effect only until the buyers have paid enough to constitute an acceptable down payment, at which time you turn over title (give them a deed).

Often a purchase-money mortgage involves a *balloon* arrangement. You may not be willing to wait 30 years for your money, yet the buyer cannot afford the large monthly payments necessary to retire the debt in five years. Payments are therefore set as if the mortgage were indeed for a 30-year period. At the end of five years, however, the entire remaining debt becomes due and payable; that large lump-sum payment is the balloon. The understanding is that either you will renew the loan or the buyer will be able, by that time, to arrange outside financing. With the average family moving every five years, the house may have changed hands and the debt may have been paid off anyway.

If you can afford to wait for your money, the advantages of holding a mortgage yourself include these:

- Your house is more easily sold in a difficult mortgage period.
- You may have income tax advantages if you receive your money over a period of years.
- You may be able to hold out for a higher sales price, because you are doing the buyers a favor.
- A house that cannot pass a lender's inspection can be sold this way with fewer complications.
- You will not owe points to a lender.

Drawbacks to Seller Financing

Drawbacks are summarized simply: Will the buyers meet their responsibilities, or will you find yourself with the house—and a host of problems—back on your hands?

If you consider taking back financing, a number of precautions are in order.

First, make sure that you receive a down payment large enough to cover the expenses of selling, the ready cash you need from the property and as much more as possible. A large down payment represents safety for you, because it means that should you ever have to foreclose, the debt may be covered by the sale of the property. A large down payment also serves to separate strong buyers from weak ones.

Next, insist upon an analysis of the borrowers' financial position in much the same way a regular lending institution would do. Your lawyer or broker can obtain a credit report on the buyers and it is essential that it be a satisfactory one, indicating that they meet their financial obligations on time. Any compromise on this point is unwise.

Analyze the buyers' present debts and income to ensure that they are not getting in over their heads. Look for job stability and prospects of advancement.

You may be asked to take a second mortgage, lending the buyers some of the money needed to assume your present loan. Second mortgages usually carry higher interest rates than first mortgages. Later, if you prefer your money in one lump sum, you can sell the second mortgage at a discount to an investor. The large discount may surprise you, though.

The second mortgage carries a higher degree of risk. In case of foreclosure, the property would be sold and the proceeds used to pay off unpaid taxes and the first mortgage, before you received payment on your second mortgage. There may not be sufficient funds, in that case, to cover your loan. Again, your best protection is a large down payment.

LEASE OPTIONS

A lease option commits you to sell the property for a given amount of money at any time within a stated term. (Other provisions may apply.) Your tenants/purchasers are usually free to buy or not to buy. If they decide not to exercise their option to purchase, they commonly remain on the property as simple tenants and may forfeit the money they put up in a lump-sum payment for the option.

From the seller's point of view, a lease option can be a fine device for securing good tenants who will consider the property their own and take good care of it. The arrangement may, however, result in no sale at all—or a forced sale you don't really want.

OTHER TYPES OF MORTGAGES

Many experts believe that the long-term, fixed rate mortgage is becoming a dinosaur. Rapidly sweeping the country are a number of innovative mortgage plans.

In certain *shared equity* or *participation* mortgages, the buyers give up a portion of their profits, when the house is sold, in return for lower interest rates along the way. The monthly subsidy can come from a lender set up for this program, a partner in the purchase or you, as seller. If you enter into such an arrangement, have a lawyer and accountant go over all the papers before you sign them.

Package mortgages cover both real and personal property. They may be found, for example, in the sale of a condominium apartment, where furniture and appliances are included.

QUALIFYING RATIOS

If you are asked to hold a mortgage yourself, you may find Table 10-1 helpful in calculating the income you might expect from your buyers.

See Table 10-2 for directions on calculating buyer's monthly payment and Table 10-3 for calculating balloon payments.

If you are selling on your own, it is wise to determine, at the start, how much income a buyer will need to qualify for your home. How much they will need to borrow, of course, depends on how much they can put down. There's no way you can guess the amount of cash your eventual buyers will have on hand, but it's safe to say that most buyers borrow as much as possible. Loans commonly run from 80 percent to, in the case of a VA loan, 100 percent of the value of your home.

Lending institutions set up *qualifying ratios* (often dictated by secondary lenders such as Fannie Mae). When a ratio of 28/36 is quoted, it means:

- Borrowers can spend up to 28 percent of their gross monthly income for mortgage payments (Principal, Interest, one-twelfth of yearly property Taxes and homeowners' Insurance, or *PITI*), or
- They may spend up to 36 percent of monthly income including other installment (debt) payments (auto loans, for example).

Every borrower's situation is different, of course. More or less cash available for a down payment makes a difference, and so does other indebtedness (car, revolving credit, student loan). And, by the time your borrower actually receives the loan, interest rates may have changed markedly.

See Table 10-4 for an approximation of the income the buyer needs to buy your house.

TABLE 10-2:   Calculating Buyer's Monthly Payment

A. Payment to amortize $1,000 (from Appendix I) $_____

B. Times number of thousands borrowed   x _____

C. Monthly payment for principal and interest $_____

   For the payment of a loan of $74,500 at 10 percent for 25 years:

- Find the monthly payment necessary to amortize $1,000. According to the chart, the figure is $9.0870.
- Multiply this by the number of thousands being borrowed: $9.087 × 74.5 = $676.9815.
- Round off to whole cents. The $676.98 amount represents the monthly payment necessary for principal and interest to retire a loan of $74,500 at 10 percent over a period of 25 years.

TABLE 10-3:   Calculating Balloon Payments

   Perhaps, with the loan in the example above, you and the buyers have set the payment as if it were going to run on a 25-year schedule, but you have agreed that at the end of 10 years the entire remaining amount will become due and payable. What will that amount be?

   Appendix II contains the factors needed to calculate the amount. The chart for 10 percent interest on a 25-year loan shows that after 10 years have elapsed, the remaining balance is .902 (90.2 percent) of the original loan.

A.   Amount of original loan $_____

B.   Multiply by factor from Appendix II   x _____

C.   Remaining principal balance $_____

   In the example given, the remaining balance, the large final payment at the end of 10 years, is $74,500 × .846 (84.6%), or $63,027. Almost 85 percent of the original loan is still due.

TABLE 10-4:   Calculating Buyer's Needed Income

Estimate of fair market value: $_____ (A)

   90 percent of value (assumes a 10-percent down payment) $_____ (B)

Current average interest rate _____ percent

Monthly payment to carry amount on line B
   (use factors in Appendix I) $_____ (C)

One-twelfth yearly property taxes $_____ (D)

One-twelfth annual insurance cost $_____ (E)

   Monthly mortgage payment (add lines C, D and E) $_____ (F)

Multiply this amount by 52 to find a rough estimate of the annual income required for the proposed mortgage loan.

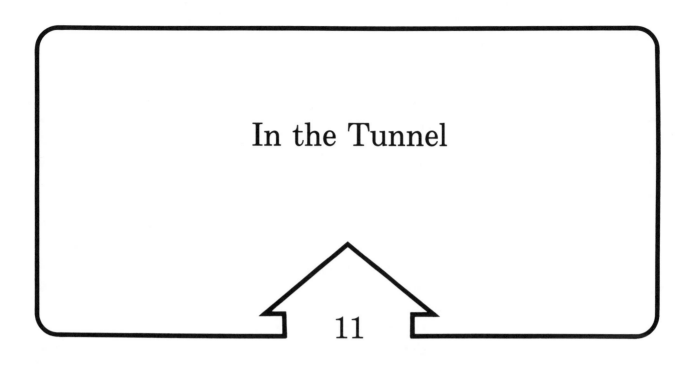

In the Tunnel

11

"We've sold our house!"

When can you joyfully spread the news to your friends? Is it the day someone first expresses an intention to buy? The time when you reach written agreement on price and terms? Or the final settlement session, when the money and the front-door key change hands?

Although most transactions do proceed smoothly from contract to eventual transfer of title, you, the agent and the buyers all have responsibilities while the sale is "in the tunnel." All of you can help ensure the successful outcome of your mutual plans.

THE AGENT'S RESPONSIBILITIES

Your agent or lawyer will furnish duplicate originals of the final purchase agreement, which has now become a binding contract to you, the buyer, the lending institution, escrow agent or other parties involved.

When a new mortgage is being placed, the agent should assist in selecting the most favorable lending institution, and may accompany the borrower to the application interview. If no agent is involved, you must take the responsibility yourself for seeing that prompt application is being made.

Unless you already know that the deposit is safely tucked into an escrow account, you are entitled to a report on its progress. If you are not notified when the check clears or the promissory note is made good do not hesitate to inquire.

Merely finding a buyer for the property will not ensure a successful sale. You, your lawyer or your agent must ride herd on the mortgage application process. You want to hear as soon as possible that the buyers' credit checked out well and the house appraised at a satisfactory figure.

Or, you may hear about holdups in the paperwork: the verification of employment form has not been returned, or a required inspection has not been documented. It may be necessary to arrange appointments for an appraiser, an inspecting engineer, a termite inspector or a surveyor.

YOU AND THE BUYERS

Remember that buyers often are jittery, worrying about whether they made the right decision. A malady known as *buyers' remorse* can set in during this period, often at 2:00 A.M. You are also facing change and upheaval and are not quite yourself. It may be advisable to talk with the buyers through your broker or lawyer. Any contact you do have should be cordial and reassuring, but also limited and noncommittal. Many queries are best answered, "I'm not sure; we're leaving that to our lawyer," or "The broker probably knows about it."

The buyers may have seen your house for half an hour at most, on only one occasion. It is understandable that they desire a closer inspection. They may want to measure for curtains, show the place to their parents or take some pictures. If there is a broker, he or she should accompany them to handle sudden doubts that may arise. Of course you have a binding contract, but the sale will go more smoothly with buyers who are eager to complete the transaction.

At this point, you may want to let the buyers know which appliances or furniture you will be selling. Keep your negotiations friendly, and remember that you can always advertise a garage sale for whatever is left.

BUYERS MOVING IN

Lawyers agree that it is a poor idea to allow the buyers to move in before closing. If circumstances dictate such an arrangement, discuss the matter thoroughly with your attorney. Among points to be considered in a moving-in agreement are these:

- The buyers must first have passed the bank's credit check.
- A high security deposit must be established. Some sellers require that all of the cash the buyers will need at closing be deposited.
- The buyers promise not to make any changes in the property until they own it.
- Rent might be set at a higher rate than the prospective mortgage payments, so that there will be an incentive to go to settlement on time.
- A written agreement should promise that the buyers will accept everything "as is" on the day they move in. Who pays for subsequent repairs should be settled in advance.
- Insurance liability must be arranged.
- Your accountant can advise whether the rental period jeopardizes your special tax treatment for profit on the sale of one's own home.

ALONG THE WAY

Your buyers must act in good faith to fulfill any conditions stipulated in the purchase contract. If a new loan is being sought, they must make application promptly at a lending institution appropriate to the financing planned, and must cooperate in securing the necessary papers.

If the purchasers must sell their present home, you may have specified in the contract that they will list it immediately in the open market. Seldom will you have control, however, over the price they ask for the property or how they answer purchase offers they receive.

The contract will contain your agreements concerning which party will arrange and pay for termite inspection, survey, engineer's report and such matters. Usually these responsibilities are established by community custom. During the waiting period, buyer or seller, their attorneys or the escrow agent will attend to these items.

Flood insurance, if it is required by the lender, must be purchased by the buyers. They will be asked by the lender to prove that they are placing adequate insurance on the property. They must arrange this before closing.

SELLER'S PROBLEMS

You may be informed, to your surprise, that the roofer with whom you quarreled last fall has filed a mechanic's lien that encumbers your title to the house. To clear this lien, pay it off. Your lawyer may be willing to convey the good news to the contractor; the worker may be so delighted at the prospect of payment that a compromise sum is agreed upon. If you prefer to challenge the lien, you can release it by posting a bond pending adjudication.

Other liens against your house must be cleared (unpaid taxes, personal judgments).

A title search may disclose unexpected claims against the property by your former spouse or by long-ago heirs of a previous owner. A simple quitclaim deed may be used in such cases. By signing this deed, the person involved waives any rights he or she might have without laying claim to the property.

If you are caught between two homes and won't receive the proceeds from the old one in time to close on the new, a specific type of short-term loan is possible. Banks call such a loan interim financing, a swing loan, a bridging loan or a turnaround. Your attorney or broker can help you investigate this.

APPRAISAL AND REPAIR OF PROPERTY

If a new mortgage loan is being sought, two hurdles must be cleared before title to a house is transferred. The house must be appraised at the agreed-upon sales price, and it must meet the lender's standards for condition.

In some areas, particularly if the house is a multiple dwelling, repairs may be required before transfer of title. When a new FHA or VA loan is being placed, the buyer pays for an appraisal and inspection. The report may stipulate specific repairs needed before the mortgage can be placed. The FHA standards deal primarily with the health and safety of the occupants and preservation of the structure. If your exterior paint is shabby, it need not be redone. If, however, bare wood is in evidence, a paint job will be required to preserve the material. Redecorating will not be required on the interior, but a handrail for the basement steps might be requested.

You are not bound to make these repairs unless specified in your contract. If you choose not to, you may void the contract and start looking for another buyer. This means, of course, that you are back to square one, with the additional handicap of not wanting to consider any further FHA or VA offers.

It is usually better to proceed with the repairs specified. With certain programs, the buyer may volunteer to assist; with others you must do the work yourself. If you cannot afford the repairs, ask your broker's help in finding a worker who will wait until the day of transfer for payment.

If the house isn't appraised favorably, the lending institution will refuse to base its loan on the sales price. With FHA or VA contracts, your buyers have the option of dropping out at this point. They may be so upset by the notification that they will do just that. Often, though, the problem is solved by renegotiation. You might drop your price to the amount of the appraisal, or the buyers might agree to make a larger down payment. Often a compromise is worked out, with each party giving up something.

BUYERS' PROBLEMS

If your purchasers plan to obtain a new mortgage loan, the progress of their application is of great importance. You can expect the broker to monitor the process, and the attorney for either party may also check up from time to time.

The application process consists mainly of assembling exhibits: various documents that will affect the lender's decision. One exhibit is the credit history of the buyers. If they are from another state, their credit report may be tardy in arriving.

The buyers' income will be verified by their employers. On the rare occasion when cooperation is not forthcoming, payroll stubs or income tax returns will be brought in by the applicant instead.

An unpleasant surprise may turn up at this point. Forgotten or unknown judgments against the buyers may surface, even as they might in your own records. These are not fatal to the application. The buyer can clear them by paying them off.

More serious is the discovery that the prospective purchasers have been less than frank about their credit history. A bankruptcy they "forgot" to mention, or several large debts presently outstanding, can seriously threaten their chances for the loan.

If such problems develop, you have a right to be notified, for time is money in your situation. If there is a chance that the transaction might fall through, you should be told at once. Your lawyer or broker can assess the chances of failure.

You can always put your house back on the market, subject to nonperformance of the existing contract. This enables you to start searching for another buyer immediately, pending the outcome of the present problem. It is, of course, a serious step and should be considered only when the outlook becomes dark.

THE DEAL THAT FAILS

If your transaction falls apart, your lawyer's help will be essential in advising you of your rights or responsibilities. Should you back out for no legally acceptable reason, you may be liable for damages, and even for a type of suit—unique to real estate—that calls for *specific performance*. The concept of specific performance is based on the fact that each property is different and that money damages may not adequately compensate the buyer who insists on purchasing your specific house.

Even if the buyers are agreeable to dropping their claims, remember that your real estate broker, having performed the services for which retained, may be entitled to full commission. Depending on circumstances, the broker may press a claim for the commission, or may waive it in favor of your goodwill and the hope of future business.

If the buyer backs out with no adequate reason, you may be entitled to damages; and your broker may be entitled to a commission, for which you are liable. Your lawyer will know whether legal action is indicated. To avoid a lawsuit, the buyer often abandons the earnest money deposit. Sometimes that sum is then divided between seller and broker.

Occasionally, a transaction falls apart with no one at fault. Certain conditions in the contract may be impossible to fulfill; the buyers may fail to secure the mortgage loan, or you may be unable to provide marketable title. In such a case, the purchase contract may specify that the buyers are to receive full return of their deposit.

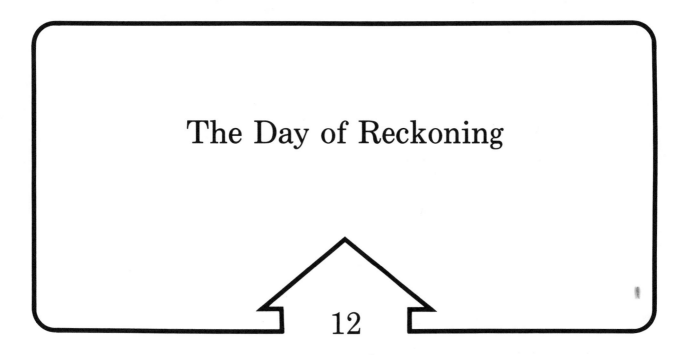

The Day of Reckoning

In your area, the process may be called settlement, transfer, closing, passing papers or going to escrow. It may be held in the county courthouse, the lending institution, a title company, a real estate office or an attorney's office. (In the latter case, etiquette may prescribe that the younger lawyer volunteer to go to the office of the older one.)

What does a typical settlement look like? In one city, buyers, sellers, attorneys, brokers and a paralegal from the lending institution may gather around a long table. In another area, there may not be a meeting at all; details are handled by mail through a special escrow company. In no aspect of real estate does local custom vary more.

Whatever the practice, however, the skeleton of the transaction remains the same.

- The seller proves marketable title.
- The buyer pays for the property.
- The seller delivers the deed.

If new financing is involved, settlement is complicated by the signing and delivery of a bond and mortgage or, in some states, a trust deed.

The deed is a bill of sale for real estate. You do not want to sign and deliver the deed until you receive your money. The buyers, on the other hand, cannot pay you until they receive their mortgage loan. The lender will not turn over the money without receiving a mortgage. But the buyers cannot sign a mortgage until they own the property. It is obvious that the various transactions must take place at one time and in precise order.

If you are unable to attend the closing, your lawyer may arrange for you to sign the deed ahead of time; this one act is your major contribution to the ceremonies. Just remember to leave the front-door key also.

THE SETTLEMENT DATE

As soon as a firm mortgage commitment has been secured by the purchasers, the person in charge of the settlement can arrange a date suitable to all parties. Additional paperwork may be required, several attorneys may need to dovetail their schedules; your moving plans and the buyers' must be considered.

If your contract stipulated a certain closing date, and that day comes and goes, the contract is still in force. In most cases, the day specified is simply a target date. Only if time is made of the essence is it an "or else" item.

PRELIMINARY PREPARATIONS

You have held your garage sale, notified the post office and magazine publishers, talked with the telephone company, secured a mover and finished your packing. What next?

Plan on leaving the house in "broom-clean" condition: if not spotless, it should be neat at least. Broom-clean condition assumes that piles of old newspapers have been removed, the refrigerator is empty, trash has been removed or left in a tidy fashion and floors have received one final sweeping.

The buyers may request a last-minute walk-through of the house. This is a reasonable and prudent step for them. They want to check for newly broken windowpanes, make sure you are leaving the stove you promised and uncover any last-minute problems before closing, rather than afterwards. As usual, it is helpful if they are accompanied by the broker, with your participation limited to a few cordial bits of information or advice about the property.

Call your utility companies and arrange for final readings of your meters. It may be practical to arrange for the fuel oil tank to be filled completely, so that you will know how much you are leaving behind. You can pay this bill and settle later with the buyers for the full tank.

Make a last-minute check of the fine print on your purchase contract to see that you have kept your promises regarding items such as fireplace equipment, smoke alarms and playground equipment.

When you go to the closing, be sure to take all door keys and remote controls for your garage doors.

ADJUSTMENTS AT CLOSING

You and the buyers have a number of financial details to settle. Property taxes will undoubtedly be adjusted. In some areas, taxes are paid in advance. In this case, if you met your last bill, you have paid for the year ahead. If you are closing at, for example, the end of the fourth month, the buyers will receive a house with taxes paid for the year, and they should reimburse you for the eight months to come.

In other areas, property taxes are paid in arrears, as opposed to in advance. The bill for the current year will not be due for eight months. Since you have lived in the house for four months, you should pay a sum equaling four months' taxes to the new owners, who will later pay for the full year.

In the same way, you will adjust water or sewer charges.

If there are tenants, you should turn over any security deposits and advance rents to the new owners, who will return these monies to the tenants when they vacate the house.

If the buyers are assuming your mortgage, interest payments will be calculated so that you pay for the days that you owned the house. The new owners will have to meet the next bill, which will cover the present month's interest.

Your present mortgage payments may include monthly charges for tax or insurance fees. Your lender sets up an escrow or reserve account for the purpose of collecting these funds for later disbursal. If the mortgage is being paid off, rather than assumed, you will receive the balance of this account directly from the lender. Otherwise, the new owners will reimburse you for monies in this account, which remains with the mortgage.

A sample RESPA settlement form is shown in Table 12-1.

You may be asked for a bill of sale on furniture or appliances being left with the property. The buyers pay for the full tank of oil you left behind; if costs have changed, custom dictates that you receive today's price.

The attorneys for both parties, or the persons in charge of the settlement session, agree upon figures for all these adjustments and gradually fill out their closing statements.

A sample closing statement is shown in Table 12-2.

SELLER'S COSTS

Some closing costs are negotiable between seller and buyer, although the last minute is not the time for doing so. Other costs are yours and may include:

Liens and claims against your property. Before the purchasers will take title, they usually insist that you clear up unpaid taxes, your present mortgage, home improvement loans, mechanics' liens, judgments and any other liens on record.

Unpaid special assessments. In the absence of any other agreement, you may be expected to pay in one lump sum special charges levied against your area for new sidewalks, street lighting or other improvements.

Transfer tax. In some states or localities, a tax is due when property is transferred, and you may find a legal provision that this one expense be paid by the seller.

Attorney or escrow agent. You owe your own attorney's fees. Beyond that, the question of who pays for settlement services is usually established by local practice.

Survey, title insurance, termite inspection. Again based on custom, the contract you sign dictates whether you or the buyer will pay.

Prepayment penalty. You may owe a penalty fee to the lender if your conventional loan is being paid off before its due date. State laws have been whittling away at these charges, however.

TABLE 12-1: RESPA Settlement Form

A. **SETTLEMENT STATEMENT** U.S. DEPARTMENT OF HOUSING AND URBAN DEVELOPMENT		
HUD-1 Rev. 3/86		OMB NO. 2502-0265 (Exp. 12-31-86)

B. TYPE OF LOAN				
1. ☐ FHA 2. ☐ FmHA 3. ☒ CONV. UNINS.	6. File Number		7. Loan Number	8.Mortgage Insurance Claim Case Number
4. ☐ VA 5. ☐ CONV. INS.				

C. NOTE: *This form is furnished to give you a statement of actual settlement costs. Amounts paid to and by the settlement agent are shown. Items marked "(p.o.c.)" were paid outside the closing; they are shown here for informational purposes and are not included in the totals.*

D. NAME AND ADDRESS OF BORROWER:	E. NAME AND ADDRESS OF SELLER:	F. NAME AND ADDRESS OF LENDER:
Brook Redemann 22 King Court Riverdale, Illinois	John and Joanne Iuro 3045 North Racine Avenue Riverdale, Illinois	Thrift Federal Savings 1100 Fountain Plaza Riverdale, Illinois

G. PROPERTY LOCATION: 3045 North Racine Avenue Riverdale, Illinois	H. SETTLEMENT AGENT: Open Door Real Estate Company PLACE OF SETTLEMENT: Open Door Real Estate Company 720 Main Street, Riverdale, Illinois	I. SETTLEMENT DATE: June 15, 19

J. SUMMARY OF BORROWER'S TRANSACTION		K. SUMMARY OF SELLER'S TRANSACTION	
100. *GROSS AMOUNT DUE FROM BORROWER:*		**400.** *GROSS AMOUNT DUE TO SELLER:*	
101. Contract sales price	$115,000.00	401. Contract sales price	$115,000.00
102. Personal property		402. Personal property	
103. Settlement charges to borrower (line 1400)	5,075.84	403.	
104.		404.	
105.		405.	
Adjustments for items paid by seller in advance		*Adjustments for items paid by seller in advance*	
106. City/town taxes to		406. City/town taxes to	
107. County taxes to		407. County taxes to	
108. Assesments to		408. Assesments to	
109.		409.	
110.		410.	
111.		411.	
112.		412.	
120. *GROSS AMOUNT DUE FROM BORROWER*	$120,075.84	**420.** *GROSS AMOUNT DUE TO SELLER*	$115,000.00
200. *AMOUNTS PAID BY OR IN BEHALF OF BORROWER:*		**500.** *REDUCTIONS IN AMOUNT DUE TO SELLER:*	
201. Deposit or earnest money	23,000.00	501. Excess deposit (see instructions)	
202. Principal amount of new loan(s)	92,000.00	502. Settlement charges to seller (line 1400)	8,080.00
203. Existing loan(s) taken subject to		503. Existing loan(s) taken subject to	
204.		504. Payoff of first mortgage loan	57,964.47
205.		505. Payoff of second mortgage loan	
206.		506.	
207.		507.	
208.		508.	
209.		509.	
Adjustments for items unpaid by seller		*Adjustments for items unpaid by seller*	
210. City/town taxes to		510. City/town taxes to	
211. County taxes to	790.63	511. County taxes to	790.63
212. Assesments to		512. Assesments to	
213.		513.	
214.		514.	
215.		515.	
216.		516.	
217.		517.	
218.		518.	
219.		519.	
220. *TOTAL PAID BY/FOR BORROWER*	$115,790.63	**520.** *TOTAL REDUCTION AMOUNT DUE SELLER*	$ 66,835.10
300. *CASH AT SETTLEMENT FROM/TO BORROWER*		**600.** *CASH AT SETTLEMENT TO/FROM SELLER*	
301. Gross amount due from borrower (line 120)	120,075.84	601. Gross amount due to seller (line 420)	115,000.00
302. Less amounts paid by/for borrower (line 220)	(115,790.63)	602. Less reductions in amount due seller (line 520)	(66,835.10)
303. *CASH (☐ FROM) (☐ TO) BORROWER*	$ 4,285.21	**603.** *CASH (☐ TO) (☐ FROM) SELLER*	$ 48,164.90

I have carefully reviewed the HUD-1 Settlement Statement and to the best of my knowledge and belief, it is a true and accurate statement of all receipts and disbursements made on my account or by me in this transaction. I further certify that I have received a copy of the HUD-1 Settlement Statement.

_____   _____
Borrower   Seller

_____   _____
Borrower   Seller

The HUD-1 Settlement Statement which I have prepared is a true and accurate account of this transaction. I have caused or will cause the funds to be disbursed in accordance with this statement.

_____   _____
Settlement Agent   Date

Warning: It is a crime to knowingly make false statements to the United States on this or any other similar form. Penalties upon conviction can include a fine and imprisonment. For details see: Title 18 U.S. Code Section 1001 and Section 1010.

2128 (6-86) 41b

TABLE 12-1:   (continued)

— 2 —

L. SETTLEMENT CHARGES			
700. TOTAL SALES/BROKER'S COMMISSION based on price $ 115,000 @ 6 % =$6,900.00		PAID FROM BORROWER'S FUNDS AT SETTLEMENT	PAID FROM SELLER'S FUNDS AT SETTLEMENT
Division of Commission (line 700) as follows:			
701. $ to			
702. $ to			
703. Commission paid at Settlement			$6,900.00
704.			
800. ITEMS PAYABLE IN CONNECTION WITH LOAN			
801. Loan Origination Fee %		$ 920.00	
802. Loan Discount 2 %		$1,840.00	
803. Appraisal Fee $125.00 to Swift Appraisal		POC	
804. Credit Report $ 60.00 to ACME Credit Bureau		POC	
805. Lender's Inspection Fee			
806. Mortgage Insurance Application Fee to			
807. Assumption Fee			
808. Application Fee			
809. Wholesale Interest Differential Fee			
810. Underwriting Fee			
811. Buydown Fee			
812. Commitment Fee			
813.			
814. Messenger Service			
815. Shortfall			
816.			
817.			
818.			
819.			
900. ITEMS REQUIRED BY LENDER TO BE PAID IN ADVANCE			
901. Interest from 6/16/88 to 6/30/88 @ $ 25.556 /day		383.34	
902. Mortgage Insurance Premium for months to			
903. Hazard Insurance Premium for 1 years to Hite Insurance Co.		345.00	
904. One-Time FHA Insurance Premium			
905. VA Funding Fee			
906.			
907.			
1000. RESERVES DEPOSITED WITH LENDER			
1001. Hazard insurance 3 months @ $ 28.75 per month		86.25	
1002. Mortgage insurance months @ $ per month			
1003. City property taxes months @ $ per month			
1004. County property taxes 7 months @ $ 143.75 per month		1,006.25	
1005. Annual assessments months @ $ per month			
1006. months @ $ per month			
1007. months @ $ per month			
1008. months @ $ per month			
1100. TITLE CHARGES			
1101. Settlement or closing fee to			
1102. Abstract or title search to			
1103. Title examination to			
1104. Title insurance binder to			10.00
1105. Document preparation to			
1106. Notary fees to			
1107. Attorney's fees to		300.00	400.00
(includes above items numbers;)			
1108. Title insurance to			540.00
(includes above items numbers;)			
1109. Lender's coverage $ 395.00			
1110. Owner's coverage $ 145.00			
1111. Tax Service Contract Fee to			
1112. Amortization Schedule to			
1113.			
1114.			
1115.			
1116.			
1200. GOVERNMENT RECORDING AND TRANSFER CHARGES			
1201. Recording Fees: Deed $ 10.00 ; Mortgage $ 10.00 ; Releases $ 10.00		20.00	10.00
1202. City/county tax/stamps: Deed $; Mortgage $			
1203. State tax/Stamps: Deed $ 115.00 ; Mortgage $			115.00
1204. Record two documents to clear title			20.00
1205.			
1300. ADDITIONAL SETTLEMENT CHARGES			
1301. Survey to		175.00	
1302. Pest inspection to			85.00
1303.			
1304.			
1305.			
1400. TOTAL SETTLEMENT CHARGES (enter on lines 103, Section J and 502, Section K)		$5,075.84	$8,080.00

2126 (6-88) 41b Reverse   HUD-1 Rev. 5/76

TABLE 12-2: Seller's Closing Statement

SELLER'S CREDITS

Sale Price _____ $ 89,500.00

ADJUSTMENT OF TAXES

School Tax	to	Amount $ 1176.35	Adj. 10	mos. 18	days $	1,039.16
City/School Tax	to	Amount $_____	Adj. _____	mos._____	days $	
County Tax 19___		Amount $ 309.06	Adj. 4	mos. 18	days $	118.52
Village Tax	to	Amount $_____	Adj. _____	mos._____	days $	
City Tax Embellishments		Amount $_____	Adj. _____	mos. _____	days $	

Total Seller's Credits $ 90,657.68

PURCHASER'S CREDITS

Deposit with Nothnagle	$ 500.00
(Assumed) (New) Mortgage with seller	$ 40,000.00
12% interest, 15 years, payments	$
$ 480.07, beginning	$
	$
	$
	$
	$

Total Purchaser's Credits $ 40,500.00

Cash (Rec'd) (Paid) at Closing $ 50,157.68

EXPENSES OF PURCHASER		**EXPENSES OF SELLER**	
Mortgage Tax .... $_____		Title Search Fee .... $ 220.00	
Recording Mortgage............. $_____		Transfer Tax on Deed .... $ 358.00	
Recording Deed.................. $_____		Filing of Gains Tax Affidavit .. $ 1.00	
		Discharge Recording Fee ...... $_____	
ESCROWS:		Mortgage Tax .... $ 100.00	
___ mos. insurance $ _____		Surveyor's Fees .... $_____	
___ mos. school tax $ _____		Points .... $_____	
___ mos. county tax $ _____		Mortgage Payoff .... $_____	
___ mos. village tax $ _____		Real Estate Commission ...... $ 487.00	
PMI FHA Insurance $ _____		Water Escrow .... $_____	
Total: $_____		19 __ school tax ...... $ 1,182.14	
Bank Attorney Fee................ $_____		Federal express.......... $ 14.00	
Points.......................... $_____		.... $_____	
Title Insurance.................... $_____		.... $_____	
Interest.......................... $_____		Legal Fee.................... $ 550.00	
.... $_____		Total....................... $ 7,295.14	
.... $_____			
.... $_____		Cash Received: $ 50,157.68	
Legal Fee........................ $_____		Less Seller's Expenses: $ 7,295.14	
Total........................... $_____		Net Proceeds: $ 42,862.54	
Cash paid to Seller: $			
Plus Purchaser's Expenses: $ _____			
Total Disbursed: $			

TAKING BACK MORTGAGE

If you will be holding a first or second mortgage or a land contract yourself, the document can be drawn up by your attorney. If the buyer offers to pay for preparing the mortgage, be sure to have your own lawyer approve or amend it. In most states, the mortgage you will receive consists of two parts: a note or bond (personal promise to pay back the loan) and the mortgage, which is a claim against the property if the promises made in the bond are not kept.

Just as the buyer is advised to put the deed on record immediately, so should you see that the mortgage is promptly entered into the public records. This will give you priority, ahead of later claims on the property, if there is trouble in the future.

If you are paying off a present mortgage, that fact, along with a certificate of satisfaction, should be filed in the public records at this time.

ACTUAL TRANSFER OF TITLE

When you are in possession of the largest check you may ever have (it should be a certified check or money order, by the way), you are ready to turn your property over to the new owner. As the seller, you sign the deed. It may take one of several forms, depending on the situation, state law and local custom:

- A quitclaim deed simply transfers any rights you may have in the property.
- A special warranty deed (or bargain and sale deed with covenants) transfers your rights and promises that you have in no undisclosed way encumbered the property.
- A full warranty deed further guarantees the buyer's protection against claims raised by any other parties.

Because the transfer of title gives the new owner your rights in the real estate, you are called the grantor. Often, only the grantor signs the deed. Title to the property transfers at the moment you place the deed into the hands of the grantee. "Signed, sealed and delivered" is the old phrase, and at the moment of physical delivery and acceptance of the deed, the property is no longer yours.

Tax Considerations When You Sell

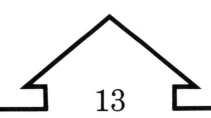

13

The sale of your home will be reported to the Internal Revenue Service (IRS) on a 1099 Form similar to those you may have received that report interest and dividend payments. This procedure has been in effect since 1987.

Responsibility for submitting the report lies with the party in charge of the closing: title or escrow company, mortgage lender, seller's or buyer's attorney, real estate broker or even, if no one else files the report, the buyer. Your social security number must be included on the report, and so you will probably be asked to furnish it at closing, along with your new address, so that you can be sent a copy of the 1099.

Even if no tax is due on your profit, and even if you have suffered a nondeductible loss, it is important that the sale be reported on your federal income tax return. If you ignore the matter, your return will not match up with the 1099 the IRS receives. Eventually the matter will come back to haunt you, with irritating paperwork and correspondence at the very least.

You report the sale of your own primary residence on Form 2119. The sale of a vacation home or rental property is reported on Schedule D. For further information, you may want to call the IRS at 800-829-3676 and ask them to send you a free copy of Publication 523, *Tax Information on Selling Your Home.* Professional assistance in preparing your tax return is usually required for the year in which you sell your home. If large sums or complicated matters are involved, it is wise to consult an accountant or lawyer who specializes in tax planning before the sale.

Free help is available from the IRS itself, either by phone or in person. As income tax time approaches, IRS and tax specialists are increasingly busy; you will receive more thorough help if you seek it as early as possible.

All of the following information applies to federal income tax. Your state may follow the federal regulations, or you may find that its rules vary considerably.

HOME SELLER'S TAX ADVANTAGES

Several favorable tax breaks are available for the treatment of profit realized on the sale of your main home, known to the IRS as your principal residence. In general, this is considered to be the place where you reside most of the time. It may be a mobile home or a houseboat, a cooperative or condominium apartment. If you own one home, but live in another, which you rent, your principal residence is the rented house, and no special tax treatment would apply to the sale of the house you own.

SELLING AT A LOSS

If you sell your own home (or a vacation home you don't rent out) at a loss, no deduction is allowed on your income tax return. You may not claim a capital loss. The rules, of course, are different for business or rental property, which qualify for capital gain or loss treatment in the ordinary way, on Schedule D.

COMPUTING YOUR COST BASIS

The first step in calculating your profit is to determine your cost basis. To the original price of your home, add certain closing costs and the money you have spent on improvements over the years. Improvements are permanent additions to the value of your property; repairs and redecorating don't count. A new roof or furnace counts as an improvement; fixing the old ones would be considered repairs and do not add to your cost basis.

If you did not buy your home, special provisions apply. If you built it, you may not include as part of cost basis the value of your labor, or any friend's labor that you did not pay for. If you received the house as a gift, your cost basis is generally the giver's cost basis. If you inherited the house, you use a *stepped-up* basis, usually the value of the property when the former owner died.

Items you must subtract from cost basis include any losses you may have deducted on income tax returns for fire or other cause, money you received in return for easements, energy improvement credits you may have claimed or depreciation you may have claimed when all or part of your home was formerly used for home office or as a rental.

Use Table 13-1 to calculate your adjusted cost basis, and Table 13-2 to calculate your gain.

SPECIAL TAX BREAKS

Two special tax treatments are available for the sale of your own home:

- Homeowners of any age must postpone tax on all or part of their profit if they purchase another main home within two years of selling the first one.
- Those aged 55 years and older at the time of sale may choose, once in a lifetime, to take up to $125,000 profit with no federal tax due ever.

TABLE 13-1:   Calculating Your Adjusted Cost Basis

Add:	Purchase price of your home	$ _____
	Attorney fees when you bought	_____
	Tax assessments for street or sidewalks	_____
	Amounts spent for:	
	Fences	_____
	Paving (not maintaining) driveway	_____
	Wall-to-wall carpeting	_____
	Permanent fixtures	_____
	New roof or furnace	_____
	Finishing basement or attic	_____
	Adding new bath	_____
	New (not repaired) plumbing	_____
	New wiring	_____
	Extensive remodeling	_____
	Building an addition	_____
	Insulation	_____
	Storm windows and screens	_____
	Permanent landscaping	_____
	Other _____	_____
	_____	_____
	Total of above Items	_____
Subtract:	Losses (fire, etc.) deducted on income tax returns	_____
	Amount received for easements, etc.	_____
	Depreciation claimed in past years	_____
	Deferred profit on previous residence(s)	_____
Adjusted Cost Basis		_____

BUYING ANOTHER HOME

If you buy another principal residence of equal or greater value within two years before or after you sell the first one, you do not owe tax immediately on your profit. Instead, your profit is subtracted from the cost basis of the next home. Here's how it works:

You buy Home A for $50,000 and sell it for $80,000. You promptly buy Home B for $100,000. The $30,000 profit you

TABLE 13-2: Calculating Your Gain

To compute the amount of your profit (known to the IRS as your gain), subtract adjusted cost basis from the sales price. You may also subtract certain costs of selling. Last-minute fix-up costs are *not* deductible at this point. Any prepayment penalty on a mortgage you pay off may be deductible as prepaid interest, elsewhere on your income tax return.

Calculating Your Profit

Sales Price	$ _____
Subtract cost basis	_____
Subtract expenses paid by seller:	_____
Real estate commissions	_____
Legal fees	_____
Advertising expenses	_____
Points paid to your buyer's lender	_____
Title insurance	_____
Survey	_____
Transfer taxes and closing costs	_____
Adjusted sales price	_____

realized on the sale of A is not presently taxed. Instead, the cost basis of Home B is considered to be $100,000 minus that untaxed $30,000. Your cost basis on B will be $70,000.

Later, you sell Home B for $125,000. Subtracting your cost basis of $70,000 gives you taxable profit of $55,000. Looking at it another way, your profit on A was $30,000, your profit on B was $25,000, giving you a combined profit of $55,000.

This process can be repeated indefinitely (not more than once every two years), piling up untaxed profits on a string of more expensive homes.

If your replacement home costs less than the first home sold for, you will defer tax on part of your profit, and pay tax only on the remainder. Here's how this might look:

You bought Home A for $50,000 and sold it for $80,000. You then move to a smaller home costing $75,000. Tax on $25,000 of your profit is deferred. You will owe income tax now on the $5,000 of your profit that actually remained in your pocket once the dust had cleared.

These examples are merely skeletal, and don't take into account any adjustments to cost basis and sales price.

Miscellaneous Provisions

If you are using part of your property for a farm, a home office, rental apartment or other business property, your sale is treated, for tax purposes, as two separate transactions. The chance to defer taxes will apply to that percentage of the real estate considered to be your residence. The balance of your proceeds will be taxed as if you had sold business property.

If your home is rented out just before you sell it (particularly for a period exceeding one year), the house may have been converted to business property and may not qualify for the special tax provisions on the sale of a residence. The law does allow a temporary period of rental simply for convenience, however, without jeopardizing the house's status as your residence.

Complex calculations apply to situations in which two homes are sold by a newly married couple, or when those recently separated replace one home with two. In each case, regulations are set up for the amount of profit on which tax may be deferred. Seek professional assistance for tax returns with any unusual conditions.

For homeowners of any age, then, and in almost every case, tax on the profit from the sale of one's home can be postponed indefinitely, probably not becoming due until one's last home is sold and no replacement home is purchased.

And, if you wait until you have turned 55, you might choose to sell your long-time home and use that $125,000 tax-free provision to cover the deferred taxes on profit from several houses back, so that you get off free in the end.

THAT $125,000 EXCLUSION

This pleasant tax provision allows for a once-in-a-lifetime sale with profit up to $125,000 and with no federal tax due, ever. This treatment can also include the untaxed profits from previous homes, to a total of $125,000. You choose the time when you want to use this tax treatment.

You qualify if:

- You have owned and occupied the property as your principal residence for at least three of the five years before the sale.

- You are aged 55 years or older on the date the sale closes.
- Neither you nor your spouse, if you have one, has ever taken advantage of this exclusion before. The exclusion applies only once in a lifetime, and only once to a couple.

If a married couple owns the house, only one need meet the age, ownership and occupancy test for the sale to qualify. Problems arise, though, if either spouse (even one not officially listed as an owner) has used the exclusion previously. Even a nonowner spouse must join in the choice to use this tax break. Neither can ever use it again, nor could a new spouse of either one in a later marriage.

Two older persons contemplating marriage, who intend to sell their homes and buy another, should consider closing both sales before their wedding date. In this case, each would be entitled to claim a full $125,000 exclusion.

More Miscellaneous Provisions

If part of your home has been used for rental or business, again you treat your sale as two separate transactions, applying the $125,000 exclusion to that fraction of your profit attributable to your own residence.

Different rules applied to a less-generous, once-in-a-lifetime opportunity before July 26, 1978. Those who took advantage of the old provision may also have one turn at the new $125,000 exclusion.

It is possible to qualify for the exclusion, in some cases, even if it was a now-deceased spouse who owned and occupied the house for the required number of years.

You may accumulate the necessary three years' occupancy even with temporary absences during the five-year period. Rental for less than two years during the five-year period will not alter your eligibility.

If you change your mind and wish you hadn't used the $125,000 exclusion, or if you pay the tax and then decide to use the exclusion, you have a three-year period in which to amend your income tax return and make the change.

Although the law makes constant reference to the role of the spouse, who must join in choosing to use the exclusion, the opportunity is, of course, available to unmarried home-owners 55 and older as well. Unmarried joint owners (brother and sister, for example, or unrelated persons) who sell their home may each use the full exclusion on his or her share of profit. This assumes, of course, that the house is the primary residence for each of them.

NO SPECIAL TAX BREAKS

If you do not buy a replacement residence, and if you do not take the 55-and-older exclusion, you will owe income tax on the profit from the sale of real estate.

Capital gains. Your profit is classified as short-term or long-term capital gains, depending on how long you have owned the house. At various times, Congress allowed you to disregard tax on 50 percent of your long-term capital gains, or 40 percent. The Tax Reform Act of 1986 reduced the untaxed amount to zero, which meant that all of your gain was taxable along with ordinary income. Starting in 1991, even if you are in a higher tax bracket, capital gains cannot be taxed at more than 28 percent.

Installment treatment. If you "take back" financing for all or part of the purchase price (hold a mortgage with the buy-ers paying you monthly), you will owe tax on your profit year by year, as you collect it, unless that profit is covered by one of the homeseller's tax breaks.

GIVING YOUR HOUSE TO THE KIDS

If you sell your home to your children, or transfer title in any way that does not involve the open market, you have a trans-action that may be ruled "not arm's length." Before you take any such action, discuss with an attorney the income or estate tax consequences. The IRS has definite ideas about the inter-est you might charge your children if you took back a mortgage from them.

The gift of one's homestead to a son or daughter may mean the elderly parent loses favorable property tax treat-ment, becomes liable for payment of state gift tax or faces an unexpected problem in the event of a child's divorce or bankruptcy. In certain circumstances, it is more prudent for children to wait to inherit property (with a stepped-up basis) than to receive it as a gift. The disposition of real estate should be considered in the wider framework of estate planning, and professional guidance is essential.

Afterword

IF YOU ARE PLEASED WITH AN AGENT

If you are pleased with the service you received from your real estate broker, there are several ways to show it. Agents are used to taking clients out to lunch or dinner; it's a real thrill when you proffer the invitation instead. Any small token—a bottle of wine, a plant for the office—will be a welcome surprise. Your agent will proudly show an invitation to your housewarming back at the office.

It is remarkable how few satisfied clients take the trouble to write to a real estate office. A letter addressed to your salesperson's supervising broker will be read aloud at a sales meeting, posted on a bulletin board and treasured by the agent involved.

Brokers work for commissions, of course, but they enjoy appreciation. Selling can be a lonely and frustrating job; complaints come in daily, but praise is rare. Particularly gratifying to any agent are future referrals. The standard answer to, "What can I do to repay your extra care?" is a cheerful, "Just send me a client!"

APPENDIX I
Monthly Payment Tables

Your buyer's monthly mortgage payment will include interest on the amount borrowed, plus a bit more intended to whittle down the principal still owed. As the loan is gradually paid, less interest is owed, and a larger portion of each payment can go toward principal.

The following tables cover loan terms of one to 40 years, with interest rates between 4 percent and 19⅞ percent.

To find your buyer's mortgage payment:

1. Search the left-hand column until you find the interest rate on your loan.

2. Search the top line for the number of years the buyer will be making payments.

3. Follow the percentage line across and the "number of years" column down until the two intersect. The figure indicated is the monthly dollar amount necessary to amortize (pay off) a loan of $1,000 in the given time, at the given rate of interest.

   Example: If a 10 percent loan has a term of 25 years, the two lines intersect at 9.0870. This means that $9.087 a month, for 25 years, would pay off a loan of $1,000 at 10 percent interest.

4. Multiply the figure indicated by the number of thousands being borrowed. This gives you the monthly payment necessary to amortize the entire loan.

    Example: If, in the example given with step 3, the loan amount is $74,500, this represents 74.5 thousands. Multiplying $9.087 by 74.5 gives you $676.9815, which would be rounded off to a monthly payment of $676.98.

The figure you have found represents principal and interest only; if a lending institution requires escrow for taxes and insurance, one-twelfth of those costs must be added to arrive at PITI payment.

MONTHLY PAYMENT TO AMORTIZE A LOAN OF $1,000

				Term of Loan				
Interest Rate	1 Year	2 Years	3 Years	4 Years	5 Years	6 Years	7 Years	8 Years
4.000%	85.1499	43.4249	29.5240	22.5791	18.4165	15.6452	13.6688	12.1893
4.125%	85.2070	43.4806	29.5796	22.6350	18.4730	15.7022	13.7264	12.2475
4.250%	85.2642	43.5363	29.6353	22.6911	18.5296	15.7593	13.7842	12.3059
4.375%	85.3213	43.5920	29.6911	22.7472	18.5862	15.8166	13.8421	12.3645
4.500%	85.3785	43.6478	29.7469	22.8035	18.6430	15.8740	13.9002	12.4232
4.625%	85.4357	43.7036	29.8028	22.8598	18.6999	15.9316	13.9584	12.4822
4.750%	85.4930	43.7595	29.8588	22.9162	18.7569	15.9892	14.0167	12.5412
4.875%	85.5502	43.8154	29.9148	22.9727	18.8140	16.0470	14.0752	12.6005
5.000%	85.6075	43.8714	29.9709	23.0293	18.8712	16.1049	14.1339	12.6599
5.125%	85.6648	43.9274	30.0271	23.0860	18.9286	16.1630	14.1927	12.7195
5.250%	85.7221	43.9834	30.0833	23.1427	18.9860	16.2212	14.2517	12.7793
5.375%	85.7794	44.0395	30.1396	23.1996	19.0435	16.2795	14.3108	12.8392
5.500%	85.8368	44.0957	30.1959	23.2565	19.1012	16.3379	14.3700	12.8993
5.625%	85.8942	44.1518	30.2523	23.3135	19.1589	16.3964	14.4294	12.9596
5.750%	85.9516	44.2080	30.3088	23.3706	19.2168	16.4551	14.4890	13.0200
5.875%	86.0090	44.2643	30.3653	23.4278	19.2747	16.5139	14.5487	13.0807
6.000%	86.0664	44.3206	30.4219	23.4850	19.3328	16.5729	14.6086	13.1414
6.125%	86.1239	44.3770	30.4786	23.5424	19.3910	16.6320	14.6686	13.2024
6.250%	86.1814	44.4333	30.5353	23.5998	19.4493	16.6912	14.7287	13.2635
6.375%	86.2389	44.4898	30.5921	23.6573	19.5077	16.7505	14.7890	13.3248
6.500%	86.2964	44.5463	30.6490	23.7150	19.5661	16.8099	14.8494	13.3862
6.625%	86.3540	44.6028	30.7059	23.7726	19.6248	16.8695	14.9100	13.4479
6.750%	86.4115	44.6593	30.7629	23.8304	19.6835	16.9292	14.9708	13.5096
6.875%	86.4691	44.7159	30.8200	23.8883	19.7423	16.9890	15.0316	13.5716
7.000%	86.5267	44.7726	30.8771	23.9462	19.8012	17.0490	15.0927	13.6337
7.125%	86.5844	44.8293	30.9343	24.0043	19.8602	17.1091	15.1539	13.6960
7.250%	86.6420	44.8860	30.9915	24.0624	19.9194	17.1693	15.2152	13.7585
7.375%	86.6997	44.9428	31.0488	24.1206	19.9786	17.2296	15.2767	13.8211
7.500%	86.7574	44.9996	31.1062	24.1789	20.0379	17.2901	15.3383	13.8839
7.625%	86.8151	45.0565	31.1637	24.2373	20.0974	17.3507	15.4000	13.9468
7.750%	86.8729	45.1134	31.2212	24.2957	20.1570	17.4114	15.4620	14.0099
7.875%	86.9306	45.1703	31.2787	24.3543	20.2166	17.4723	15.5240	14.0732
8.000%	86.9884	45.2273	31.3364	24.4129	20.2764	17.5332	15.5862	14.1367
8.125%	87.0462	45.2843	31.3941	24.4716	20.3363	17.5943	15.6486	14.2003
8.250%	87.1041	45.3414	31.4518	24.5304	20.3963	17.6556	15.7111	14.2641
8.375%	87.1619	45.3985	31.5096	24.5893	20.4563	17.7169	15.7737	14.3280
8.500%	87.2198	45.4557	31.5675	24.6483	20.5165	17.7784	15.8365	14.3921
8.625%	87.2777	45.5129	31.6255	24.7074	20.5768	17.8400	15.8994	14.4564
8.750%	87.3356	45.5701	31.6835	24.7665	20.6372	17.9017	15.9625	14.5208
8.875%	87.3935	45.6274	31.7416	24.8257	20.6977	17.9636	16.0257	14.5854
9.000%	87.4515	45.6847	31.7997	24.8850	20.7584	18.0255	16.0891	14.6502
9.125%	87.5095	45.7421	31.8579	24.9444	20.8191	18.0876	16.1526	14.7151
9.250%	87.5675	45.7995	31.9162	25.0039	20.8799	18.1499	16.2162	14.7802
9.375%	87.6255	45.8570	31.9745	25.0635	20.9408	18.2122	16.2800	14.8455
9.500%	87.6835	45.9145	32.0329	25.1231	21.0019	18.2747	16.3440	14.9109
9.625%	87.7416	45.9720	32.0914	25.1829	21.0630	18.3373	16.4081	14.9765
9.750%	87.7997	46.0296	32.1499	25.2427	21.1242	18.4000	16.4723	15.0422
9.875%	87.8578	46.0873	32.2085	25.3026	21.1856	18.4629	16.5367	15.1081

MONTHLY PAYMENT TO AMORTIZE A LOAN OF $1,000

Term of Loan

Interest Rate	9 Years	10 Years	11 Years	12 Years	13 Years	14 Years	15 Years	16 Years
4.000%	11.0410	10.1245	9.3767	8.7553	8.2312	7.7835	7.3969	7.0600
4.125%	11.0998	10.1840	9.4368	8.8161	8.2926	7.8456	7.4597	7.1234
4.250%	11.1589	10.2438	9.4972	8.8772	8.3544	7.9080	7.5228	7.1872
4.375%	11.2181	10.3037	9.5579	8.9385	8.4164	7.9707	7.5862	7.2513
4.500%	11.2776	10.3638	9.6187	9.0001	8.4787	8.0338	7.6499	7.3158
4.625%	11.3372	10.4242	9.6798	9.0619	8.5413	8.0971	7.7140	7.3805
4.750%	11.3971	10.4848	9.7411	9.1240	8.6041	8.1607	7.7783	7.4456
4.875%	11.4571	10.5456	9.8027	9.1863	8.6672	8.2245	7.8430	7.5111
5.000%	11.5173	10.6066	9.8645	9.2489	8.7306	8.2887	7.9079	7.5768
5.125%	11.5777	10.6678	9.9265	9.3117	8.7942	8.3532	7.9732	7.6429
5.250%	11.6383	10.7292	9.9888	9.3748	8.8582	8.4179	8.0388	7.7093
5.375%	11.6990	10.7908	10.0512	9.4381	8.9223	8.4829	8.1047	7.7760
5.500%	11.7600	10.8526	10.1139	9.5017	8.9868	8.5483	8.1708	7.8430
5.625%	11.8212	10.9147	10.1769	9.5655	9.0515	8.6139	8.2373	7.9104
5.750%	11.8825	10.9769	10.2400	9.6296	9.1165	8.6797	8.3041	7.9781
5.875%	11.9440	11.0394	10.3034	9.6939	9.1817	8.7459	8.3712	8.0461
6.000%	12.0057	11.1021	10.3670	9.7585	9.2472	8.8124	8.4386	8.1144
6.125%	12.0677	11.1649	10.4309	9.8233	9.3130	8.8791	8.5062	8.1830
6.250%	12.1298	11.2280	10.4949	9.8884	9.3790	8.9461	8.5742	8.2519
6.375%	12.1920	11.2913	10.5592	9.9537	9.4453	9.0134	8.6425	8.3212
6.500%	12.2545	11.3548	10.6238	10.0192	9.5119	9.0810	8.7111	8.3908
6.625%	12.3172	11.4185	10.6885	10.0850	9.5787	9.1488	8.7799	8.4606
6.750%	12.3800	11.4824	10.7535	10.1510	9.6458	9.2169	8.8491	8.5308
6.875%	12.4431	11.5465	10.8187	10.2173	9.7131	9.2853	8.9185	8.6013
7.000%	12.5063	11.6108	10.8841	10.2838	9.7807	9.3540	8.9883	8.6721
7.125%	12.5697	11.6754	10.9497	10.3506	9.8486	9.4230	9.0583	8.7432
7.250%	12.6333	11.7401	11.0156	10.4176	9.9167	9.4922	9.1286	8.8146
7.375%	12.6971	11.8050	11.0817	10.4848	9.9851	9.5617	9.1992	8.8863
7.500%	12.7610	11.8702	11.1480	10.5523	10.0537	9.6314	9.2701	8.9583
7.625%	12.8252	11.9355	11.2145	10.6200	10.1226	9.7015	9.3413	9.0306
7.750%	12.8895	12.0011	11.2813	10.6879	10.1917	9.7718	9.4128	9.1032
7.875%	12.9540	12.0668	11.3483	10.7561	10.2611	9.8423	9.4845	9.1761
8.000%	13.0187	12.1328	11.4154	10.8245	10.3307	9.9132	9.5565	9.2493
8.125%	13.0836	12.1989	11.4829	10.8932	10.4006	9.9843	9.6288	9.3227
8.250%	13.1487	12.2653	11.5505	10.9621	10.4708	10.0557	9.7014	9.3965
8.375%	13.2139	12.3318	11.6183	11.0312	10.5412	10.1273	9.7743	9.4706
8.500%	13.2794	12.3986	11.6864	11.1006	10.6118	10.1992	9.8474	9.5449
8.625%	13.3450	12.4655	11.7547	11.1701	10.6827	10.2713	9.9208	9.6195
8.750%	13.4108	12.5327	11.8232	11.2400	10.7538	10.3438	9.9945	9.6945
8.875%	13.4767	12.6000	11.8919	11.3100	10.8252	10.4164	10.0684	9.7697
9.000%	13.5429	12.6676	11.9608	11.3803	10.8968	10.4894	10.1427	9.8452
9.125%	13.6093	12.7353	12.0299	11.4508	10.9687	10.5626	10.2172	9.9209
9.250%	13.6758	12.8033	12.0993	11.5216	11.0408	10.6360	10.2919	9.9970
9.375%	13.7425	12.8714	12.1689	11.5925	11.1131	10.7097	10.3670	10.0733
9.500%	13.8094	12.9398	12.2386	11.6637	11.1857	10.7837	10.4422	10.1499
9.625%	13.8764	13.0083	12.3086	11.7352	11.2586	10.8579	10.5178	10.2268
9.750%	13.9437	13.0770	12.3788	11.8068	11.3316	10.9324	10.5936	10.3039
9.875%	14.0111	13.1460	12.4493	11.8787	11.4049	11.0071	10.6697	10.3813

MONTHLY PAYMENT TO AMORTIZE A LOAN OF $1,000

Term of Loan

Interest Rate	17 Years	18 Years	19 Years	20 Years	21 Years	22 Years	23 Years	24 Years
4.000%	6.7639	6.5020	6.2687	6.0598	5.8718	5.7018	5.5475	5.4069
4.125%	6.8280	6.5667	6.3341	6.1259	5.9385	5.7692	5.6155	5.4755
4.250%	6.8925	6.6319	6.3999	6.1923	6.0056	5.8370	5.6840	5.5446
4.375%	6.9573	6.6974	6.4661	6.2592	6.0732	5.9052	5.7529	5.6142
4.500%	7.0225	6.7632	6.5327	6.3265	6.1412	5.9739	5.8222	5.6842
4.625%	7.0880	6.8295	6.5996	6.3942	6.2096	6.0430	5.8920	5.7547
4.750%	7.1538	6.8961	6.6670	6.4622	6.2784	6.1125	5.9623	5.8257
4.875%	7.2200	6.9630	6.7347	6.5307	6.3476	6.1824	6.0329	5.8971
5.000%	7.2866	7.0303	6.8028	6.5996	6.4172	6.2528	6.1041	5.9690
5.125%	7.3534	7.0980	6.8712	6.6688	6.4872	6.3236	6.1756	6.0413
5.250%	7.4206	7.1660	6.9401	6.7384	6.5576	6.3948	6.2476	6.1140
5.375%	7.4882	7.2344	7.0093	6.8085	6.6285	6.4664	6.3200	6.1872
5.500%	7.5561	7.3032	7.0789	6.8789	6.6997	6.5385	6.3929	6.2609
5.625%	7.6243	7.3723	7.1488	6.9497	6.7713	6.6109	6.4661	6.3350
5.750%	7.6929	7.4417	7.2191	7.0208	6.8434	6.6838	6.5398	6.4095
5.875%	7.7618	7.5115	7.2898	7.0924	6.9158	6.7571	6.6139	6.4844
6.000%	7.8310	7.5816	7.3608	7.1643	6.9886	6.8307	6.6885	6.5598
6.125%	7.9006	7.6521	7.4322	7.2366	7.0618	6.9048	6.7634	6.6356
6.250%	7.9705	7.7229	7.5040	7.3093	7.1353	6.9793	6.8387	6.7118
6.375%	8.0407	7.7941	7.5761	7.3823	7.2093	7.0541	6.9145	6.7884
6.500%	8.1112	7.8656	7.6486	7.4557	7.2836	7.1294	6.9906	6.8654
6.625%	8.1821	7.9375	7.7214	7.5295	7.3583	7.2050	7.0672	6.9429
6.750%	8.2533	8.0096	7.7945	7.6036	7.4334	7.2811	7.1441	7.0207
6.875%	8.3248	8.0822	7.8681	7.6781	7.5089	7.3575	7.2215	7.0990
7.000%	8.3966	8.1550	7.9419	7.7530	7.5847	7.4342	7.2992	7.1776
7.125%	8.4688	8.2282	8.0161	7.8282	7.6609	7.5114	7.3773	7.2566
7.250%	8.5412	8.3017	8.0907	7.9038	7.7375	7.5889	7.4558	7.3361
7.375%	8.6140	8.3756	8.1656	7.9797	7.8144	7.6668	7.5347	7.4159
7.500%	8.6871	8.4497	8.2408	8.0559	7.8917	7.7451	7.6139	7.4960
7.625%	8.7605	8.5242	8.3163	8.1325	7.9693	7.8237	7.6935	7.5766
7.750%	8.8342	8.5990	8.3922	8.2095	8.0473	7.9027	7.7735	7.6576
7.875%	8.9082	8.6742	8.4685	8.2868	8.1256	7.9821	7.8538	7.7389
8.000%	8.9826	8.7496	8.5450	8.3644	8.2043	8.0618	7.9345	7.8205
8.125%	9.0572	8.8254	8.6219	8.4424	8.2833	8.1418	8.0156	7.9026
8.250%	9.1321	8.9015	8.6991	8.5207	8.3627	8.2222	8.0970	7.9850
8.375%	9.2074	8.9779	8.7766	8.5993	8.4424	8.3030	8.1788	8.0677
8.500%	9.2829	9.0546	8.8545	8.6782	8.5224	8.3841	8.2609	8.1508
8.625%	9.3588	9.1316	8.9326	8.7575	8.6028	8.4655	8.3433	8.2343
8.750%	9.4349	9.2089	9.0111	8.8371	8.6834	8.5472	8.4261	8.3181
8.875%	9.5113	9.2865	9.0899	8.9170	8.7645	8.6293	8.5092	8.4022
9.000%	9.5880	9.3644	9.1690	8.9973	8.8458	8.7117	8.5927	8.4866
9.125%	9.6650	9.4427	9.2484	9.0778	8.9275	8.7945	8.6765	8.5714
9.250%	9.7423	9.5212	9.3281	9.1587	9.0094	8.8775	8.7606	8.6566
9.375%	9.8199	9.6000	9.4081	9.2398	9.0917	8.9609	8.8450	8.7420
9.500%	9.8978	9.6791	9.4884	9.3213	9.1743	9.0446	8.9297	8.8277
9.625%	9.9760	9.7585	9.5690	9.4031	9.2573	9.1286	9.0148	8.9138
9.750%	10.0544	9.8382	9.6499	9.4852	9.3405	9.2129	9.1002	9.0002
9.875%	10.1331	9.9182	9.7311	9.5675	9.4240	9.2975	9.1858	9.0869

MONTHLY PAYMENT TO AMORTIZE A LOAN OF $1,000

Term of Loan

Interest Rate	25 Years	26 Years	27 Years	28 Years	29 Years	30 Years	35 Years	40 Years
4.000%	5.2784	5.1605	5.0521	4.9521	4.8597	4.7742	4.4277	4.1794
4.125%	5.3476	5.2304	5.1226	5.0233	4.9315	4.8465	4.5030	4.2575
4.250%	5.4174	5.3008	5.1936	5.0949	5.0038	4.9194	4.5789	4.3362
4.375%	5.4876	5.3717	5.2652	5.1671	5.0766	4.9929	4.6555	4.4156
4.500%	5.5583	5.4430	5.3372	5.2398	5.1499	5.0669	4.7326	4.4956
4.625%	5.6295	5.5149	5.4098	5.3130	5.2238	5.1414	4.8103	4.5763
4.750%	5.7012	5.5873	5.4828	5.3868	5.2982	5.2165	4.8886	4.6576
4.875%	5.7733	5.6601	5.5564	5.4610	5.3732	5.2921	4.9674	4.7395
5.000%	5.8459	5.7334	5.6304	5.5357	5.4486	5.3682	5.0469	4.8220
5.125%	5.9190	5.8072	5.7049	5.6110	5.5246	5.4449	5.1269	4.9050
5.250%	5.9925	5.8815	5.7799	5.6867	5.6010	5.5220	5.2074	4.9887
5.375%	6.0665	5.9562	5.8554	5.7629	5.6780	5.5997	5.2885	5.0729
5.500%	6.1409	6.0314	5.9314	5.8397	5.7554	5.6779	5.3702	5.1577
5.625%	6.2157	6.1071	6.0078	5.9168	5.8334	5.7566	5.4523	5.2430
5.750%	6.2911	6.1832	6.0847	5.9945	5.9118	5.8357	5.5350	5.3289
5.875%	6.3668	6.2598	6.1620	6.0726	5.9907	5.9154	5.6182	5.4153
6.000%	6.4430	6.3368	6.2399	6.1512	6.0700	5.9955	5.7019	5.5021
6.125%	6.5196	6.4142	6.3181	6.2303	6.1499	6.0761	5.7861	5.5895
6.250%	6.5967	6.4921	6.3968	6.3098	6.2302	6.1572	5.8708	5.6774
6.375%	6.6742	6.5704	6.4760	6.3898	6.3109	6.2387	5.9559	5.7657
6.500%	6.7521	6.6492	6.5555	6.4702	6.3921	6.3207	6.0415	5.8546
6.625%	6.8304	6.7284	6.6356	6.5510	6.4738	6.4031	6.1276	5.9438
6.750%	6.9091	6.8079	6.7160	6.6323	6.5558	6.4860	6.2142	6.0336
6.875%	6.9883	6.8880	6.7969	6.7140	6.6384	6.5693	6.3011	6.1237
7.000%	7.0678	6.9684	6.8781	6.7961	6.7213	6.6530	6.3886	6.2143
7.125%	7.1477	7.0492	6.9598	6.8786	6.8047	6.7372	6.4764	6.3053
7.250%	7.2281	7.1304	7.0419	6.9616	6.8884	6.8218	6.5647	6.3967
7.375%	7.3088	7.2121	7.1244	7.0449	6.9726	6.9068	6.6533	6.4885
7.500%	7.3899	7.2941	7.2073	7.1287	7.0572	6.9921	6.7424	6.5807
7.625%	7.4714	7.3765	7.2906	7.2128	7.1422	7.0779	6.8319	6.6733
7.750%	7.5533	7.4593	7.3743	7.2974	7.2276	7.1641	6.9218	6.7662
7.875%	7.6355	7.5424	7.4584	7.3823	7.3133	7.2507	7.0120	6.8595
8.000%	7.7182	7.6260	7.5428	7.4676	7.3995	7.3376	7.1026	6.9531
8.125%	7.8012	7.7099	7.6276	7.5533	7.4860	7.4250	7.1936	7.0471
8.250%	7.8845	7.7942	7.7128	7.6393	7.5729	7.5127	7.2849	7.1414
8.375%	7.9682	7.8788	7.7983	7.7257	7.6601	7.6007	7.3766	7.2360
8.500%	8.0523	7.9638	7.8842	7.8125	7.7477	7.6891	7.4686	7.3309
8.625%	8.1367	8.0491	7.9705	7.8996	7.8357	7.7779	7.5610	7.4262
8.750%	8.2214	8.1348	8.0570	7.9871	7.9240	7.8670	7.6536	7.5217
8.875%	8.3065	8.2209	8.1440	8.0749	8.0126	7.9564	7.7466	7.6175
9.000%	8.3920	8.3072	8.2313	8.1630	8.1016	8.0462	7.8399	7.7136
9.125%	8.4777	8.3939	8.3189	8.2515	8.1909	8.1363	7.9335	7.8100
9.250%	8.5638	8.4810	8.4068	8.3403	8.2805	8.2268	8.0274	7.9066
9.375%	8.6502	8.5683	8.4950	8.4294	8.3705	8.3175	8.1216	8.0035
9.500%	8.7370	8.6560	8.5836	8.5188	8.4607	8.4085	8.2161	8.1006
9.625%	8.8240	8.7440	8.6725	8.6086	8.5513	8.4999	8.3109	8.1980
9.750%	8.9114	8.8323	8.7617	8.6986	8.6421	8.5915	8.4059	8.2956
9.875%	8.9990	8.9209	8.8512	8.7890	8.7333	8.6835	8.5012	8.3934

MONTHLY PAYMENT TO AMORTIZE A LOAN OF $1,000

				Term of Loan				
Interest Rate	1 Year	2 Years	3 Years	4 Years	5 Years	6 Years	7 Years	8 Years
10.000%	87.9159	46.1449	32.2672	25.3626	21.2470	18.5258	16.6012	15.1742
10.125%	87.9740	46.2026	32.3259	25.4227	21.3086	18.5889	16.6658	15.2404
10.250%	88.0322	46.2604	32.3847	25.4828	21.3703	18.6522	16.7306	15.3068
10.375%	88.0904	46.3182	32.4435	25.5431	21.4320	18.7155	16.7956	15.3733
10.500%	88.1486	46.3760	32.5024	25.6034	21.4939	18.7790	16.8607	15.4400
10.625%	88.2068	46.4339	32.5614	25.6638	21.5559	18.8426	16.9259	15.5069
10.750%	88.2651	46.4919	32.6205	25.7243	21.6180	18.9063	16.9913	15.5739
10.875%	88.3234	46.5498	32.6796	25.7849	21.6801	18.9701	17.0568	15.6411
11.000%	88.3817	46.6078	32.7387	25.8455	21.7424	19.0341	17.1224	15.7084
11.125%	88.4400	46.6659	32.7979	25.9063	21.8048	19.0982	17.1882	15.7759
11.250%	88.4983	46.7240	32.8572	25.9671	21.8673	19.1624	17.2542	15.8436
11.375%	88.5567	46.7821	32.9166	26.0280	21.9299	19.2267	17.3202	15.9114
11.500%	88.6151	46.8403	32.9760	26.0890	21.9926	19.2912	17.3865	15.9794
11.625%	88.6735	46.8985	33.0355	26.1501	22.0554	19.3557	17.4528	16.0475
11.750%	88.7319	46.9568	33.0950	26.2113	22.1183	19.4204	17.5193	16.1158
11.875%	88.7903	47.0151	33.1546	26.2725	22.1813	19.4853	17.5860	16.1842
12.000%	88.8488	47.0735	33.2143	26.3338	22.2444	19.5502	17.6527	16.2528
12.125%	88.9073	47.1319	33.2740	26.3953	22.3077	19.6153	17.7197	16.3216
12.250%	88.9658	47.1903	33.3338	26.4568	22.3710	19.6804	17.7867	16.3905
12.375%	89.0243	47.2488	33.3937	26.5183	22.4344	19.7457	17.8539	16.4596
12.500%	89.0829	47.3073	33.4536	26.5800	22.4979	19.8112	17.9212	16.5288
12.625%	89.1414	47.3659	33.5136	26.6417	22.5616	19.8767	17.9887	16.5982
12.750%	89.2000	47.4245	33.5737	26.7036	22.6253	19.9424	18.0563	16.6677
12.875%	89.2586	47.4831	33.6338	26.7655	22.6891	20.0082	18.1241	16.7374
13.000%	89.3173	47.5418	33.6940	26.8275	22.7531	20.0741	18.1920	16.8073
13.125%	89.3759	47.6006	33.7542	26.8896	22.8171	20.1401	18.2600	16.8773
13.250%	89.4346	47.6593	33.8145	26.9517	22.8813	20.2063	18.3282	16.9474
13.375%	89.4933	47.7182	33.8749	27.0140	22.9455	20.2726	18.3965	17.0177
13.500%	89.5520	47.7770	33.9353	27.0763	23.0098	20.3390	18.4649	17.0882
13.625%	89.6108	47.8359	33.9958	27.1387	23.0743	20.4055	18.5335	17.1588
13.750%	89.6695	47.8949	34.0563	27.2012	23.1388	20.4721	18.6022	17.2295
13.875%	89.7283	47.9539	34.1169	27.2638	23.2035	20.5389	18.6710	17.3004
14.000%	89.7871	48.0129	34.1776	27.3265	23.2683	20.6057	18.7400	17.3715
14.125%	89.8459	48.0720	34.2384	27.3892	23.3331	20.6727	18.8091	17.4427
14.250%	89.9048	48.1311	34.2992	27.4520	23.3981	20.7398	18.8784	17.5141
14.375%	89.9637	48.1902	34.3600	27.5150	23.4631	20.8071	18.9478	17.5856
14.500%	90.0225	48.2494	34.4210	27.5780	23.5283	20.8744	19.0173	17.6573
14.625%	90.0815	48.3087	34.4820	27.6410	23.5935	20.9419	19.0870	17.7291
14.750%	90.1404	48.3680	34.5430	27.7042	23.6589	21.0095	19.1568	17.8010
14.875%	90.1993	48.4273	34.6041	27.7674	23.7244	21.0772	19.2267	17.8731
15.000%	90.2583	48.4866	34.6653	27.8307	23.7899	21.1450	19.2968	17.9454
15.125%	90.3173	48.5461	34.7266	27.8942	23.8556	21.2130	19.3670	18.0178
15.250%	90.3763	48.6055	34.7879	27.9576	23.9214	21.2810	19.4373	18.0904
15.375%	90.4354	48.6650	34.8492	28.0212	23.9872	21.3492	19.5077	18.1631
15.500%	90.4944	48.7245	34.9107	28.0849	24.0532	21.4175	19.5783	18.2359
15.625%	90.5535	48.7841	34.9722	28.1486	24.1193	21.4859	19.6491	18.3089
15.750%	90.6126	48.8437	35.0337	28.2124	24.1854	21.5544	19.7199	18.3821
15.875%	90.6717	48.9034	35.0954	28.2763	24.2517	21.6231	19.7909	18.4554

MONTHLY PAYMENT TO AMORTIZE A LOAN OF $1,000

Term of Loan

Interest Rate	9 Years	10 Years	11 Years	12 Years	13 Years	14 Years	15 Years	16 Years
10.000%	14.0787	13.2151	12.5199	11.9508	11.4785	11.0820	10.7461	10.4590
10.125%	14.1465	13.2844	12.5907	12.0231	11.5523	11.1572	10.8227	10.5370
10.250%	14.2144	13.3539	12.6618	12.0957	11.6263	11.2327	10.8995	10.6152
10.375%	14.2826	13.4236	12.7330	12.1684	11.7005	11.3084	10.9766	10.6937
10.500%	14.3509	13.4935	12.8045	12.2414	11.7750	11.3843	11.0540	10.7724
10.625%	14.4193	13.5636	12.8761	12.3146	11.8497	11.4605	11.1316	10.8514
10.750%	14.4880	13.6339	12.9480	12.3880	11.9247	11.5370	11.2095	10.9307
10.875%	14.5568	13.7043	13.0201	12.4617	11.9999	11.6136	11.2876	11.0102
11.000%	14.6259	13.7750	13.0923	12.5356	12.0753	11.6905	11.3660	11.0900
11.125%	14.6950	13.8459	13.1648	12.6096	12.1509	11.7677	11.4446	11.1700
11.250%	14.7644	13.9169	13.2375	12.6839	12.2268	11.8451	11.5234	11.2503
11.375%	14.8339	13.9881	13.3104	12.7584	12.3029	11.9227	11.6026	11.3309
11.500%	14.9037	14.0595	13.3835	12.8332	12.3792	12.0006	11.6819	11.4116
11.625%	14.9735	14.1312	13.4568	12.9081	12.4557	12.0786	11.7615	11.4927
11.750%	15.0436	14.2029	13.5303	12.9833	12.5325	12.1570	11.8413	11.5740
11.875%	15.1138	14.2749	13.6040	13.0586	12.6095	12.2355	11.9214	11.6555
12.000%	15.1842	14.3471	13.6779	13.1342	12.6867	12.3143	12.0017	11.7373
12.125%	15.2548	14.4194	13.7520	13.2100	12.7641	12.3933	12.0822	11.8193
12.250%	15.3256	14.4920	13.8263	13.2860	12.8417	12.4725	12.1630	11.9015
12.375%	15.3965	14.5647	13.9007	13.3622	12.9196	12.5520	12.2440	11.9840
12.500%	15.4676	14.6376	13.9754	13.4386	12.9977	12.6317	12.3252	12.0667
12.625%	15.5388	14.7107	14.0503	13.5152	13.0760	12.7116	12.4067	12.1496
12.750%	15.6102	14.7840	14.1254	13.5920	13.1545	12.7917	12.4884	12.2328
12.875%	15.6818	14.8574	14.2006	13.6690	13.2332	12.8721	12.5703	12.3162
13.000%	15.7536	14.9311	14.2761	13.7463	13.3121	12.9526	12.6524	12.3999
13.125%	15.8255	15.0049	14.3518	13.8237	13.3912	13.0334	12.7348	12.4837
13.250%	15.8976	15.0789	14.4276	13.9013	13.4706	13.1144	12.8174	12.5678
13.375%	15.9699	15.1531	14.5036	13.9791	13.5502	13.1956	12.9002	12.6521
13.500%	16.0423	15.2274	14.5799	14.0572	13.6299	13.2771	12.9832	12.7367
13.625%	16.1149	15.3020	14.6563	14.1354	13.7099	13.3587	13.0664	12.8214
13.750%	16.1877	15.3767	14.7329	14.2138	13.7901	13.4406	13.1499	12.9064
13.875%	16.2606	15.4516	14.8097	14.2925	13.8704	13.5226	13.2335	12.9916
14.000%	16.3337	15.5266	14.8867	14.3713	13.9510	13.6049	13.3174	13.0770
14.125%	16.4070	15.6019	14.9638	14.4503	14.0318	13.6874	13.4015	13.1626
14.250%	16.4804	15.6773	15.0412	14.5295	14.1128	13.7701	13.4858	13.2484
14.375%	16.5540	15.7529	15.1187	14.6089	14.1940	13.8529	13.5703	13.3345
14.500%	16.6277	15.8287	15.1964	14.6885	14.2754	13.9360	13.6550	13.4207
14.625%	16.7016	15.9046	15.2743	14.7683	14.3570	14.0193	13.7399	13.5071
14.750%	16.7757	15.9807	15.3524	14.8483	14.4387	14.1028	13.8250	13.5938
14.875%	16.8499	16.0570	15.4307	14.9284	14.5207	14.1865	13.9104	13.6806
15.000%	16.9243	16.1335	15.5091	15.0088	14.6029	14.2704	13.9959	13.7677
15.125%	16.9989	16.2101	15.5878	15.0893	14.6852	14.3545	14.0816	13.8549
15.250%	17.0736	16.2869	15.6666	15.1700	14.7678	14.4388	14.1675	13.9424
15.375%	17.1485	16.3639	15.7456	15.2509	14.8505	14.5232	14.2536	14.0300
15.500%	17.2235	16.4411	15.8247	15.3320	14.9335	14.6079	14.3399	14.1179
15.625%	17.2987	16.5184	15.9041	15.4133	15.0166	14.6928	14.4264	14.2059
15.750%	17.3741	16.5958	15.9836	15.4948	15.0999	14.7778	14.5131	14.2941
15.875%	17.4496	16.6735	16.0633	15.5764	15.1834	14.8630	14.5999	14.3825

MONTHLY PAYMENT TO AMORTIZE A LOAN OF $1,000

Term of Loan

Interest Rate	17 Years	18 Years	19 Years	20 Years	21 Years	22 Years	23 Years	24 Years
10.000%	10.2121	9.9984	9.8126	9.6502	9.5078	9.3825	9.2718	9.1739
10.125%	10.2914	10.0790	9.8944	9.7332	9.5919	9.4677	9.3581	9.2612
10.250%	10.3709	10.1598	9.9764	9.8164	9.6763	9.5532	9.4447	9.3488
10.375%	10.4507	10.2409	10.0588	9.9000	9.7610	9.6390	9.5315	9.4366
10.500%	10.5308	10.3223	10.1414	9.9838	9.8460	9.7251	9.6187	9.5248
10.625%	10.6112	10.4039	10.2243	10.0679	9.9312	9.8114	9.7061	9.6133
10.750%	10.6918	10.4858	10.3075	10.1523	10.0168	9.8981	9.7938	9.7020
10.875%	10.7727	10.5680	10.3909	10.2370	10.1026	9.9850	9.8818	9.7910
11.000%	10.8538	10.6505	10.4746	10.3219	10.1887	10.0722	9.9701	9.8803
11.125%	10.9352	10.7332	10.5586	10.4071	10.2751	10.1597	10.0586	9.9698
11.250%	11.0169	10.8162	10.6429	10.4926	10.3617	10.2475	10.1474	10.0596
11.375%	11.0988	10.8994	10.7274	10.5783	10.4486	10.3355	10.2365	10.1497
11.500%	11.1810	10.9830	10.8122	10.6643	10.5358	10.4237	10.3258	10.2400
11.625%	11.2634	11.0667	10.8972	10.7506	10.6232	10.5123	10.4154	10.3306
11.750%	11.3461	11.1507	10.9825	10.8371	10.7109	10.6011	10.5052	10.4214
11.875%	11.4290	11.2350	11.0681	10.9238	10.7988	10.6901	10.5953	10.5125
12.000%	11.5122	11.3195	11.1539	11.0109	10.8870	10.7794	10.6856	10.6038
12.125%	11.5956	11.4043	11.2399	11.0981	10.9754	10.8689	10.7762	10.6954
12.250%	11.6792	11.4893	11.3262	11.1856	11.0641	10.9587	10.8670	10.7872
12.375%	11.7631	11.5745	11.4127	11.2734	11.1530	11.0487	10.9581	10.8792
12.500%	11.8473	11.6600	11.4995	11.3614	11.2422	11.1390	11.0494	10.9714
12.625%	11.9316	11.7457	11.5865	11.4496	11.3316	11.2294	11.1409	11.0639
12.750%	12.0162	11.8317	11.6738	11.5381	11.4212	11.3202	11.2326	11.1566
12.875%	12.1011	11.9179	11.7613	11.6268	11.5111	11.4111	11.3246	11.2495
13.000%	12.1861	12.0043	11.8490	11.7158	11.6011	11.5023	11.4168	11.3427
13.125%	12.2714	12.0910	11.9369	11.8049	11.6915	11.5937	11.5092	11.4360
13.250%	12.3570	12.1779	12.0251	11.8943	11.7820	11.6853	11.6018	11.5296
13.375%	12.4427	12.2650	12.1135	11.9839	11.8727	11.7771	11.6946	11.6233
13.500%	12.5287	12.3523	12.2021	12.0737	11.9637	11.8691	11.7876	11.7173
13.625%	12.6149	12.4399	12.2910	12.1638	12.0549	11.9613	11.8808	11.8114
13.750%	12.7013	12.5276	12.3800	12.2541	12.1463	12.0538	11.9743	11.9058
13.875%	12.7879	12.6156	12.4693	12.3445	12.2379	12.1464	12.0679	12.0003
14.000%	12.8748	12.7038	12.5588	12.4352	12.3297	12.2393	12.1617	12.0950
14.125%	12.9618	12.7922	12.6485	12.5261	12.4217	12.3323	12.2557	12.1900
14.250%	13.0491	12.8809	12.7384	12.6172	12.5139	12.4256	12.3500	12.2851
14.375%	13.1366	12.9697	12.8285	12.7085	12.6063	12.5190	12.4443	12.3803
14.500%	13.2242	13.0587	12.9188	12.8000	12.6989	12.6126	12.5389	12.4758
14.625%	13.3121	13.1480	13.0093	12.8917	12.7917	12.7065	12.6337	12.5714
14.750%	13.4002	13.2374	13.1000	12.9836	12.8847	12.8004	12.7286	12.6672
14.875%	13.4885	13.3271	13.1909	13.0756	12.9778	12.8946	12.8237	12.7632
15.000%	13.5770	13.4169	13.2820	13.1679	13.0712	12.9890	12.9190	12.8593
15.125%	13.6657	13.5069	13.3733	13.2603	13.1647	13.0835	13.0144	12.9556
15.250%	13.7546	13.5972	13.4647	13.3530	13.2584	13.1782	13.1100	13.0520
15.375%	13.8437	13.6876	13.5564	13.4458	13.3523	13.2731	13.2058	13.1486
15.500%	13.9329	13.7782	13.6483	13.5388	13.4464	13.3681	13.3018	13.2454
15.625%	14.0224	13.8690	13.7403	13.6320	13.5406	13.4633	13.3979	13.3423
15.750%	14.1120	13.9600	13.8325	13.7253	13.6350	13.5587	13.4941	13.4394
15.875%	14.2019	14.0511	13.9249	13.8189	13.7296	13.6542	13.5905	13.5366

MONTHLY PAYMENT TO AMORTIZE A LOAN OF $1,000

				Term of Loan				
Interest Rate	25 Years	26 Years	27 Years	28 Years	29 Years	30 Years	35 Years	40 Years
10.000%	9.0870	9.0098	8.9410	8.8796	8.8248	8.7757	8.5967	8.4915
10.125%	9.1753	9.0990	9.0311	8.9705	8.9165	8.8682	8.6925	8.5897
10.250%	9.2638	9.1885	9.1214	9.0618	9.0085	8.9610	8.7886	8.6882
10.375%	9.3527	9.2782	9.2121	9.1533	9.1008	9.0541	8.8848	8.7868
10.500%	9.4418	9.3683	9.3030	9.2450	9.1934	9.1474	8.9813	8.8857
10.625%	9.5312	9.4586	9.3943	9.3371	9.2862	9.2410	9.0781	8.9847
10.750%	9.6209	9.5492	9.4857	9.4294	9.3793	9.3348	9.1750	9.0840
10.875%	9.7109	9.6401	9.5775	9.5220	9.4727	9.4289	9.2722	9.1834
11.000%	9.8011	9.7313	9.6695	9.6148	9.5663	9.5232	9.3696	9.2829
11.125%	9.8916	9.8227	9.7618	9.7079	9.6601	9.6178	9.4672	9.3827
11.250%	9.9824	9.9143	9.8543	9.8012	9.7542	9.7126	9.5649	9.4826
11.375%	10.0734	10.0063	9.9471	9.8948	9.8486	9.8077	9.6629	9.5826
11.500%	10.1647	10.0984	10.0401	9.9886	9.9431	9.9029	9.7611	9.6828
11.625%	10.2562	10.1909	10.1333	10.0826	10.0379	9.9984	9.8594	9.7832
11.750%	10.3480	10.2835	10.2268	10.1769	10.1329	10.0941	9.9579	9.8836
11.875%	10.4400	10.3764	10.3205	10.2714	10.2281	10.1900	10.0566	9.9843
12.000%	10.5322	10.4695	10.4145	10.3661	10.3236	10.2861	10.1555	10.0850
12.125%	10.6247	10.5629	10.5087	10.4611	10.4192	10.3824	10.2545	10.1859
12.250%	10.7174	10.6565	10.6030	10.5562	10.5151	10.4790	10.3537	10.2869
12.375%	10.8104	10.7503	10.6977	10.6516	10.6112	10.5757	10.4531	10.3880
12.500%	10.9035	10.8443	10.7925	10.7471	10.7074	10.6726	10.5525	10.4892
12.625%	10.9969	10.9385	10.8875	10.8429	10.8039	10.7697	10.6522	10.5905
12.750%	11.0905	11.0329	10.9827	10.9388	10.9005	10.8669	10.7520	10.6920
12.875%	11.1843	11.1276	11.0781	11.0350	10.9973	10.9644	10.8519	10.7935
13.000%	11.2784	11.2224	11.1738	11.1313	11.0943	11.0620	10.9519	10.8951
13.125%	11.3726	11.3175	11.2696	11.2279	11.1915	11.1598	11.0521	10.9969
13.250%	11.4670	11.4127	11.3656	11.3246	11.2888	11.2577	11.1524	11.0987
13.375%	11.5616	11.5082	11.4618	11.4214	11.3864	11.3558	11.2529	11.2006
13.500%	11.6564	11.6038	11.5581	11.5185	11.4841	11.4541	11.3534	11.3026
13.625%	11.7515	11.6996	11.6547	11.6157	11.5819	11.5525	11.4541	11.4047
13.750%	11.8467	11.7956	11.7514	11.7131	11.6799	11.6511	11.5549	11.5069
13.875%	11.9420	11.8917	11.8483	11.8107	11.7781	11.7498	11.6557	11.6091
14.000%	12.0376	11.9881	11.9453	11.9084	11.8764	11.8487	11.7567	11.7114
14.125%	12.1334	12.0846	12.0425	12.0062	11.9749	11.9477	11.8578	11.8138
14.250%	12.2293	12.1813	12.1399	12.1043	12.0735	12.0469	11.9590	11.9162
14.375%	12.3254	12.2781	12.2375	12.2024	12.1722	12.1461	12.0603	12.0187
14.500%	12.4216	12.3751	12.3351	12.3007	12.2711	12.2456	12.1617	12.1213
14.625%	12.5181	12.4723	12.4330	12.3992	12.3701	12.3451	12.2632	12.2240
14.750%	12.6146	12.5696	12.5310	12.4978	12.4693	12.4448	12.3647	12.3267
14.875%	12.7114	12.6671	12.6291	12.5965	12.5686	12.5445	12.4664	12.4294
15.000%	12.8083	12.7647	12.7274	12.6954	12.6680	12.6444	12.5681	12.5322
15.125%	12.9054	12.8625	12.8258	12.7944	12.7675	12.7445	12.6699	12.6351
15.250%	13.0026	12.9604	12.9243	12.8935	12.8672	12.8446	12.7718	12.7380
15.375%	13.0999	13.0584	13.0230	12.9928	12.9669	12.9448	12.8738	12.8410
15.500%	13.1975	13.1566	13.1218	13.0922	13.0668	13.0452	12.9758	12.9440
15.625%	13.2951	13.2550	13.2208	13.1916	13.1668	13.1456	13.0780	13.0471
15.750%	13.3929	13.3534	13.3198	13.2913	13.2669	13.2462	13.1801	13.1502
15.875%	13.4908	13.4520	13.4190	13.3910	13.3671	13.3468	13.2824	13.2533

MONTHLY PAYMENT TO AMORTIZE A LOAN OF $1,000

				Term of Loan				
Interest Rate	1 Year	2 Years	3 Years	4 Years	5 Years	6 Years	7 Years	8 Years
16.000%	90.7309	48.9631	35.1570	28.3403	24.3181	21.6918	19.8621	18.5288
16.125%	90.7900	49.0229	35.2188	28.4043	24.3845	21.7607	19.9333	18.6024
16.250%	90.8492	49.0826	35.2806	28.4685	24.4511	21.8297	20.0047	18.6761
16.375%	90.9084	49.1425	35.3425	28.5327	24.5178	21.8988	20.0762	18.7500
16.500%	90.9676	49.2024	35.4044	28.5970	24.5845	21.9681	20.1479	18.8240
16.625%	91.0269	49.2623	35.4664	28.6614	24.6514	22.0374	20.2197	18.8981
16.750%	91.0862	49.3222	35.5284	28.7259	24.7184	22.1069	20.2916	18.9724
16.875%	91.1454	49.3822	35.5905	28.7904	24.7854	22.1764	20.3636	19.0469
17.000%	91.2048	49.4423	35.6527	28.8550	24.8526	22.2461	20.4358	19.1215
17.125%	91.2641	49.5023	35.7150	28.9198	24.9198	22.3159	20.5081	19.1962
17.250%	91.3234	49.5625	35.7773	28.9845	24.9872	22.3859	20.5805	19.2710
17.375%	91.3828	49.6226	35.8396	29.0494	25.0547	22.4559	20.6531	19.3461
17.500%	91.4422	49.6828	35.9021	29.1144	25.1222	22.5260	20.7258	19.4212
17.625%	91.5016	49.7431	35.9646	29.1794	25.1899	22.5963	20.7986	19.4965
17.750%	91.5611	49.8034	36.0271	29.2445	25.2576	22.6667	20.8716	19.5719
17.875%	91.6205	49.8637	36.0897	29.3097	25.3255	22.7372	20.9446	19.6475
18.000%	91.6800	49.9241	36.1524	29.3750	25.3934	22.8078	21.0178	19.7232
18.125%	91.7395	49.9845	36.2151	29.4404	25.4615	22.8785	21.0912	19.7991
18.250%	91.7990	50.0450	36.2779	29.5058	25.5296	22.9493	21.1646	19.8751
18.375%	91.8586	50.1055	36.3408	29.5713	25.5979	23.0203	21.2382	19.9512
18.500%	91.9181	50.1660	36.4037	29.6369	25.6662	23.0914	21.3119	20.0274
18.625%	91.9777	50.2266	36.4667	29.7026	25.7346	23.1625	21.3858	20.1038
18.750%	92.0373	50.2872	36.5297	29.7684	25.8032	23.2338	21.4597	20.1804
18.875%	92.0969	50.3479	36.5929	29.8342	25.8718	23.3052	21.5338	20.2571
19.000%	92.1566	50.4086	36.6560	29.9001	25.9406	23.3767	21.6080	20.3339
19.125%	92.2162	50.4694	36.7193	29.9661	26.0094	23.4483	21.6824	20.4108
19.250%	92.2759	50.5302	36.7825	30.0322	26.0783	23.5201	21.7568	20.4879
19.375%	92.3356	50.5910	36.8459	30.0984	26.1473	23.5919	21.8314	20.5651
19.500%	92.3954	50.6519	36.9093	30.1646	26.2164	23.6639	21.9061	20.6425
19.625%	92.4551	50.7128	36.9728	30.2309	26.2857	23.7360	21.9810	20.7199
19.750%	92.5149	50.7738	37.0363	30.2973	26.3550	23.8081	22.0559	20.7976
19.875%	92.5747	50.8348	37.0999	30.3638	26.4244	23.8804	22.1310	20.8753

MONTHLY PAYMENT TO AMORTIZE A LOAN OF $1,000

				Term of Loan				
Interest Rate	9 Years	10 Years	11 Years	12 Years	13 Years	14 Years	15 Years	16 Years
16.000%	17.5253	16.7513	16.1432	15.6583	15.2670	14.9485	14.6870	14.4711
16.125%	17.6011	16.8293	16.2232	15.7403	15.3509	15.0341	14.7743	14.5599
16.250%	17.6771	16.9074	16.3034	15.8224	15.4349	15.1199	14.8617	14.6488
16.375%	17.7532	16.9858	16.3838	15.9048	15.5192	15.2058	14.9493	14.7380
16.500%	17.8295	17.0642	16.4644	15.9873	15.6036	15.2920	15.0371	14.8273
16.625%	17.9059	17.1429	16.5451	16.0700	15.6881	15.3783	15.1251	14.9168
16.750%	17.9825	17.2217	16.6260	16.1529	15.7729	15.4648	15.2132	15.0065
16.875%	18.0593	17.3006	16.7071	16.2360	15.8578	15.5515	15.3015	15.0963
17.000%	18.1362	17.3798	16.7883	16.3192	15.9430	15.6384	15.3900	15.1863
17.125%	18.2132	17.4591	16.8697	16.4026	16.0282	15.7254	15.4787	15.2765
17.250%	18.2905	17.5385	16.9513	16.4862	16.1137	15.8126	15.5676	15.3669
17.375%	18.3678	17.6181	17.0330	16.5700	16.1993	15.9000	15.6566	15.4574
17.500%	18.4453	17.6979	17.1149	16.6539	16.2851	15.9876	15.7458	15.5481
17.625%	18.5230	17.7778	17.1970	16.7380	16.3711	16.0753	15.8351	15.6390
17.750%	18.6008	17.8579	17.2792	16.8222	16.4572	16.1632	15.9247	15.7300
17.875%	18.6788	17.9381	17.3616	16.9066	16.5435	16.2513	16.0144	15.8212
18.000%	18.7569	18.0185	17.4442	16.9912	16.6300	16.3395	16.1042	15.9126
18.125%	18.8351	18.0991	17.5269	17.0759	16.7166	16.4279	16.1942	16.0041
18.250%	18.9136	18.1798	17.6098	17.1608	16.8034	16.5165	16.2844	16.0957
18.375%	18.9921	18.2606	17.6928	17.2459	16.8904	16.6052	16.3747	16.1875
18.500%	19.0708	18.3417	17.7760	17.3311	16.9775	16.6941	16.4652	16.2795
18.625%	19.1497	18.4228	17.8593	17.4165	17.0648	16.7831	16.5559	16.3716
18.750%	19.2287	18.5041	17.9428	17.5021	17.1523	16.8723	16.6467	16.4639
18.875%	19.3078	18.5856	18.0265	17.5878	17.2399	16.9616	16.7376	16.5564
19.000%	19.3871	18.6672	18.1103	17.6736	17.3276	17.0511	16.8288	16.6489
19.125%	19.4665	18.7490	18.1943	17.7597	17.4155	17.1408	16.9200	16.7416
19.250%	19.5461	18.8309	18.2784	17.8458	17.5036	17.2306	17.0114	16.8345
19.375%	19.6258	18.9130	18.3627	17.9322	17.5918	17.3206	17.1030	16.9275
19.500%	19.7057	18.9952	18.4471	18.0186	17.6802	17.4107	17.1947	17.0207
19.625%	19.7857	19.0776	18.5317	18.1053	17.7687	17.5010	17.2866	17.1140
19.750%	19.8658	19.1601	18.6164	18.1921	17.8574	17.5914	17.3785	17.2074
19.875%	19.9461	19.2428	18.7013	18.2790	17.9462	17.6819	17.4707	17.3010

MONTHLY PAYMENT TO AMORTIZE A LOAN OF $1,000

				Term of Loan				
Interest Rate	17 Years	18 Years	19 Years	20 Years	21 Years	22 Years	23 Years	24 Years
16.000%	14.2919	14.1425	14.0175	13.9126	13.8243	13.7499	13.6871	13.6339
16.125%	14.3821	14.2340	14.1102	14.0064	13.9192	13.8457	13.7838	13.7314
16.250%	14.4725	14.3257	14.2031	14.1005	14.0143	13.9417	13.8806	13.8290
16.375%	14.5630	14.4176	14.2962	14.1946	14.1095	14.0379	13.9776	13.9268
16.500%	14.6538	14.5096	14.3894	14.2890	14.2048	14.1342	14.0747	14.0247
16.625%	14.7447	14.6018	14.4829	14.3835	14.3004	14.2306	14.1720	14.1227
16.750%	14.8358	14.6942	14.5764	14.4782	14.3960	14.3272	14.2694	14.2208
16.875%	14.9270	14.7868	14.6702	14.5730	14.4919	14.4239	14.3669	14.3191
17.000%	15.0184	14.8795	14.7641	14.6680	14.5878	14.5208	14.4646	14.4175
17.125%	15.1100	14.9724	14.8581	14.7631	14.6839	14.6178	14.5624	14.5160
17.250%	15.2018	15.0654	14.9524	14.8584	14.7802	14.7149	14.6603	14.6147
17.375%	15.2937	15.1586	15.0467	14.9538	14.8766	14.8122	14.7584	14.7134
17.500%	15.3858	15.2519	15.1412	15.0494	14.9731	14.9095	14.8565	14.8123
17.625%	15.4780	15.3455	15.2359	15.1451	15.0698	15.0071	14.9548	14.9113
17.750%	15.5704	15.4391	15.3307	15.2410	15.1666	15.1047	15.0532	15.0104
17.875%	15.6630	15.5329	15.4257	15.3370	15.2635	15.2025	15.1518	15.1096
18.000%	15.7557	15.6269	15.5208	15.4331	15.3605	15.3004	15.2504	15.2089
18.125%	15.8486	15.7210	15.6160	15.5294	15.4577	15.3984	15.3492	15.3083
18.250%	15.9416	15.8153	15.7114	15.6258	15.5550	15.4965	15.4480	15.4078
18.375%	16.0348	15.9097	15.8069	15.7223	15.6525	15.5948	15.5470	15.5074
18.500%	16.1281	16.0042	15.9026	15.8190	15.7500	15.6931	15.6461	15.6071
18.625%	16.2216	16.0989	15.9984	15.9158	15.8477	15.7916	15.7452	15.7069
18.750%	16.3152	16.1938	16.0943	16.0127	15.9455	15.8902	15.8445	15.8068
18.875%	16.4090	16.2887	16.1904	16.1097	16.0434	15.9889	15.9439	15.9068
19.000%	16.5029	16.3838	16.2866	16.2068	16.1414	16.0876	16.0434	16.0069
19.125%	16.5969	16.4791	16.3829	16.3041	16.2396	16.1865	16.1429	16.1071
19.250%	16.6911	16.5745	16.4793	16.4015	16.3378	16.2855	16.2426	16.2073
19.375%	16.7854	16.6700	16.5759	16.4990	16.4362	16.3846	16.3424	16.3077
19.500%	16.8799	16.7656	16.6725	16.5966	16.5346	16.4838	16.4422	16.4081
19.625%	16.9745	16.8613	16.7693	16.6944	16.6332	16.5831	16.5422	16.5086
19.750%	17.0692	16.9572	16.8663	16.7922	16.7318	16.6825	16.6422	16.6092
19.875%	17.1640	17.0532	16.9633	16.8902	16.8306	16.7820	16.7423	16.7099

MONTHLY PAYMENT TO AMORTIZE A LOAN OF $1,000

Term of Loan

Interest Rate	25 Years	26 Years	27 Years	28 Years	29 Years	30 Years	35 Years	40 Years
16.000%	13.5889	13.5507	13.5183	13.4908	13.4674	13.4476	13.3847	13.3565
16.125%	13.6871	13.6496	13.6178	13.5908	13.5679	13.5484	13.4871	13.4597
16.250%	13.7854	13.7485	13.7173	13.6908	13.6684	13.6493	13.5895	13.5630
16.375%	13.8839	13.8476	13.8169	13.7910	13.7690	13.7504	13.6920	13.6663
16.500%	13.9824	13.9468	13.9167	13.8912	13.8697	13.8515	13.7945	13.7696
16.625%	14.0811	14.0461	14.0166	13.9916	13.9705	13.9527	13.8971	13.8730
16.750%	14.1800	14.1456	14.1165	14.0921	14.0714	14.0540	13.9998	13.9764
16.875%	14.2789	14.2451	14.2166	14.1926	14.1724	14.1553	14.1025	14.0798
17.000%	14.3780	14.3447	14.3168	14.2933	14.2734	14.2568	14.2053	14.1832
17.125%	14.4771	14.4445	14.4171	14.3940	14.3746	14.3583	14.3081	14.2867
17.250%	14.5764	14.5443	14.5174	14.4948	14.4758	14.4599	14.4109	14.3902
17.375%	14.6758	14.6443	14.6179	14.5957	14.5771	14.5615	14.5138	14.4938
17.500%	14.7753	14.7443	14.7184	14.6967	14.6785	14.6633	14.6168	14.5973
17.625%	14.8749	14.8445	14.8191	14.7978	14.7800	14.7651	14.7197	14.7009
17.750%	14.9746	14.9447	14.9198	14.8989	14.8815	14.8669	14.8228	14.8045
17.875%	15.0744	15.0451	15.0206	15.0002	14.9831	14.9689	14.9258	14.9082
18.000%	15.1743	15.1455	15.1215	15.1015	15.0848	15.0709	15.0289	15.0118
18.125%	15.2743	15.2460	15.2225	15.2029	15.1865	15.1729	15.1321	15.1155
18.250%	15.3744	15.3466	15.3235	15.3043	15.2883	15.2750	15.2352	15.2192
18.375%	15.4746	15.4473	15.4247	15.4059	15.3902	15.3772	15.3384	15.3229
18.500%	15.5748	15.5481	15.5259	15.5075	15.4922	15.4794	15.4417	15.4266
18.625%	15.6752	15.6489	15.6272	15.6091	15.5942	15.5817	15.5449	15.5304
18.750%	15.7757	15.7499	15.7285	15.7109	15.6962	15.6841	15.6483	15.6342
18.875%	15.8762	15.8509	15.8300	15.8127	15.7983	15.7865	15.7516	15.7379
19.000%	15.9768	15.9520	15.9315	15.9145	15.9005	15.8889	15.8549	15.8417
19.125%	16.0775	16.0531	16.0330	16.0164	16.0027	15.9914	15.9583	15.9456
19.250%	16.1783	16.1544	16.1347	16.1184	16.1050	16.0940	16.0618	16.0494
19.375%	16.2791	16.2557	16.2364	16.2204	16.2074	16.1966	16.1652	16.1532
19.500%	16.3801	16.3570	16.3381	16.3225	16.3097	16.2992	16.2687	16.2571
19.625%	16.4811	16.4585	16.4399	16.4247	16.4122	16.4019	16.3722	16.3610
19.750%	16.5821	16.5600	16.5418	16.5269	16.5147	16.5046	16.4757	16.4648
19.875%	16.6833	16.6616	16.6437	16.6292	16.6172	16.6074	16.5792	16.5687

APPENDIX II
Remaining Principal Balance

If you arrange a balloon mortgage with your buyer, monthly payments will be set on a long-term schedule. At some point during the life of the loan, though, the entire remaining balance will suddenly become due and payable.

How much will that final (balloon) payment be? In the early years of a loan, interest charges absorb most of the monthly payment, and little is left to reduce the principal. It is not unusual for the final payment to be almost as much as the original debt.

To calculate the amount:

1. Find the table with the interest rate on your mortgage.

2. Follow across the top line until you find the original term of the loan (the number of years that were used to calculate the monthly payment).

3. Go down the left-hand column until you find the number of years the loan will actually last (the age of the loan when you will receive that balloon payment).

4. Find the spot where the two lines intersect.

    Example: On the chart for 10 percent loans, with an original term of 25 years, a 10-year balloon has a factor of .846. Almost 85 percent of the original loan is still due.

5. Multiply the original loan amount by the factor.
    Example: A loan of $74,500 × .846 (84.6%) = $63,027. This represents the remaining balance after ten years' payments have been made, and it represents the final balloon payment.

Remaining Principal Balance Factors

For Mortgages with an Interest Rate of 6.00% and an Original Term of:

Age of Loan in Years	5 Years	6 Years	7 Years	8 Years	9 Years	10 Years	11 Years	12 Years	15 Years	20 Years	25 Years	30 Years	35 Years	40 Years
1	0.823	0.857	0.881	0.900	0.914	0.925	0.934	0.941	0.958	0.973	0.982	0.988	0.991	0.994
2	0.635	0.706	0.756	0.793	0.822	0.845	0.864	0.879	0.913	0.945	0.963	0.975	0.982	0.987
3	0.436	0.545	0.622	0.680	0.724	0.760	0.789	0.813	0.865	0.915	0.943	0.961	0.972	0.980
4	0.225	0.374	0.480	0.560	0.621	0.670	0.710	0.743	0.814	0.883	0.922	0.946	0.962	0.973
5	0.000	0.193	0.330	0.432	0.511	0.574	0.626	0.668	0.760	0.849	0.899	0.931	0.951	0.965
6		0.000	0.170	0.297	0.395	0.473	0.536	0.589	0.703	0.813	0.875	0.914	0.939	0.957
7			0.000	0.153	0.271	0.365	0.441	0.505	0.642	0.775	0.850	0.896	0.927	0.948
8				0.000	0.139	0.250	0.341	0.416	0.578	0.734	0.823	0.878	0.914	0.938
9					0.000	0.129	0.234	0.321	0.509	0.691	0.794	0.858	0.900	0.928
10						0.000	0.120	0.220	0.436	0.645	0.764	0.837	0.885	0.918
11							0.000	0.113	0.359	0.597	0.731	0.815	0.869	0.906
12								0.000	0.277	0.545	0.697	0.791	0.852	0.894
15									0.000	0.371	0.580	0.710	0.796	0.854
20										0.000	0.333	0.540	0.676	0.768
25											0.000	0.310	0.514	0.652
30												0.000	0.295	0.496
35													0.000	0.285
40														0.000

For Mortgages with an Interest Rate of 6.25% and an Original Term of:

Age of Loan in Years	5 Years	6 Years	7 Years	8 Years	9 Years	10 Years	11 Years	12 Years	15 Years	20 Years	25 Years	30 Years	35 Years	40 Years
1	0.824	0.858	0.882	0.901	0.915	0.926	0.935	0.942	0.958	0.974	0.983	0.988	0.992	0.994
2	0.637	0.707	0.757	0.795	0.824	0.847	0.865	0.881	0.914	0.946	0.965	0.976	0.983	0.988
3	0.438	0.547	0.624	0.682	0.727	0.762	0.791	0.815	0.867	0.917	0.945	0.963	0.974	0.981
4	0.226	0.376	0.482	0.562	0.624	0.673	0.713	0.746	0.817	0.886	0.925	0.948	0.964	0.974
5	0.000	0.194	0.331	0.434	0.514	0.577	0.629	0.671	0.764	0.852	0.903	0.933	0.953	0.967
6		0.000	0.171	0.299	0.397	0.476	0.540	0.592	0.707	0.817	0.879	0.917	0.942	0.959
7			0.000	0.154	0.273	0.368	0.445	0.508	0.646	0.779	0.854	0.900	0.930	0.951
8				0.000	0.141	0.253	0.344	0.419	0.582	0.739	0.828	0.882	0.918	0.942
9					0.000	0.130	0.236	0.324	0.514	0.696	0.799	0.863	0.904	0.932
10						0.000	0.122	0.223	0.441	0.651	0.769	0.842	0.890	0.922
11							0.000	0.115	0.363	0.603	0.737	0.821	0.875	0.911
12								0.000	0.281	0.551	0.703	0.797	0.858	0.900
15									0.000	0.376	0.588	0.718	0.803	0.861
20										0.000	0.339	0.548	0.685	0.777
25											0.000	0.317	0.523	0.662
30												0.000	0.302	0.506
35													0.000	0.292
40														0.000

Remaining Principal Balance Factors

For Mortgages with an Interest Rate of 6.50% and an Original Term of:

Age of Loan in Years	5 Years	6 Years	7 Years	8 Years	9 Years	10 Years	11 Years	12 Years	15 Years	20 Years	25 Years	30 Years	35 Years	40 Years
1	0.825	0.859	0.883	0.901	0.915	0.927	0.936	0.943	0.959	0.975	0.983	0.989	0.992	0.995
2	0.638	0.709	0.759	0.796	0.825	0.848	0.867	0.882	0.916	0.948	0.966	0.977	0.984	0.989
3	0.439	0.548	0.626	0.684	0.729	0.765	0.794	0.818	0.869	0.919	0.947	0.964	0.975	0.983
4	0.227	0.377	0.484	0.564	0.626	0.675	0.715	0.748	0.820	0.889	0.927	0.951	0.966	0.976
5	0.000	0.195	0.333	0.437	0.517	0.580	0.632	0.675	0.767	0.856	0.906	0.936	0.956	0.969
6		0.000	0.172	0.301	0.400	0.479	0.543	0.596	0.711	0.821	0.883	0.921	0.945	0.962
7			0.000	0.155	0.275	0.370	0.448	0.512	0.651	0.784	0.858	0.904	0.934	0.954
8				0.000	0.142	0.255	0.347	0.422	0.587	0.744	0.832	0.887	0.922	0.945
9					0.000	0.132	0.238	0.327	0.518	0.702	0.805	0.868	0.909	0.936
10						0.000	0.123	0.225	0.445	0.657	0.775	0.848	0.895	0.926
11							0.000	0.116	0.367	0.608	0.744	0.826	0.880	0.916
12								0.000	0.284	0.557	0.710	0.804	0.864	0.905
15									0.000	0.381	0.595	0.726	0.810	0.867
20										0.000	0.345	0.557	0.694	0.785
25											0.000	0.323	0.532	0.672
30												0.000	0.309	0.516
35													0.000	0.299
40														0.000

For Mortgages with an Interest Rate of 6.75% and an Original Term of:

Age of Loan in Years	5 Years	6 Years	7 Years	8 Years	9 Years	10 Years	11 Years	12 Years	15 Years	20 Years	25 Years	30 Years	35 Years	40 Years
1	0.826	0.860	0.884	0.902	0.916	0.927	0.937	0.944	0.960	0.976	0.984	0.989	0.993	0.995
2	0.640	0.710	0.761	0.798	0.827	0.850	0.869	0.884	0.917	0.949	0.967	0.978	0.985	0.990
3	0.441	0.550	0.628	0.686	0.731	0.767	0.796	0.820	0.872	0.921	0.949	0.966	0.977	0.984
4	0.228	0.379	0.487	0.567	0.629	0.678	0.718	0.751	0.823	0.891	0.929	0.953	0.968	0.978
5	0.000	0.196	0.335	0.439	0.520	0.583	0.635	0.678	0.771	0.859	0.909	0.939	0.958	0.971
6		0.000	0.173	0.303	0.402	0.482	0.546	0.600	0.715	0.825	0.886	0.924	0.948	0.964
7			0.000	0.156	0.277	0.373	0.451	0.516	0.655	0.788	0.863	0.908	0.937	0.956
8				0.000	0.143	0.257	0.350	0.426	0.591	0.749	0.837	0.891	0.925	0.948
9					0.000	0.133	0.241	0.330	0.523	0.707	0.810	0.873	0.913	0.940
10						0.000	0.124	0.227	0.450	0.662	0.781	0.853	0.899	0.930
11							0.000	0.117	0.371	0.614	0.750	0.832	0.885	0.920
12								0.000	0.288	0.563	0.716	0.810	0.870	0.910
15									0.000	0.386	0.602	0.733	0.817	0.873
20										0.000	0.351	0.565	0.702	0.794
25											0.000	0.330	0.541	0.682
30												0.000	0.316	0.525
35													0.000	0.307
40														0.000

Remaining Principal Balance Factors

For Mortgages with an Interest Rate of 7.00% and an Original Term of:

Age of Loan in Years	5 Years	6 Years	7 Years	8 Years	9 Years	10 Years	11 Years	12 Years	15 Years	20 Years	25 Years	30 Years	35 Years	40 Years
1	0.827	0.861	0.885	0.903	0.917	0.928	0.937	0.945	0.961	0.976	0.985	0.990	0.993	0.995
2	0.641	0.712	0.762	0.800	0.829	0.852	0.870	0.886	0.919	0.951	0.968	0.979	0.986	0.990
3	0.442	0.552	0.630	0.689	0.734	0.769	0.798	0.822	0.874	0.923	0.951	0.967	0.978	0.985
4	0.229	0.381	0.489	0.569	0.632	0.681	0.721	0.754	0.826	0.894	0.932	0.955	0.969	0.979
5	0.000	0.197	0.337	0.442	0.522	0.586	0.638	0.681	0.774	0.863	0.912	0.941	0.960	0.973
6		0.000	0.174	0.305	0.405	0.485	0.550	0.603	0.719	0.829	0.890	0.927	0.950	0.966
7			0.000	0.158	0.279	0.376	0.455	0.519	0.659	0.793	0.867	0.911	0.940	0.959
8				0.000	0.145	0.259	0.352	0.429	0.596	0.754	0.842	0.895	0.929	0.951
9					0.000	0.134	0.243	0.333	0.527	0.712	0.815	0.877	0.917	0.943
10						0.000	0.126	0.230	0.454	0.668	0.786	0.858	0.904	0.934
11							0.000	0.119	0.375	0.620	0.756	0.838	0.890	0.925
12								0.000	0.291	0.569	0.723	0.816	0.875	0.914
15									0.000	0.392	0.609	0.740	0.824	0.879
20										0.000	0.357	0.573	0.711	0.802
25											0.000	0.336	0.550	0.691
30												0.000	0.323	0.535
35													0.000	0.314
40														0.000

For Mortgages with an Interest Rate of 7.25% and an Original Term of:

Age of Loan in Years	5 Years	6 Years	7 Years	8 Years	9 Years	10 Years	11 Years	12 Years	15 Years	20 Years	25 Years	30 Years	35 Years	40 Years
1	0.828	0.862	0.886	0.904	0.918	0.929	0.938	0.946	0.962	0.977	0.985	0.990	0.994	0.996
2	0.643	0.714	0.764	0.801	0.830	0.853	0.872	0.887	0.921	0.952	0.969	0.980	0.987	0.991
3	0.444	0.554	0.632	0.691	0.736	0.772	0.801	0.825	0.876	0.925	0.952	0.969	0.979	0.986
4	0.230	0.383	0.491	0.572	0.634	0.684	0.724	0.757	0.829	0.897	0.934	0.957	0.971	0.980
5	0.000	0.198	0.339	0.444	0.525	0.589	0.642	0.685	0.778	0.866	0.915	0.944	0.962	0.974
6		0.000	0.176	0.307	0.408	0.488	0.553	0.607	0.723	0.833	0.893	0.930	0.953	0.968
7			0.000	0.159	0.281	0.379	0.458	0.523	0.663	0.797	0.871	0.915	0.943	0.961
8				0.000	0.146	0.262	0.355	0.433	0.600	0.759	0.846	0.899	0.932	0.954
9					0.000	0.136	0.245	0.336	0.532	0.718	0.820	0.882	0.921	0.946
10						0.000	0.127	0.232	0.458	0.673	0.792	0.863	0.908	0.938
11							0.000	0.120	0.379	0.626	0.761	0.843	0.895	0.929
12								0.000	0.295	0.574	0.729	0.822	0.880	0.919
15									0.000	0.397	0.616	0.747	0.831	0.885
20										0.000	0.363	0.581	0.719	0.809
25											0.000	0.342	0.559	0.701
30												0.000	0.330	0.545
35													0.000	0.321
40														0.000

Remaining Principal Balance Factors

For Mortgages with an Interest Rate of 7.50% and an Original Term of:

Age of Loan in Years	5 Years	6 Years	7 Years	8 Years	9 Years	10 Years	11 Years	12 Years	15 Years	20 Years	25 Years	30 Years	35 Years	40 Years
1	0.829	0.863	0.887	0.905	0.919	0.930	0.939	0.947	0.962	0.978	0.986	0.991	0.994	0.996
2	0.644	0.715	0.765	0.803	0.832	0.855	0.874	0.889	0.922	0.953	0.971	0.981	0.987	0.991
3	0.445	0.556	0.634	0.693	0.738	0.774	0.803	0.827	0.878	0.927	0.954	0.970	0.980	0.987
4	0.231	0.384	0.493	0.574	0.637	0.687	0.727	0.760	0.832	0.899	0.936	0.959	0.973	0.982
5	0.000	0.199	0.341	0.446	0.528	0.592	0.645	0.688	0.781	0.869	0.917	0.946	0.964	0.976
6		0.000	0.177	0.309	0.410	0.491	0.556	0.610	0.726	0.836	0.897	0.933	0.955	0.970
7			0.000	0.160	0.284	0.382	0.461	0.527	0.668	0.801	0.875	0.918	0.946	0.964
8				0.000	0.147	0.264	0.358	0.436	0.604	0.763	0.851	0.903	0.935	0.957
9					0.000	0.137	0.248	0.339	0.536	0.723	0.825	0.886	0.924	0.949
10						0.000	0.128	0.234	0.463	0.679	0.797	0.868	0.912	0.941
11							0.000	0.122	0.383	0.631	0.767	0.848	0.899	0.932
12								0.000	0.298	0.580	0.735	0.827	0.886	0.923
15									0.000	0.402	0.623	0.754	0.837	0.890
20										0.000	0.369	0.589	0.727	0.817
25											0.000	0.349	0.568	0.710
30												0.000	0.336	0.554
35													0.000	0.328
40														0.000

For Mortgages with an Interest Rate of 7.75% and an Original Term of:

Age of Loan in Years	5 Years	6 Years	7 Years	8 Years	9 Years	10 Years	11 Years	12 Years	15 Years	20 Years	25 Years	30 Years	35 Years	40 Years
1	0.830	0.864	0.888	0.906	0.920	0.931	0.940	0.947	0.963	0.978	0.986	0.991	0.994	0.996
2	0.646	0.717	0.767	0.805	0.834	0.857	0.875	0.891	0.924	0.955	0.972	0.982	0.988	0.992
3	0.447	0.558	0.636	0.695	0.740	0.776	0.805	0.829	0.881	0.929	0.956	0.971	0.981	0.988
4	0.232	0.386	0.495	0.577	0.639	0.689	0.730	0.763	0.834	0.902	0.939	0.960	0.974	0.983
5	0.000	0.200	0.343	0.449	0.531	0.595	0.648	0.691	0.784	0.872	0.920	0.948	0.966	0.978
6		0.000	0.178	0.311	0.413	0.494	0.560	0.614	0.730	0.840	0.900	0.936	0.958	0.972
7			0.000	0.161	0.286	0.384	0.464	0.530	0.672	0.806	0.878	0.922	0.949	0.966
8				0.000	0.148	0.266	0.361	0.440	0.609	0.768	0.855	0.907	0.939	0.959
9					0.000	0.138	0.250	0.342	0.541	0.728	0.830	0.890	0.928	0.952
10						0.000	0.130	0.237	0.467	0.684	0.802	0.873	0.916	0.944
11							0.000	0.123	0.387	0.637	0.773	0.854	0.904	0.936
12								0.000	0.301	0.586	0.741	0.833	0.890	0.927
15									0.000	0.407	0.629	0.761	0.843	0.896
20										0.000	0.375	0.597	0.735	0.824
25											0.000	0.355	0.577	0.719
30												0.000	0.343	0.564
35													0.000	0.336
40														0.000

Remaining Principal Balance Factors

For Mortgages with an Interest Rate of 8.00% and an Original Term of:

Age of Loan in Years	5 Years	6 Years	7 Years	8 Years	9 Years	10 Years	11 Years	12 Years	15 Years	20 Years	25 Years	30 Years	35 Years	40 Years
1	0.831	0.865	0.889	0.907	0.921	0.932	0.941	0.948	0.964	0.979	0.987	0.992	0.995	0.996
2	0.647	0.718	0.769	0.806	0.835	0.858	0.877	0.892	0.925	0.956	0.973	0.983	0.989	0.993
3	0.448	0.560	0.638	0.697	0.743	0.778	0.808	0.831	0.883	0.931	0.957	0.973	0.982	0.988
4	0.233	0.388	0.497	0.579	0.642	0.692	0.732	0.766	0.837	0.904	0.941	0.962	0.975	0.984
5	0.000	0.202	0.345	0.451	0.533	0.598	0.651	0.694	0.788	0.875	0.923	0.951	0.968	0.979
6		0.000	0.179	0.313	0.415	0.497	0.563	0.617	0.734	0.844	0.903	0.938	0.960	0.974
7			0.000	0.163	0.288	0.387	0.468	0.534	0.676	0.810	0.882	0.925	0.951	0.968
8				0.000	0.150	0.268	0.364	0.443	0.613	0.773	0.859	0.910	0.942	0.962
9					0.000	0.139	0.252	0.345	0.545	0.733	0.834	0.894	0.931	0.955
10						0.000	0.131	0.239	0.471	0.689	0.808	0.877	0.920	0.948
11							0.000	0.124	0.391	0.642	0.779	0.859	0.908	0.940
12								0.000	0.305	0.592	0.747	0.839	0.895	0.931
15									0.000	0.413	0.636	0.768	0.849	0.901
20										0.000	0.381	0.605	0.743	0.831
25											0.000	0.362	0.585	0.728
30												0.000	0.350	0.573
35													0.000	0.343
40														0.000

For Mortgages with an Interest Rate of 8.25% and an Original Term of:

Age of Loan in Years	5 Years	6 Years	7 Years	8 Years	9 Years	10 Years	11 Years	12 Years	15 Years	20 Years	25 Years	30 Years	35 Years	40 Years
1	0.831	0.866	0.890	0.908	0.922	0.933	0.942	0.949	0.965	0.979	0.987	0.992	0.995	0.997
2	0.648	0.720	0.770	0.808	0.837	0.860	0.878	0.894	0.927	0.957	0.974	0.983	0.989	0.993
3	0.450	0.561	0.640	0.699	0.745	0.781	0.810	0.834	0.885	0.933	0.959	0.974	0.983	0.989
4	0.234	0.389	0.500	0.581	0.645	0.695	0.735	0.769	0.840	0.907	0.943	0.964	0.977	0.985
5	0.000	0.203	0.347	0.454	0.536	0.601	0.654	0.698	0.791	0.878	0.925	0.953	0.970	0.980
6		0.000	0.180	0.315	0.418	0.500	0.566	0.621	0.738	0.847	0.906	0.941	0.962	0.975
7			0.000	0.164	0.290	0.390	0.471	0.537	0.680	0.814	0.886	0.928	0.954	0.970
8				0.000	0.151	0.271	0.367	0.447	0.617	0.777	0.863	0.914	0.945	0.964
9					0.000	0.141	0.255	0.349	0.549	0.738	0.839	0.898	0.935	0.958
10						0.000	0.133	0.242	0.476	0.695	0.813	0.882	0.924	0.951
11							0.000	0.126	0.395	0.648	0.784	0.864	0.912	0.943
12								0.000	0.308	0.597	0.753	0.844	0.900	0.935
15									0.000	0.418	0.643	0.774	0.855	0.906
20										0.000	0.387	0.613	0.751	0.838
25											0.000	0.368	0.594	0.736
30												0.000	0.357	0.582
35													0.000	0.350
40														0.000

Remaining Principal Balance Factors

For Mortgages with an Interest Rate of 8.50% and an Original Term of:

Age of Loan in Years	5 Years	6 Years	7 Years	8 Years	9 Years	10 Years	11 Years	12 Years	15 Years	20 Years	25 Years	30 Years	35 Years	40 Years
1	0.832	0.867	0.891	0.909	0.923	0.934	0.943	0.950	0.966	0.980	0.988	0.992	0.995	0.997
2	0.650	0.721	0.772	0.810	0.839	0.861	0.880	0.895	0.928	0.958	0.975	0.984	0.990	0.994
3	0.451	0.563	0.642	0.701	0.747	0.783	0.812	0.836	0.887	0.935	0.960	0.975	0.984	0.990
4	0.235	0.391	0.502	0.584	0.647	0.697	0.738	0.771	0.843	0.909	0.945	0.966	0.978	0.986
5	0.000	0.204	0.348	0.456	0.539	0.604	0.657	0.701	0.794	0.881	0.928	0.955	0.971	0.982
6		0.000	0.182	0.317	0.421	0.503	0.570	0.624	0.742	0.851	0.909	0.943	0.964	0.977
7			0.000	0.165	0.292	0.393	0.474	0.541	0.684	0.818	0.889	0.931	0.956	0.972
8				0.000	0.152	0.273	0.370	0.450	0.622	0.782	0.867	0.917	0.947	0.966
9					0.000	0.142	0.257	0.352	0.554	0.743	0.844	0.902	0.938	0.960
10						0.000	0.134	0.244	0.480	0.700	0.818	0.886	0.928	0.953
11							0.000	0.127	0.400	0.654	0.790	0.868	0.916	0.946
12								0.000	0.312	0.603	0.759	0.849	0.904	0.938
15									0.000	0.423	0.649	0.781	0.861	0.910
20										0.000	0.392	0.620	0.758	0.845
25											0.000	0.375	0.602	0.744
30												0.000	0.364	0.591
35													0.000	0.357
40														0.000

For Mortgages with an Interest Rate of 8.75% and an Original Term of:

Age of Loan in Years	5 Years	6 Years	7 Years	8 Years	9 Years	10 Years	11 Years	12 Years	15 Years	20 Years	25 Years	30 Years	35 Years	40 Years
1	0.833	0.867	0.892	0.910	0.924	0.935	0.943	0.951	0.966	0.981	0.988	0.993	0.995	0.997
2	0.651	0.723	0.773	0.811	0.840	0.863	0.882	0.897	0.929	0.960	0.976	0.985	0.991	0.994
3	0.453	0.565	0.645	0.704	0.749	0.785	0.814	0.838	0.889	0.937	0.962	0.976	0.985	0.991
4	0.236	0.393	0.504	0.586	0.650	0.700	0.741	0.774	0.845	0.912	0.947	0.967	0.979	0.987
5	0.000	0.205	0.350	0.458	0.541	0.607	0.660	0.704	0.797	0.884	0.930	0.957	0.973	0.983
6		0.000	0.183	0.319	0.423	0.506	0.573	0.628	0.745	0.854	0.912	0.946	0.966	0.978
7			0.000	0.166	0.294	0.396	0.477	0.545	0.688	0.822	0.893	0.934	0.958	0.973
8				0.000	0.154	0.275	0.373	0.454	0.626	0.786	0.871	0.920	0.950	0.968
9					0.000	0.144	0.259	0.355	0.558	0.747	0.848	0.906	0.941	0.962
10						0.000	0.135	0.247	0.484	0.705	0.823	0.890	0.931	0.956
11							0.000	0.129	0.404	0.659	0.795	0.873	0.920	0.949
12								0.000	0.315	0.609	0.765	0.854	0.908	0.942
15									0.000	0.428	0.656	0.787	0.866	0.915
20										0.000	0.398	0.628	0.766	0.851
25											0.000	0.381	0.611	0.753
30												0.000	0.371	0.600
35													0.000	0.364
40														0.000

Remaining Principal Balance Factors

For Mortgages with an Interest Rate of 9.00% and an Original Term of:

Age of Loan in Years	5 Years	6 Years	7 Years	8 Years	9 Years	10 Years	11 Years	12 Years	15 Years	20 Years	25 Years	30 Years	35 Years	40 Years
1	0.834	0.868	0.893	0.911	0.924	0.935	0.944	0.951	0.967	0.981	0.989	0.993	0.996	0.997
2	0.653	0.724	0.775	0.813	0.842	0.865	0.883	0.898	0.931	0.961	0.977	0.986	0.991	0.994
3	0.454	0.567	0.647	0.706	0.751	0.787	0.816	0.840	0.891	0.938	0.963	0.978	0.986	0.991
4	0.237	0.395	0.506	0.589	0.652	0.703	0.743	0.777	0.848	0.914	0.949	0.969	0.980	0.988
5	0.000	0.206	0.352	0.461	0.544	0.610	0.664	0.707	0.801	0.887	0.933	0.959	0.974	0.984
6		0.000	0.184	0.321	0.426	0.509	0.576	0.631	0.749	0.858	0.915	0.948	0.968	0.980
7			0.000	0.168	0.296	0.398	0.481	0.548	0.692	0.826	0.896	0.936	0.960	0.975
8				0.000	0.155	0.277	0.376	0.457	0.630	0.791	0.875	0.924	0.952	0.970
9					0.000	0.145	0.262	0.358	0.563	0.752	0.852	0.910	0.944	0.965
10						0.000	0.137	0.249	0.489	0.710	0.827	0.894	0.934	0.959
11							0.000	0.130	0.408	0.664	0.800	0.878	0.924	0.952
12								0.000	0.319	0.614	0.770	0.859	0.912	0.945
15									0.000	0.433	0.662	0.793	0.871	0.919
20										0.000	0.404	0.635	0.773	0.857
25											0.000	0.388	0.619	0.761
30												0.000	0.378	0.609
35													0.000	0.372
40														0.000

For Mortgages with an Interest Rate of 9.25% and an Original Term of:

Age of Loan in Years	5 Years	6 Years	7 Years	8 Years	9 Years	10 Years	11 Years	12 Years	15 Years	20 Years	25 Years	30 Years	35 Years	40 Years
1	0.835	0.869	0.893	0.911	0.925	0.936	0.945	0.952	0.968	0.982	0.989	0.994	0.996	0.998
2	0.654	0.726	0.777	0.814	0.843	0.866	0.885	0.900	0.932	0.962	0.978	0.986	0.992	0.995
3	0.456	0.569	0.649	0.708	0.753	0.790	0.819	0.842	0.893	0.940	0.965	0.979	0.987	0.992
4	0.238	0.396	0.508	0.591	0.655	0.705	0.746	0.780	0.851	0.916	0.951	0.970	0.982	0.989
5	0.000	0.207	0.354	0.463	0.547	0.613	0.667	0.710	0.804	0.890	0.935	0.961	0.976	0.985
6		0.000	0.185	0.323	0.428	0.512	0.579	0.635	0.753	0.861	0.918	0.950	0.969	0.981
7			0.000	0.169	0.299	0.401	0.484	0.552	0.696	0.830	0.899	0.939	0.962	0.977
8				0.000	0.156	0.280	0.379	0.461	0.635	0.795	0.879	0.927	0.955	0.972
9					0.000	0.146	0.264	0.361	0.567	0.757	0.857	0.913	0.947	0.967
10						0.000	0.138	0.252	0.493	0.715	0.832	0.898	0.937	0.961
11							0.000	0.132	0.412	0.670	0.805	0.882	0.927	0.955
12								0.000	0.322	0.620	0.776	0.864	0.916	0.948
15									0.000	0.439	0.669	0.799	0.876	0.923
20										0.000	0.410	0.643	0.780	0.863
25											0.000	0.394	0.627	0.768
30												0.000	0.384	0.618
35													0.000	0.379
40														0.000

Remaining Principal Balance Factors

For Mortgages with an Interest Rate of 9.50% and an Original Term of:

Age of Loan in Years	5 Years	6 Years	7 Years	8 Years	9 Years	10 Years	11 Years	12 Years	15 Years	20 Years	25 Years	30 Years	35 Years	40 Years
1	0.836	0.870	0.894	0.912	0.926	0.937	0.946	0.953	0.968	0.982	0.990	0.994	0.996	0.998
2	0.656	0.727	0.778	0.816	0.845	0.868	0.886	0.901	0.934	0.963	0.978	0.987	0.992	0.995
3	0.457	0.570	0.651	0.710	0.756	0.792	0.821	0.845	0.895	0.942	0.966	0.980	0.988	0.992
4	0.240	0.398	0.510	0.594	0.658	0.708	0.749	0.782	0.853	0.918	0.952	0.971	0.983	0.989
5	0.000	0.208	0.356	0.465	0.550	0.616	0.670	0.714	0.807	0.893	0.937	0.962	0.977	0.986
6		0.000	0.186	0.325	0.431	0.515	0.583	0.638	0.756	0.864	0.921	0.953	0.971	0.982
7			0.000	0.170	0.301	0.404	0.487	0.555	0.700	0.833	0.903	0.942	0.964	0.978
8				0.000	0.157	0.282	0.382	0.464	0.639	0.799	0.883	0.930	0.957	0.974
9					0.000	0.148	0.267	0.364	0.571	0.762	0.861	0.917	0.949	0.969
10						0.000	0.140	0.254	0.497	0.720	0.837	0.902	0.940	0.963
11							0.000	0.133	0.416	0.675	0.810	0.886	0.931	0.957
12								0.000	0.326	0.625	0.781	0.869	0.920	0.951
15									0.000	0.444	0.675	0.805	0.881	0.927
20										0.000	0.416	0.650	0.787	0.869
25											0.000	0.400	0.635	0.776
30												0.000	0.391	0.626
35													0.000	0.386
40														0.000

For Mortgages with an Interest Rate of 9.75% and an Original Term of:

Age of Loan in Years	5 Years	6 Years	7 Years	8 Years	9 Years	10 Years	11 Years	12 Years	15 Years	20 Years	25 Years	30 Years	35 Years	40 Years
1	0.837	0.871	0.895	0.913	0.927	0.938	0.947	0.954	0.969	0.983	0.990	0.994	0.996	0.998
2	0.657	0.729	0.780	0.818	0.846	0.869	0.888	0.903	0.935	0.964	0.979	0.988	0.993	0.995
3	0.459	0.572	0.653	0.712	0.758	0.794	0.823	0.847	0.897	0.943	0.967	0.981	0.988	0.993
4	0.241	0.400	0.512	0.596	0.660	0.711	0.751	0.785	0.856	0.921	0.954	0.973	0.984	0.990
5	0.000	0.210	0.358	0.468	0.552	0.619	0.673	0.717	0.810	0.895	0.940	0.964	0.978	0.987
6		0.000	0.188	0.327	0.434	0.518	0.586	0.642	0.760	0.868	0.923	0.955	0.973	0.983
7			0.000	0.171	0.303	0.407	0.490	0.559	0.704	0.837	0.906	0.944	0.966	0.980
8				0.000	0.159	0.284	0.385	0.468	0.643	0.803	0.886	0.933	0.959	0.975
9					0.000	0.149	0.269	0.367	0.576	0.766	0.865	0.920	0.952	0.971
10						0.000	0.141	0.257	0.501	0.725	0.841	0.906	0.943	0.966
11							0.000	0.134	0.420	0.680	0.815	0.890	0.934	0.960
12								0.000	0.330	0.631	0.786	0.873	0.924	0.954
15									0.000	0.449	0.681	0.811	0.886	0.931
20										0.000	0.422	0.657	0.793	0.875
25											0.000	0.407	0.643	0.783
30												0.000	0.398	0.634
35													0.000	0.393
40														0.000

Remaining Principal Balance Factors

For Mortgages with an Interest Rate of 10.00% and an Original Term of:

Age of Loan in Years	5 Years	6 Years	7 Years	8 Years	9 Years	10 Years	11 Years	12 Years	15 Years	20 Years	25 Years	30 Years	35 Years	40 Years
1	0.838	0.872	0.896	0.914	0.928	0.939	0.947	0.955	0.970	0.983	0.991	0.994	0.997	0.998
2	0.658	0.730	0.781	0.819	0.848	0.871	0.889	0.904	0.936	0.965	0.980	0.988	0.993	0.996
3	0.460	0.574	0.655	0.714	0.760	0.796	0.825	0.849	0.899	0.945	0.969	0.982	0.989	0.993
4	0.242	0.401	0.514	0.598	0.663	0.713	0.754	0.788	0.858	0.923	0.956	0.974	0.985	0.991
5	0.000	0.211	0.360	0.470	0.555	0.622	0.676	0.720	0.813	0.898	0.942	0.966	0.980	0.988
6		0.000	0.189	0.329	0.436	0.521	0.589	0.645	0.763	0.871	0.926	0.957	0.974	0.984
7			0.000	0.173	0.305	0.410	0.494	0.562	0.708	0.841	0.909	0.946	0.968	0.981
8				0.000	0.160	0.286	0.388	0.471	0.647	0.807	0.890	0.935	0.961	0.977
9					0.000	0.150	0.271	0.370	0.580	0.771	0.869	0.923	0.954	0.972
10						0.000	0.142	0.259	0.506	0.730	0.846	0.909	0.946	0.968
11							0.000	0.136	0.424	0.685	0.820	0.894	0.937	0.962
12								0.000	0.333	0.636	0.792	0.878	0.927	0.956
15									0.000	0.454	0.688	0.817	0.891	0.934
20										0.000	0.428	0.664	0.800	0.880
25											0.000	0.413	0.651	0.790
30												0.000	0.405	0.643
35													0.000	0.400
40														0.000

For Mortgages with an Interest Rate of 10.25% and an Original Term of:

Age of Loan in Years	5 Years	6 Years	7 Years	8 Years	9 Years	10 Years	11 Years	12 Years	15 Years	20 Years	25 Years	30 Years	35 Years	40 Years
1	0.839	0.873	0.897	0.915	0.929	0.939	0.948	0.955	0.970	0.984	0.991	0.995	0.997	0.998
2	0.660	0.732	0.783	0.821	0.850	0.872	0.891	0.906	0.937	0.966	0.981	0.989	0.993	0.996
3	0.462	0.576	0.657	0.716	0.762	0.798	0.827	0.851	0.901	0.947	0.970	0.982	0.990	0.994
4	0.243	0.403	0.517	0.601	0.665	0.716	0.757	0.790	0.861	0.925	0.957	0.975	0.985	0.991
5	0.000	0.212	0.362	0.473	0.558	0.625	0.679	0.723	0.816	0.901	0.944	0.967	0.981	0.989
6		0.000	0.190	0.331	0.439	0.524	0.592	0.648	0.767	0.874	0.929	0.959	0.976	0.986
7			0.000	0.174	0.307	0.412	0.497	0.566	0.712	0.844	0.912	0.949	0.970	0.982
8				0.000	0.161	0.289	0.391	0.475	0.651	0.812	0.893	0.938	0.964	0.978
9					0.000	0.152	0.274	0.373	0.584	0.775	0.873	0.926	0.956	0.974
10						0.000	0.144	0.261	0.510	0.735	0.850	0.913	0.949	0.970
11							0.000	0.137	0.428	0.691	0.825	0.898	0.940	0.964
12								0.000	0.337	0.641	0.797	0.882	0.931	0.959
15									0.000	0.459	0.694	0.822	0.895	0.938
20										0.000	0.433	0.671	0.806	0.885
25											0.000	0.419	0.658	0.797
30												0.000	0.411	0.651
35													0.000	0.407
40														0.000

Remaining Principal Balance Factors

For Mortgages with an Interest Rate of 10.50% and an Original Term of:

Age of Loan in Years	5 Years	6 Years	7 Years	8 Years	9 Years	10 Years	11 Years	12 Years	15 Years	20 Years	25 Years	30 Years	35 Years	40 Years
1	0.839	0.874	0.898	0.916	0.929	0.940	0.949	0.956	0.971	0.984	0.991	0.995	0.997	0.998
2	0.661	0.733	0.784	0.822	0.851	0.874	0.892	0.907	0.939	0.967	0.982	0.989	0.994	0.996
3	0.463	0.578	0.659	0.718	0.764	0.800	0.829	0.853	0.903	0.948	0.971	0.983	0.990	0.994
4	0.244	0.405	0.519	0.603	0.668	0.719	0.759	0.793	0.863	0.927	0.959	0.976	0.986	0.992
5	0.000	0.213	0.364	0.475	0.561	0.628	0.682	0.726	0.819	0.903	0.946	0.969	0.982	0.989
6		0.000	0.191	0.333	0.442	0.527	0.596	0.652	0.770	0.877	0.931	0.960	0.977	0.986
7			0.000	0.175	0.309	0.415	0.500	0.570	0.716	0.848	0.915	0.951	0.971	0.983
8				0.000	0.163	0.291	0.394	0.478	0.656	0.816	0.897	0.941	0.965	0.980
9					0.000	0.153	0.276	0.377	0.589	0.780	0.876	0.929	0.959	0.976
10						0.000	0.145	0.264	0.514	0.740	0.854	0.916	0.951	0.971
11							0.000	0.139	0.432	0.696	0.829	0.902	0.943	0.967
12								0.000	0.340	0.647	0.802	0.886	0.934	0.961
15									0.000	0.464	0.700	0.828	0.900	0.941
20										0.000	0.439	0.678	0.812	0.890
25											0.000	0.426	0.666	0.804
30												0.000	0.418	0.659
35													0.000	0.413
40														0.000

For Mortgages with an Interest Rate of 10.75% and an Original Term of:

Age of Loan in Years	5 Years	6 Years	7 Years	8 Years	9 Years	10 Years	11 Years	12 Years	15 Years	20 Years	25 Years	30 Years	35 Years	40 Years
1	0.840	0.875	0.899	0.917	0.930	0.941	0.950	0.957	0.972	0.985	0.992	0.995	0.997	0.998
2	0.663	0.735	0.786	0.824	0.853	0.875	0.894	0.909	0.940	0.968	0.982	0.990	0.994	0.997
3	0.465	0.580	0.661	0.720	0.766	0.802	0.831	0.855	0.905	0.950	0.972	0.984	0.991	0.995
4	0.245	0.407	0.521	0.605	0.670	0.721	0.762	0.795	0.866	0.929	0.960	0.978	0.987	0.993
5	0.000	0.214	0.365	0.477	0.563	0.631	0.685	0.729	0.822	0.906	0.948	0.970	0.983	0.990
6		0.000	0.193	0.335	0.444	0.530	0.599	0.655	0.774	0.880	0.933	0.962	0.978	0.987
7			0.000	0.176	0.312	0.418	0.503	0.573	0.720	0.851	0.918	0.953	0.973	0.984
8				0.000	0.164	0.293	0.397	0.482	0.660	0.820	0.900	0.943	0.967	0.981
9					0.000	0.154	0.279	0.380	0.593	0.784	0.880	0.932	0.961	0.977
10						0.000	0.147	0.266	0.519	0.745	0.858	0.919	0.954	0.973
11							0.000	0.140	0.436	0.701	0.834	0.906	0.946	0.969
12								0.000	0.344	0.652	0.807	0.890	0.937	0.963
15									0.000	0.470	0.706	0.833	0.904	0.944
20										0.000	0.445	0.685	0.819	0.895
25											0.000	0.432	0.673	0.810
30												0.000	0.424	0.666
35													0.000	0.420
40														0.000

Remaining Principal Balance Factors

For Mortgages with an Interest Rate of 11.00% and an Original Term of:

Age of Loan in Years	5 Years	6 Years	7 Years	8 Years	9 Years	10 Years	11 Years	12 Years	15 Years	20 Years	25 Years	30 Years	35 Years	40 Years
1	0.841	0.875	0.900	0.917	0.931	0.942	0.950	0.957	0.972	0.985	0.992	0.995	0.997	0.999
2	0.664	0.736	0.788	0.825	0.854	0.877	0.895	0.910	0.941	0.969	0.983	0.990	0.995	0.997
3	0.466	0.581	0.662	0.722	0.768	0.805	0.833	0.857	0.907	0.951	0.973	0.985	0.991	0.995
4	0.246	0.408	0.523	0.608	0.673	0.724	0.765	0.798	0.868	0.931	0.962	0.979	0.988	0.993
5	0.000	0.215	0.367	0.480	0.566	0.634	0.688	0.732	0.825	0.908	0.950	0.972	0.984	0.991
6		0.000	0.194	0.337	0.447	0.533	0.602	0.659	0.777	0.883	0.936	0.964	0.979	0.988
7			0.000	0.178	0.314	0.421	0.507	0.577	0.724	0.855	0.920	0.955	0.974	0.985
8				0.000	0.165	0.296	0.400	0.485	0.664	0.823	0.903	0.945	0.969	0.982
9					0.000	0.156	0.281	0.383	0.597	0.788	0.884	0.935	0.963	0.979
10						0.000	0.148	0.269	0.523	0.749	0.862	0.923	0.956	0.975
11							0.000	0.142	0.440	0.706	0.838	0.909	0.948	0.970
12								0.000	0.347	0.657	0.812	0.894	0.940	0.965
15									0.000	0.475	0.712	0.838	0.908	0.947
20										0.000	0.451	0.691	0.824	0.899
25											0.000	0.438	0.680	0.817
30												0.000	0.431	0.674
35													0.000	0.427
40														0.000

For Mortgages with an Interest Rate of 11.25% and an Original Term of:

Age of Loan in Years	5 Years	6 Years	7 Years	8 Years	9 Years	10 Years	11 Years	12 Years	15 Years	20 Years	25 Years	30 Years	35 Years	40 Years
1	0.842	0.876	0.900	0.918	0.932	0.943	0.951	0.958	0.973	0.986	0.992	0.996	0.998	0.999
2	0.666	0.738	0.789	0.827	0.856	0.878	0.897	0.911	0.942	0.970	0.984	0.991	0.995	0.997
3	0.468	0.583	0.664	0.725	0.770	0.807	0.836	0.859	0.909	0.952	0.974	0.986	0.992	0.995
4	0.247	0.410	0.525	0.610	0.675	0.726	0.767	0.801	0.871	0.933	0.963	0.980	0.989	0.994
5	0.000	0.217	0.369	0.482	0.569	0.636	0.691	0.735	0.828	0.911	0.951	0.973	0.985	0.991
6		0.000	0.195	0.339	0.449	0.536	0.605	0.662	0.780	0.886	0.938	0.966	0.981	0.989
7			0.000	0.179	0.316	0.424	0.510	0.580	0.727	0.858	0.923	0.957	0.976	0.986
8				0.000	0.167	0.298	0.403	0.488	0.668	0.827	0.906	0.948	0.971	0.983
9					0.000	0.157	0.283	0.386	0.601	0.793	0.887	0.937	0.965	0.980
10						0.000	0.150	0.271	0.527	0.754	0.866	0.926	0.958	0.976
11							0.000	0.143	0.444	0.711	0.843	0.913	0.951	0.972
12								0.000	0.351	0.662	0.816	0.898	0.943	0.967
15									0.000	0.480	0.717	0.843	0.912	0.950
20										0.000	0.456	0.698	0.830	0.904
25											0.000	0.444	0.687	0.823
30												0.000	0.437	0.681
35													0.000	0.434
40														0.000

Remaining Principal Balance Factors

For Mortgages with an Interest Rate of 11.50% and an Original Term of:

Age of Loan in Years	5 Years	6 Years	7 Years	8 Years	9 Years	10 Years	11 Years	12 Years	15 Years	20 Years	25 Years	30 Years	35 Years	40 Years
1	0.843	0.877	0.901	0.919	0.933	0.943	0.952	0.959	0.973	0.986	0.993	0.996	0.998	0.999
2	0.667	0.739	0.791	0.828	0.857	0.880	0.898	0.913	0.944	0.971	0.984	0.991	0.995	0.997
3	0.470	0.585	0.666	0.727	0.773	0.809	0.838	0.861	0.910	0.954	0.975	0.986	0.992	0.996
4	0.248	0.412	0.527	0.612	0.678	0.729	0.770	0.803	0.873	0.935	0.965	0.981	0.989	0.994
5	0.000	0.218	0.371	0.485	0.571	0.639	0.694	0.738	0.831	0.913	0.953	0.974	0.986	0.992
6		0.000	0.196	0.341	0.452	0.539	0.609	0.665	0.784	0.889	0.940	0.967	0.982	0.990
7			0.000	0.180	0.318	0.426	0.513	0.584	0.731	0.861	0.925	0.959	0.977	0.987
8				0.000	0.168	0.300	0.406	0.492	0.672	0.831	0.909	0.950	0.972	0.984
9					0.000	0.159	0.286	0.389	0.606	0.797	0.891	0.940	0.967	0.981
10						0.000	0.151	0.274	0.531	0.759	0.870	0.929	0.960	0.978
11							0.000	0.145	0.448	0.716	0.847	0.916	0.953	0.974
12								0.000	0.354	0.667	0.821	0.902	0.945	0.969
15									0.000	0.485	0.723	0.848	0.915	0.953
20										0.000	0.462	0.704	0.836	0.908
25											0.000	0.450	0.694	0.829
30												0.000	0.444	0.689
35													0.000	0.440
40														0.000

For Mortgages with an Interest Rate of 11.75% and an Original Term of:

Age of Loan in Years	5 Years	6 Years	7 Years	8 Years	9 Years	10 Years	11 Years	12 Years	15 Years	20 Years	25 Years	30 Years	35 Years	40 Years
1	0.844	0.878	0.902	0.920	0.933	0.944	0.953	0.960	0.974	0.987	0.993	0.996	0.998	0.999
2	0.668	0.741	0.792	0.830	0.859	0.881	0.899	0.914	0.945	0.972	0.985	0.992	0.996	0.998
3	0.471	0.587	0.668	0.729	0.775	0.811	0.840	0.863	0.912	0.955	0.976	0.987	0.993	0.996
4	0.249	0.414	0.529	0.615	0.680	0.731	0.772	0.806	0.875	0.936	0.966	0.982	0.990	0.994
5	0.000	0.219	0.373	0.487	0.574	0.642	0.697	0.741	0.834	0.915	0.955	0.975	0.987	0.993
6		0.000	0.197	0.343	0.455	0.542	0.612	0.669	0.787	0.891	0.942	0.969	0.983	0.990
7			0.000	0.182	0.320	0.429	0.516	0.587	0.735	0.865	0.928	0.961	0.978	0.988
8				0.000	0.170	0.302	0.409	0.495	0.676	0.835	0.912	0.952	0.974	0.985
9					0.000	0.160	0.288	0.392	0.610	0.801	0.894	0.942	0.968	0.982
10						0.000	0.152	0.276	0.535	0.763	0.874	0.931	0.962	0.979
11							0.000	0.146	0.452	0.720	0.851	0.919	0.956	0.975
12								0.000	0.358	0.672	0.826	0.905	0.948	0.971
15									0.000	0.490	0.729	0.852	0.919	0.955
20										0.000	0.468	0.711	0.841	0.912
25											0.000	0.456	0.701	0.835
30												0.000	0.450	0.696
35													0.000	0.447
40														0.000

Remaining Principal Balance Factors

For Mortgages with an Interest Rate of 12.00% and an Original Term of:

Age of Loan in Years	5 Years	6 Years	7 Years	8 Years	9 Years	10 Years	11 Years	12 Years	15 Years	20 Years	25 Years	30 Years	35 Years	40 Years
1	0.845	0.879	0.903	0.921	0.934	0.945	0.953	0.960	0.975	0.987	0.993	0.996	0.998	0.999
2	0.670	0.742	0.794	0.831	0.860	0.883	0.901	0.915	0.946	0.973	0.986	0.992	0.996	0.998
3	0.473	0.589	0.670	0.731	0.777	0.813	0.842	0.865	0.914	0.956	0.977	0.988	0.993	0.996
4	0.250	0.415	0.531	0.617	0.683	0.734	0.775	0.808	0.877	0.938	0.967	0.982	0.990	0.995
5	0.000	0.220	0.375	0.489	0.577	0.645	0.700	0.744	0.837	0.917	0.957	0.977	0.987	0.993
6		0.000	0.199	0.345	0.457	0.545	0.615	0.672	0.790	0.894	0.944	0.970	0.984	0.991
7			0.000	0.183	0.323	0.432	0.519	0.590	0.738	0.868	0.930	0.963	0.980	0.989
8				0.000	0.171	0.305	0.412	0.499	0.680	0.838	0.915	0.954	0.975	0.986
9					0.000	0.161	0.291	0.395	0.614	0.805	0.897	0.945	0.970	0.984
10						0.000	0.154	0.279	0.540	0.767	0.878	0.934	0.964	0.980
11							0.000	0.148	0.456	0.725	0.855	0.922	0.958	0.977
12								0.000	0.361	0.677	0.830	0.909	0.950	0.973
15									0.000	0.495	0.734	0.857	0.922	0.958
20										0.000	0.473	0.717	0.846	0.916
25											0.000	0.462	0.708	0.840
30												0.000	0.457	0.703
35													0.000	0.453
40														0.000

For Mortgages with an Interest Rate of 12.25% and an Original Term of:

Age of Loan in Years	5 Years	6 Years	7 Years	8 Years	9 Years	10 Years	11 Years	12 Years	15 Years	20 Years	25 Years	30 Years	35 Years	40 Years
1	0.846	0.880	0.904	0.922	0.935	0.946	0.954	0.961	0.975	0.988	0.994	0.997	0.998	0.999
2	0.671	0.744	0.795	0.833	0.862	0.884	0.902	0.917	0.947	0.974	0.986	0.993	0.996	0.998
3	0.474	0.590	0.672	0.733	0.779	0.815	0.844	0.867	0.915	0.958	0.978	0.988	0.994	0.997
4	0.251	0.417	0.534	0.620	0.685	0.736	0.777	0.811	0.880	0.940	0.969	0.983	0.991	0.995
5	0.000	0.221	0.377	0.492	0.579	0.648	0.703	0.747	0.839	0.920	0.958	0.978	0.988	0.994
6		0.000	0.200	0.347	0.460	0.548	0.618	0.675	0.794	0.897	0.946	0.971	0.985	0.992
7			0.000	0.184	0.325	0.435	0.523	0.594	0.742	0.871	0.933	0.964	0.981	0.990
8				0.000	0.172	0.307	0.415	0.502	0.684	0.842	0.918	0.956	0.976	0.987
9					0.000	0.163	0.293	0.399	0.618	0.809	0.901	0.947	0.972	0.985
10						0.000	0.155	0.282	0.544	0.772	0.881	0.937	0.966	0.982
11							0.000	0.149	0.460	0.730	0.859	0.925	0.960	0.978
12								0.000	0.365	0.682	0.835	0.912	0.953	0.974
15									0.000	0.500	0.740	0.862	0.926	0.960
20										0.000	0.479	0.723	0.851	0.920
25											0.000	0.468	0.714	0.846
30												0.000	0.463	0.710
35													0.000	0.460
40														0.000

Remaining Principal Balance Factors

For Mortgages with an Interest Rate of 12.50% and an Original Term of:

Age of Loan in Years	5 Years	6 Years	7 Years	8 Years	9 Years	10 Years	11 Years	12 Years	15 Years	20 Years	25 Years	30 Years	35 Years	40 Years
1	0.846	0.881	0.905	0.922	0.936	0.946	0.955	0.962	0.976	0.988	0.994	0.997	0.998	0.999
2	0.673	0.745	0.797	0.834	0.863	0.886	0.904	0.918	0.948	0.974	0.987	0.993	0.996	0.998
3	0.476	0.592	0.674	0.735	0.781	0.817	0.846	0.869	0.917	0.959	0.979	0.989	0.994	0.997
4	0.253	0.419	0.536	0.622	0.688	0.739	0.780	0.813	0.882	0.942	0.970	0.984	0.992	0.996
5	0.000	0.222	0.379	0.494	0.582	0.651	0.705	0.750	0.842	0.922	0.960	0.979	0.989	0.994
6		0.000	0.201	0.349	0.462	0.551	0.621	0.678	0.797	0.899	0.948	0.973	0.986	0.992
7			0.000	0.186	0.327	0.438	0.526	0.597	0.746	0.874	0.935	0.966	0.982	0.990
8				0.000	0.174	0.309	0.418	0.506	0.688	0.845	0.920	0.958	0.978	0.988
9					0.000	0.164	0.295	0.402	0.622	0.813	0.904	0.949	0.973	0.986
10						0.000	0.157	0.284	0.548	0.776	0.885	0.939	0.968	0.983
11							0.000	0.151	0.464	0.735	0.863	0.928	0.962	0.980
12								0.000	0.368	0.687	0.839	0.915	0.955	0.976
15									0.000	0.505	0.745	0.866	0.929	0.962
20										0.000	0.485	0.729	0.856	0.923
25											0.000	0.474	0.721	0.851
30												0.000	0.469	0.717
35													0.000	0.466
40														0.000

For Mortgages with an Interest Rate of 12.75% and an Original Term of:

Age of Loan in Years	5 Years	6 Years	7 Years	8 Years	9 Years	10 Years	11 Years	12 Years	15 Years	20 Years	25 Years	30 Years	35 Years	40 Years
1	0.847	0.881	0.905	0.923	0.937	0.947	0.955	0.962	0.976	0.988	0.994	0.997	0.998	0.999
2	0.674	0.747	0.798	0.836	0.865	0.887	0.905	0.919	0.949	0.975	0.987	0.993	0.997	0.998
3	0.477	0.594	0.676	0.737	0.783	0.819	0.847	0.871	0.919	0.960	0.980	0.989	0.994	0.997
4	0.254	0.421	0.538	0.624	0.690	0.741	0.782	0.815	0.884	0.943	0.971	0.985	0.992	0.996
5	0.000	0.224	0.381	0.496	0.585	0.653	0.708	0.753	0.845	0.924	0.961	0.980	0.989	0.994
6		0.000	0.202	0.351	0.465	0.554	0.624	0.682	0.800	0.902	0.950	0.974	0.986	0.993
7			0.000	0.187	0.329	0.440	0.529	0.601	0.749	0.877	0.937	0.967	0.983	0.991
8				0.000	0.175	0.312	0.421	0.509	0.692	0.849	0.923	0.960	0.979	0.989
9					0.000	0.166	0.298	0.405	0.626	0.817	0.907	0.951	0.975	0.987
10						0.000	0.158	0.287	0.552	0.780	0.888	0.942	0.969	0.984
11							0.000	0.152	0.468	0.739	0.867	0.931	0.964	0.981
12								0.000	0.372	0.692	0.843	0.918	0.957	0.977
15									0.000	0.510	0.750	0.870	0.932	0.964
20										0.000	0.490	0.735	0.861	0.927
25											0.000	0.480	0.727	0.856
30												0.000	0.475	0.723
35													0.000	0.473
40														0.000

Remaining Principal Balance Factors

For Mortgages with an Interest Rate of 13.00% and an Original Term of:

Age of Loan in Years	5 Years	6 Years	7 Years	8 Years	9 Years	10 Years	11 Years	12 Years	15 Years	20 Years	25 Years	30 Years	35 Years	40 Years
1	0.848	0.882	0.906	0.924	0.937	0.948	0.956	0.963	0.977	0.989	0.994	0.997	0.998	0.999
2	0.675	0.748	0.800	0.837	0.866	0.888	0.906	0.921	0.950	0.976	0.988	0.994	0.997	0.998
3	0.479	0.596	0.678	0.739	0.785	0.821	0.849	0.873	0.920	0.961	0.981	0.990	0.995	0.997
4	0.255	0.422	0.540	0.626	0.692	0.744	0.785	0.818	0.886	0.945	0.972	0.986	0.993	0.996
5	0.000	0.225	0.383	0.499	0.587	0.656	0.711	0.756	0.847	0.926	0.963	0.981	0.990	0.995
6		0.000	0.204	0.354	0.468	0.557	0.627	0.685	0.803	0.905	0.952	0.975	0.987	0.993
7			0.000	0.188	0.331	0.443	0.532	0.604	0.753	0.880	0.940	0.969	0.984	0.992
8				0.000	0.176	0.314	0.424	0.512	0.695	0.852	0.926	0.962	0.980	0.990
9					0.000	0.167	0.300	0.408	0.630	0.821	0.910	0.954	0.976	0.987
10						0.000	0.160	0.289	0.556	0.785	0.891	0.944	0.971	0.985
11							0.000	0.154	0.472	0.744	0.871	0.934	0.966	0.982
12								0.000	0.376	0.697	0.847	0.922	0.959	0.979
15									0.000	0.515	0.755	0.874	0.935	0.966
20										0.000	0.496	0.741	0.866	0.930
25											0.000	0.486	0.733	0.861
30												0.000	0.481	0.730
35													0.000	0.479
40														0.000

For Mortgages with an Interest Rate of 13.25% and an Original Term of:

Age of Loan in Years	5 Years	6 Years	7 Years	8 Years	9 Years	10 Years	11 Years	12 Years	15 Years	20 Years	25 Years	30 Years	35 Years	40 Years
1	0.849	0.883	0.907	0.925	0.938	0.949	0.957	0.964	0.977	0.989	0.995	0.997	0.999	0.999
2	0.677	0.750	0.801	0.839	0.867	0.890	0.908	0.922	0.952	0.977	0.988	0.994	0.997	0.998
3	0.480	0.598	0.680	0.741	0.787	0.823	0.851	0.874	0.922	0.963	0.981	0.991	0.995	0.997
4	0.256	0.424	0.542	0.629	0.695	0.746	0.787	0.820	0.888	0.946	0.973	0.986	0.993	0.996
5	0.000	0.226	0.385	0.501	0.590	0.659	0.714	0.758	0.850	0.928	0.964	0.982	0.991	0.995
6		0.000	0.205	0.356	0.470	0.559	0.631	0.688	0.806	0.907	0.954	0.976	0.988	0.994
7			0.000	0.189	0.334	0.446	0.535	0.608	0.756	0.883	0.942	0.970	0.985	0.992
8				0.000	0.178	0.316	0.427	0.516	0.699	0.856	0.928	0.963	0.981	0.990
9					0.000	0.169	0.303	0.411	0.634	0.824	0.912	0.956	0.977	0.988
10						0.000	0.161	0.292	0.560	0.789	0.895	0.946	0.973	0.986
11							0.000	0.155	0.476	0.748	0.874	0.936	0.967	0.983
12								0.000	0.379	0.702	0.851	0.924	0.961	0.980
15									0.000	0.520	0.760	0.878	0.938	0.968
20										0.000	0.501	0.747	0.870	0.933
25											0.000	0.492	0.740	0.866
30												0.000	0.487	0.736
35													0.000	0.485
40														0.000

Remaining Principal Balance Factors

For Mortgages with an Interest Rate of 13.50% and an Original Term of:

Age of Loan in Years	5 Years	6 Years	7 Years	8 Years	9 Years	10 Years	11 Years	12 Years	15 Years	20 Years	25 Years	30 Years	35 Years	40 Years
1	0.850	0.884	0.908	0.925	0.939	0.949	0.957	0.964	0.978	0.989	0.995	0.997	0.999	0.999
2	0.678	0.751	0.802	0.840	0.869	0.891	0.909	0.923	0.953	0.977	0.989	0.994	0.997	0.999
3	0.482	0.599	0.682	0.743	0.789	0.825	0.853	0.876	0.924	0.964	0.982	0.991	0.995	0.998
4	0.257	0.426	0.544	0.631	0.697	0.749	0.790	0.823	0.890	0.948	0.974	0.987	0.993	0.997
5	0.000	0.227	0.386	0.504	0.592	0.662	0.717	0.761	0.853	0.930	0.965	0.983	0.991	0.996
6		0.000	0.206	0.358	0.473	0.562	0.634	0.691	0.809	0.909	0.955	0.978	0.989	0.994
7			0.000	0.191	0.336	0.449	0.538	0.611	0.760	0.886	0.944	0.972	0.986	0.993
8				0.000	0.179	0.319	0.430	0.519	0.703	0.859	0.930	0.965	0.982	0.991
9					0.000	0.170	0.305	0.414	0.638	0.828	0.915	0.957	0.978	0.989
10						0.000	0.163	0.294	0.564	0.793	0.898	0.949	0.974	0.987
11							0.000	0.157	0.480	0.753	0.878	0.939	0.969	0.984
12								0.000	0.383	0.707	0.855	0.927	0.963	0.981
15									0.000	0.525	0.765	0.882	0.940	0.970
20										0.000	0.507	0.752	0.874	0.936
25											0.000	0.498	0.746	0.871
30												0.000	0.493	0.742
35													0.000	0.491
40														0.000

For Mortgages with an Interest Rate of 13.75% and an Original Term of:

Age of Loan in Years	5 Years	6 Years	7 Years	8 Years	9 Years	10 Years	11 Years	12 Years	15 Years	20 Years	25 Years	30 Years	35 Years	40 Years
1	0.851	0.885	0.909	0.926	0.940	0.950	0.958	0.965	0.978	0.990	0.995	0.998	0.999	0.999
2	0.679	0.753	0.804	0.842	0.870	0.892	0.910	0.924	0.954	0.978	0.989	0.995	0.997	0.999
3	0.483	0.601	0.684	0.745	0.791	0.827	0.855	0.878	0.925	0.965	0.983	0.991	0.996	0.998
4	0.258	0.427	0.546	0.633	0.700	0.751	0.792	0.825	0.893	0.949	0.975	0.988	0.994	0.997
5	0.000	0.228	0.388	0.506	0.595	0.665	0.720	0.764	0.855	0.932	0.967	0.983	0.992	0.996
6		0.000	0.207	0.360	0.475	0.565	0.637	0.694	0.812	0.912	0.957	0.979	0.989	0.995
7			0.000	0.192	0.338	0.452	0.542	0.614	0.763	0.889	0.946	0.973	0.986	0.993
8				0.000	0.181	0.321	0.433	0.523	0.707	0.862	0.933	0.967	0.983	0.992
9					0.000	0.171	0.308	0.417	0.642	0.832	0.918	0.959	0.980	0.990
10						0.000	0.164	0.297	0.568	0.797	0.901	0.951	0.975	0.988
11							0.000	0.159	0.483	0.757	0.881	0.941	0.971	0.985
12								0.000	0.386	0.711	0.859	0.930	0.965	0.982
15									0.000	0.530	0.770	0.886	0.943	0.971
20										0.000	0.512	0.758	0.879	0.939
25											0.000	0.504	0.751	0.875
30												0.000	0.499	0.748
35													0.000	0.497
40														0.000

Remaining Principal Balance Factors

For Mortgages with an Interest Rate of 14.00% and an Original Term of:

Age of Loan in Years	5 Years	6 Years	7 Years	8 Years	9 Years	10 Years	11 Years	12 Years	15 Years	20 Years	25 Years	30 Years	35 Years	40 Years
1	0.851	0.886	0.909	0.927	0.940	0.951	0.959	0.965	0.979	0.990	0.995	0.998	0.999	0.999
2	0.681	0.754	0.805	0.843	0.872	0.894	0.911	0.926	0.955	0.979	0.990	0.995	0.998	0.999
3	0.485	0.603	0.686	0.747	0.793	0.829	0.857	0.880	0.927	0.966	0.984	0.992	0.996	0.998
4	0.259	0.429	0.548	0.636	0.702	0.754	0.794	0.827	0.895	0.951	0.976	0.988	0.994	0.997
5	0.000	0.229	0.390	0.508	0.598	0.667	0.722	0.767	0.858	0.934	0.968	0.984	0.992	0.996
6		0.000	0.209	0.362	0.478	0.568	0.640	0.697	0.815	0.914	0.959	0.980	0.990	0.995
7			0.000	0.193	0.340	0.454	0.545	0.618	0.767	0.891	0.948	0.974	0.987	0.994
8				0.000	0.182	0.323	0.436	0.526	0.711	0.865	0.935	0.968	0.984	0.992
9					0.000	0.173	0.310	0.420	0.646	0.835	0.921	0.961	0.981	0.990
10						0.000	0.166	0.299	0.572	0.801	0.904	0.953	0.977	0.988
11							0.000	0.160	0.487	0.761	0.885	0.943	0.972	0.986
12								0.000	0.390	0.716	0.863	0.933	0.967	0.983
15									0.000	0.534	0.775	0.890	0.945	0.973
20										0.000	0.517	0.763	0.883	0.942
25											0.000	0.509	0.757	0.879
30												0.000	0.505	0.754
35													0.000	0.503
40														0.000

For Mortgages with an Interest Rate of 14.25% and an Original Term of:

Age of Loan in Years	5 Years	6 Years	7 Years	8 Years	9 Years	10 Years	11 Years	12 Years	15 Years	20 Years	25 Years	30 Years	35 Years	40 Years
1	0.852	0.886	0.910	0.928	0.941	0.951	0.959	0.966	0.979	0.990	0.995	0.998	0.999	0.999
2	0.682	0.755	0.807	0.844	0.873	0.895	0.913	0.927	0.956	0.980	0.990	0.995	0.998	0.999
3	0.486	0.605	0.688	0.749	0.795	0.830	0.859	0.882	0.928	0.967	0.984	0.992	0.996	0.998
4	0.260	0.431	0.550	0.638	0.704	0.756	0.797	0.830	0.897	0.952	0.977	0.989	0.995	0.997
5	0.000	0.231	0.392	0.511	0.600	0.670	0.725	0.770	0.860	0.936	0.969	0.985	0.993	0.996
6		0.000	0.210	0.364	0.480	0.571	0.643	0.701	0.818	0.916	0.960	0.981	0.991	0.995
7			0.000	0.195	0.342	0.457	0.548	0.621	0.770	0.894	0.949	0.975	0.988	0.994
8				0.000	0.183	0.326	0.439	0.529	0.714	0.868	0.937	0.970	0.985	0.993
9					0.000	0.174	0.313	0.424	0.650	0.839	0.923	0.963	0.982	0.991
10						0.000	0.167	0.302	0.576	0.805	0.907	0.955	0.978	0.989
11							0.000	0.162	0.491	0.766	0.888	0.946	0.973	0.987
12								0.000	0.393	0.720	0.867	0.935	0.968	0.984
15									0.000	0.539	0.780	0.893	0.948	0.974
20										0.000	0.523	0.768	0.887	0.944
25											0.000	0.515	0.763	0.884
30												0.000	0.511	0.760
35													0.000	0.509
40														0.000

Remaining Principal Balance Factors

For Mortgages with an Interest Rate of 14.50% and an Original Term of:

Age of Loan in Years	5 Years	6 Years	7 Years	8 Years	9 Years	10 Years	11 Years	12 Years	15 Years	20 Years	25 Years	30 Years	35 Years	40 Years
1	0.853	0.887	0.911	0.928	0.942	0.952	0.960	0.967	0.980	0.991	0.996	0.998	0.999	1.000
2	0.684	0.757	0.808	0.846	0.874	0.896	0.914	0.928	0.957	0.980	0.991	0.996	0.998	0.999
3	0.488	0.606	0.690	0.750	0.797	0.832	0.861	0.883	0.930	0.968	0.985	0.993	0.996	0.998
4	0.261	0.433	0.552	0.640	0.707	0.758	0.799	0.832	0.899	0.954	0.978	0.990	0.995	0.998
5	0.000	0.232	0.394	0.513	0.603	0.673	0.728	0.772	0.863	0.937	0.970	0.986	0.993	0.997
6		0.000	0.211	0.366	0.483	0.574	0.646	0.704	0.821	0.918	0.962	0.982	0.991	0.996
7			0.000	0.196	0.345	0.460	0.551	0.624	0.773	0.897	0.951	0.977	0.989	0.995
8				0.000	0.185	0.328	0.441	0.533	0.718	0.871	0.939	0.971	0.986	0.993
9					0.000	0.176	0.315	0.427	0.654	0.842	0.926	0.964	0.983	0.992
10						0.000	0.169	0.304	0.580	0.809	0.910	0.957	0.979	0.990
11							0.000	0.163	0.495	0.770	0.891	0.948	0.975	0.988
12								0.000	0.397	0.725	0.870	0.938	0.970	0.985
15									0.000	0.544	0.785	0.897	0.950	0.976
20										0.000	0.528	0.774	0.891	0.947
25											0.000	0.520	0.768	0.888
30												0.000	0.517	0.766
35													0.000	0.515
40														0.000

For Mortgages with an Interest Rate of 14.75% and an Original Term of:

Age of Loan in Years	5 Years	6 Years	7 Years	8 Years	9 Years	10 Years	11 Years	12 Years	15 Years	20 Years	25 Years	30 Years	35 Years	40 Years
1	0.854	0.888	0.912	0.929	0.942	0.953	0.961	0.967	0.980	0.991	0.996	0.998	0.999	1.000
2	0.685	0.758	0.810	0.847	0.876	0.898	0.915	0.929	0.957	0.981	0.991	0.996	0.998	0.999
3	0.489	0.608	0.691	0.752	0.798	0.834	0.862	0.885	0.931	0.969	0.985	0.993	0.997	0.998
4	0.262	0.434	0.555	0.643	0.709	0.761	0.801	0.834	0.901	0.955	0.979	0.990	0.995	0.998
5	0.000	0.233	0.396	0.515	0.606	0.675	0.731	0.775	0.865	0.939	0.972	0.987	0.994	0.997
6		0.000	0.213	0.368	0.486	0.577	0.649	0.707	0.824	0.921	0.963	0.982	0.992	0.996
7			0.000	0.197	0.347	0.463	0.554	0.628	0.777	0.899	0.953	0.978	0.989	0.995
8				0.000	0.186	0.330	0.444	0.536	0.722	0.874	0.941	0.972	0.987	0.994
9					0.000	0.177	0.317	0.430	0.658	0.846	0.928	0.966	0.984	0.992
10						0.000	0.170	0.307	0.584	0.812	0.912	0.959	0.980	0.991
11							0.000	0.165	0.499	0.774	0.894	0.950	0.976	0.989
12								0.000	0.400	0.729	0.874	0.940	0.971	0.986
15									0.000	0.549	0.789	0.900	0.952	0.977
20										0.000	0.533	0.779	0.894	0.949
25											0.000	0.526	0.774	0.892
30												0.000	0.523	0.771
35													0.000	0.521
40														0.000

Remaining Principal Balance Factors

For Mortgages with an Interest Rate of 15.00% and an Original Term of:

Age of Loan in Years	5 Years	6 Years	7 Years	8 Years	9 Years	10 Years	11 Years	12 Years	15 Years	20 Years	25 Years	30 Years	35 Years	40 Years
1	0.855	0.889	0.913	0.930	0.943	0.953	0.961	0.968	0.981	0.991	0.996	0.998	0.999	1.000
2	0.686	0.760	0.811	0.849	0.877	0.899	0.916	0.930	0.958	0.981	0.991	0.996	0.998	0.999
3	0.491	0.610	0.693	0.754	0.800	0.836	0.864	0.887	0.933	0.970	0.986	0.993	0.997	0.999
4	0.264	0.436	0.557	0.645	0.711	0.763	0.804	0.836	0.902	0.956	0.980	0.991	0.996	0.998
5	0.000	0.234	0.398	0.518	0.608	0.678	0.733	0.778	0.868	0.941	0.973	0.987	0.994	0.997
6		0.000	0.214	0.370	0.488	0.580	0.652	0.710	0.827	0.923	0.964	0.983	0.992	0.996
7			0.000	0.199	0.349	0.465	0.557	0.631	0.780	0.902	0.955	0.979	0.990	0.995
8				0.000	0.188	0.333	0.447	0.539	0.725	0.877	0.943	0.973	0.987	0.994
9					0.000	0.179	0.320	0.433	0.662	0.849	0.930	0.967	0.985	0.993
10						0.000	0.172	0.310	0.588	0.816	0.915	0.960	0.981	0.991
11							0.000	0.166	0.503	0.778	0.898	0.952	0.977	0.989
12								0.000	0.404	0.734	0.877	0.942	0.973	0.987
15									0.000	0.554	0.794	0.903	0.954	0.978
20										0.000	0.538	0.784	0.898	0.952
25											0.000	0.532	0.779	0.895
30												0.000	0.528	0.777
35													0.000	0.527
40														0.000

For Mortgages with an Interest Rate of 15.25% and an Original Term of:

Age of Loan in Years	5 Years	6 Years	7 Years	8 Years	9 Years	10 Years	11 Years	12 Years	15 Years	20 Years	25 Years	30 Years	35 Years	40 Years
1	0.856	0.890	0.913	0.931	0.944	0.954	0.962	0.968	0.981	0.992	0.996	0.998	0.999	1.000
2	0.688	0.761	0.813	0.850	0.878	0.900	0.918	0.931	0.959	0.982	0.992	0.996	0.998	0.999
3	0.492	0.612	0.695	0.756	0.802	0.838	0.866	0.889	0.934	0.971	0.987	0.994	0.997	0.999
4	0.265	0.438	0.559	0.647	0.714	0.765	0.806	0.839	0.904	0.958	0.981	0.991	0.996	0.998
5	0.000	0.235	0.400	0.520	0.611	0.681	0.736	0.780	0.870	0.943	0.974	0.988	0.994	0.997
6		0.000	0.215	0.372	0.491	0.583	0.655	0.713	0.830	0.925	0.966	0.984	0.993	0.997
7			0.000	0.200	0.351	0.468	0.560	0.634	0.783	0.904	0.956	0.980	0.991	0.996
8				0.000	0.189	0.335	0.450	0.543	0.729	0.880	0.945	0.975	0.988	0.994
9					0.000	0.180	0.322	0.436	0.666	0.852	0.933	0.969	0.985	0.993
10						0.000	0.173	0.312	0.592	0.820	0.918	0.962	0.982	0.992
11							0.000	0.168	0.507	0.782	0.901	0.954	0.979	0.990
12								0.000	0.407	0.738	0.880	0.945	0.974	0.988
15									0.000	0.558	0.798	0.907	0.956	0.980
20										0.000	0.544	0.789	0.901	0.954
25											0.000	0.537	0.784	0.899
30												0.000	0.534	0.782
35													0.000	0.532
40														0.000

Remaining Principal Balance Factors

For Mortgages with an Interest Rate of 15.50% and an Original Term of:

Age of Loan in Years	5 Years	6 Years	7 Years	8 Years	9 Years	10 Years	11 Years	12 Years	15 Years	20 Years	25 Years	30 Years	35 Years	40 Years
1	0.856	0.890	0.914	0.931	0.944	0.955	0.963	0.969	0.982	0.992	0.996	0.998	0.999	1.000
2	0.689	0.763	0.814	0.851	0.880	0.902	0.919	0.933	0.960	0.983	0.992	0.996	0.998	0.999
3	0.494	0.613	0.697	0.758	0.804	0.840	0.868	0.890	0.935	0.972	0.987	0.994	0.997	0.999
4	0.266	0.440	0.561	0.649	0.716	0.768	0.808	0.841	0.906	0.959	0.981	0.992	0.996	0.998
5	0.000	0.237	0.402	0.522	0.613	0.684	0.739	0.783	0.872	0.944	0.975	0.988	0.995	0.998
6		0.000	0.216	0.374	0.493	0.585	0.658	0.716	0.833	0.927	0.967	0.985	0.993	0.997
7			0.000	0.202	0.353	0.471	0.563	0.637	0.786	0.907	0.958	0.981	0.991	0.996
8				0.000	0.190	0.337	0.453	0.546	0.732	0.883	0.947	0.976	0.989	0.995
9					0.000	0.182	0.325	0.439	0.670	0.856	0.935	0.970	0.986	0.994
10						0.000	0.175	0.315	0.596	0.823	0.920	0.964	0.983	0.992
11							0.000	0.169	0.511	0.786	0.903	0.956	0.980	0.991
12								0.000	0.411	0.742	0.884	0.947	0.975	0.989
15									0.000	0.563	0.803	0.910	0.958	0.981
20										0.000	0.549	0.793	0.905	0.956
25											0.000	0.542	0.789	0.903
30												0.000	0.539	0.787
35													0.000	0.538
40														0.000

For Mortgages with an Interest Rate of 15.75% and an Original Term of:

Age of Loan in Years	5 Years	6 Years	7 Years	8 Years	9 Years	10 Years	11 Years	12 Years	15 Years	20 Years	25 Years	30 Years	35 Years	40 Years
1	0.857	0.891	0.915	0.932	0.945	0.955	0.963	0.969	0.982	0.992	0.997	0.998	0.999	1.000
2	0.690	0.764	0.815	0.853	0.881	0.903	0.920	0.934	0.961	0.983	0.992	0.997	0.998	0.999
3	0.495	0.615	0.699	0.760	0.806	0.842	0.870	0.892	0.937	0.973	0.988	0.994	0.997	0.999
4	0.267	0.441	0.563	0.652	0.718	0.770	0.811	0.843	0.908	0.960	0.982	0.992	0.996	0.998
5	0.000	0.238	0.404	0.525	0.616	0.686	0.742	0.786	0.875	0.946	0.976	0.989	0.995	0.998
6		0.000	0.218	0.376	0.496	0.588	0.661	0.719	0.835	0.929	0.968	0.986	0.993	0.997
7			0.000	0.203	0.356	0.474	0.567	0.641	0.790	0.909	0.959	0.982	0.992	0.996
8				0.000	0.192	0.340	0.456	0.549	0.736	0.886	0.949	0.977	0.990	0.995
9					0.000	0.183	0.327	0.442	0.673	0.859	0.937	0.971	0.987	0.994
10						0.000	0.176	0.317	0.600	0.827	0.923	0.965	0.984	0.993
11							0.000	0.171	0.514	0.790	0.906	0.958	0.981	0.991
12								0.000	0.414	0.747	0.887	0.949	0.977	0.989
15									0.000	0.568	0.807	0.913	0.960	0.982
20										0.000	0.554	0.798	0.908	0.958
25											0.000	0.548	0.794	0.906
30												0.000	0.545	0.792
35													0.000	0.544
40														0.000

Remaining Principal Balance Factors

For Mortgages with an Interest Rate of 16.00% and an Original Term of:

Age of Loan in Years	5 Years	6 Years	7 Years	8 Years	9 Years	10 Years	11 Years	12 Years	15 Years	20 Years	25 Years	30 Years	35 Years	40 Years
1	0.858	0.892	0.916	0.933	0.946	0.956	0.964	0.970	0.983	0.993	0.997	0.999	0.999	1.000
2	0.692	0.765	0.817	0.854	0.882	0.904	0.921	0.935	0.962	0.984	0.993	0.997	0.999	0.999
3	0.497	0.617	0.701	0.762	0.808	0.843	0.871	0.893	0.938	0.973	0.988	0.995	0.998	0.999
4	0.268	0.443	0.565	0.654	0.721	0.772	0.813	0.845	0.910	0.961	0.983	0.992	0.997	0.998
5	0.000	0.239	0.406	0.527	0.618	0.689	0.744	0.788	0.877	0.947	0.977	0.990	0.995	0.998
6		0.000	0.219	0.378	0.498	0.591	0.664	0.722	0.838	0.931	0.969	0.986	0.994	0.997
7			0.000	0.204	0.358	0.476	0.570	0.644	0.793	0.911	0.961	0.983	0.992	0.996
8				0.000	0.193	0.342	0.459	0.553	0.739	0.889	0.951	0.978	0.990	0.996
9					0.000	0.185	0.330	0.445	0.677	0.862	0.939	0.973	0.988	0.994
10						0.000	0.178	0.320	0.604	0.831	0.925	0.967	0.985	0.993
11							0.000	0.173	0.518	0.794	0.909	0.959	0.982	0.992
12								0.000	0.418	0.751	0.890	0.951	0.978	0.990
15									0.000	0.572	0.811	0.916	0.962	0.983
20										0.000	0.559	0.803	0.911	0.960
25											0.000	0.553	0.799	0.909
30												0.000	0.550	0.797
35													0.000	0.549
40														0.000

For Mortgages with an Interest Rate of 16.25% and an Original Term of:

Age of Loan in Years	5 Years	6 Years	7 Years	8 Years	9 Years	10 Years	11 Years	12 Years	15 Years	20 Years	25 Years	30 Years	35 Years	40 Years
1	0.859	0.893	0.916	0.934	0.947	0.956	0.964	0.970	0.983	0.993	0.997	0.999	0.999	1.000
2	0.693	0.767	0.818	0.856	0.884	0.905	0.922	0.936	0.963	0.984	0.993	0.997	0.999	0.999
3	0.498	0.619	0.703	0.764	0.810	0.845	0.873	0.895	0.939	0.974	0.989	0.995	0.998	0.999
4	0.269	0.445	0.567	0.656	0.723	0.775	0.815	0.847	0.912	0.963	0.984	0.993	0.997	0.999
5	0.000	0.240	0.408	0.529	0.621	0.691	0.747	0.791	0.879	0.949	0.978	0.990	0.996	0.998
6		0.000	0.220	0.381	0.501	0.594	0.667	0.725	0.841	0.933	0.971	0.987	0.994	0.997
7			0.000	0.206	0.360	0.479	0.573	0.647	0.796	0.914	0.962	0.983	0.993	0.997
8				0.000	0.195	0.344	0.462	0.556	0.743	0.891	0.953	0.979	0.991	0.996
9					0.000	0.186	0.332	0.448	0.681	0.865	0.941	0.974	0.988	0.995
10						0.000	0.179	0.322	0.608	0.834	0.928	0.968	0.986	0.994
11							0.000	0.174	0.522	0.798	0.912	0.961	0.983	0.992
12								0.000	0.421	0.755	0.893	0.953	0.979	0.991
15									0.000	0.577	0.815	0.918	0.964	0.984
20										0.000	0.564	0.807	0.914	0.962
25											0.000	0.558	0.804	0.913
30												0.000	0.556	0.802
35													0.000	0.555
40														0.000

Remaining Principal Balance Factors

For Mortgages with an Interest Rate of 16.50% and an Original Term of:

Age of Loan in Years	5 Years	6 Years	7 Years	8 Years	9 Years	10 Years	11 Years	12 Years	15 Years	20 Years	25 Years	30 Years	35 Years	40 Years
1	0.860	0.894	0.917	0.934	0.947	0.957	0.965	0.971	0.983	0.993	0.997	0.999	0.999	1.000
2	0.694	0.768	0.820	0.857	0.885	0.907	0.923	0.937	0.964	0.985	0.993	0.997	0.999	0.999
3	0.500	0.620	0.705	0.766	0.812	0.847	0.875	0.897	0.941	0.975	0.989	0.995	0.998	0.999
4	0.270	0.446	0.569	0.658	0.725	0.777	0.817	0.849	0.913	0.964	0.984	0.993	0.997	0.999
5	0.000	0.241	0.409	0.532	0.623	0.694	0.749	0.793	0.881	0.950	0.979	0.991	0.996	0.998
6		0.000	0.221	0.383	0.504	0.597	0.670	0.728	0.843	0.934	0.972	0.988	0.995	0.998
7			0.000	0.207	0.362	0.482	0.576	0.650	0.799	0.916	0.964	0.984	0.993	0.997
8				0.000	0.196	0.347	0.465	0.559	0.746	0.894	0.954	0.980	0.991	0.996
9					0.000	0.188	0.335	0.452	0.684	0.868	0.943	0.975	0.989	0.995
10						0.000	0.181	0.325	0.612	0.837	0.930	0.969	0.987	0.994
11							0.000	0.176	0.526	0.801	0.914	0.963	0.984	0.993
12								0.000	0.425	0.759	0.896	0.955	0.980	0.991
15									0.000	0.581	0.819	0.921	0.965	0.985
20										0.000	0.569	0.812	0.917	0.964
25											0.000	0.563	0.808	0.916
30												0.000	0.561	0.807
35													0.000	0.560
40														0.000

For Mortgages with an Interest Rate of 16.75% and an Original Term of:

Age of Loan in Years	5 Years	6 Years	7 Years	8 Years	9 Years	10 Years	11 Years	12 Years	15 Years	20 Years	25 Years	30 Years	35 Years	40 Years
1	0.860	0.894	0.918	0.935	0.948	0.958	0.965	0.972	0.984	0.993	0.997	0.999	0.999	1.000
2	0.696	0.770	0.821	0.858	0.886	0.908	0.925	0.938	0.965	0.985	0.994	0.997	0.999	0.999
3	0.501	0.622	0.706	0.768	0.813	0.849	0.876	0.898	0.942	0.976	0.990	0.996	0.998	0.999
4	0.271	0.448	0.571	0.660	0.727	0.779	0.819	0.851	0.915	0.965	0.985	0.994	0.997	0.999
5	0.000	0.243	0.411	0.534	0.626	0.697	0.752	0.796	0.883	0.952	0.979	0.991	0.996	0.998
6		0.000	0.223	0.385	0.506	0.600	0.673	0.731	0.846	0.936	0.973	0.988	0.995	0.998
7			0.000	0.208	0.365	0.485	0.579	0.653	0.802	0.918	0.965	0.985	0.993	0.997
8				0.000	0.197	0.349	0.468	0.562	0.750	0.896	0.956	0.981	0.992	0.996
9					0.000	0.189	0.337	0.455	0.688	0.871	0.945	0.976	0.990	0.996
10						0.000	0.183	0.327	0.615	0.841	0.932	0.971	0.987	0.994
11							0.000	0.177	0.530	0.805	0.917	0.964	0.984	0.993
12								0.000	0.428	0.763	0.899	0.956	0.981	0.992
15									0.000	0.586	0.823	0.924	0.967	0.986
20										0.000	0.574	0.816	0.920	0.965
25											0.000	0.569	0.813	0.919
30												0.000	0.566	0.812
35													0.000	0.565
40														0.000

Remaining Principal Balance Factors

For Mortgages with an Interest Rate of 17.00% and an Original Term of:

Age of Loan in Years	5 Years	6 Years	7 Years	8 Years	9 Years	10 Years	11 Years	12 Years	15 Years	20 Years	25 Years	30 Years	35 Years	40 Years
1	0.861	0.895	0.919	0.936	0.948	0.958	0.966	0.972	0.984	0.993	0.997	0.999	0.999	1.000
2	0.697	0.771	0.822	0.860	0.887	0.909	0.926	0.939	0.965	0.986	0.994	0.997	0.999	1.000
3	0.503	0.624	0.708	0.769	0.815	0.850	0.878	0.900	0.943	0.977	0.990	0.996	0.998	0.999
4	0.272	0.450	0.573	0.663	0.730	0.781	0.822	0.853	0.917	0.966	0.986	0.994	0.997	0.999
5	0.000	0.244	0.413	0.536	0.629	0.699	0.755	0.799	0.886	0.953	0.980	0.992	0.996	0.998
6		0.000	0.224	0.387	0.509	0.602	0.676	0.734	0.849	0.938	0.974	0.989	0.995	0.998
7			0.000	0.210	0.367	0.487	0.582	0.657	0.805	0.920	0.966	0.986	0.994	0.997
8				0.000	0.199	0.352	0.471	0.566	0.753	0.899	0.957	0.982	0.992	0.997
9					0.000	0.191	0.340	0.458	0.692	0.874	0.947	0.977	0.990	0.996
10						0.000	0.184	0.330	0.619	0.844	0.934	0.972	0.988	0.995
11							0.000	0.179	0.533	0.809	0.919	0.966	0.985	0.994
12								0.000	0.432	0.767	0.902	0.958	0.982	0.992
15									0.000	0.590	0.827	0.926	0.968	0.986
20										0.000	0.579	0.820	0.923	0.967
25											0.000	0.574	0.817	0.922
30												0.000	0.572	0.816
35													0.000	0.571
40														0.000

For Mortgages with an Interest Rate of 17.25% and an Original Term of:

Age of Loan in Years	5 Years	6 Years	7 Years	8 Years	9 Years	10 Years	11 Years	12 Years	15 Years	20 Years	25 Years	30 Years	35 Years	40 Years
1	0.862	0.896	0.919	0.936	0.949	0.959	0.967	0.973	0.985	0.994	0.997	0.999	1.000	1.000
2	0.698	0.772	0.824	0.861	0.889	0.910	0.927	0.940	0.966	0.986	0.994	0.998	0.999	1.000
3	0.504	0.626	0.710	0.771	0.817	0.852	0.880	0.901	0.944	0.977	0.991	0.996	0.998	0.999
4	0.274	0.452	0.575	0.665	0.732	0.783	0.824	0.855	0.918	0.967	0.986	0.994	0.998	0.999
5	0.000	0.245	0.415	0.539	0.631	0.702	0.757	0.801	0.888	0.954	0.981	0.992	0.997	0.999
6		0.000	0.225	0.389	0.511	0.605	0.678	0.736	0.851	0.940	0.975	0.989	0.996	0.998
7			0.000	0.211	0.369	0.490	0.585	0.660	0.808	0.922	0.968	0.986	0.994	0.998
8				0.000	0.200	0.354	0.474	0.569	0.756	0.901	0.959	0.983	0.993	0.997
9					0.000	0.192	0.342	0.461	0.695	0.877	0.949	0.978	0.991	0.996
10						0.000	0.186	0.333	0.623	0.847	0.936	0.973	0.989	0.995
11							0.000	0.181	0.537	0.812	0.922	0.967	0.986	0.994
12								0.000	0.435	0.771	0.905	0.960	0.983	0.993
15									0.000	0.595	0.831	0.929	0.970	0.987
20										0.000	0.583	0.824	0.926	0.968
25											0.000	0.579	0.822	0.924
30												0.000	0.577	0.820
35													0.000	0.576
40														0.000

Remaining Principal Balance Factors

For Mortgages with an Interest Rate of 17.50% and an Original Term of:

Age of Loan in Years	5 Years	6 Years	7 Years	8 Years	9 Years	10 Years	11 Years	12 Years	15 Years	20 Years	25 Years	30 Years	35 Years	40 Years
1	0.863	0.897	0.920	0.937	0.950	0.959	0.967	0.973	0.985	0.994	0.998	0.999	1.000	1.000
2	0.700	0.774	0.825	0.862	0.890	0.911	0.928	0.941	0.967	0.987	0.995	0.998	0.999	1.000
3	0.506	0.627	0.712	0.773	0.819	0.854	0.881	0.903	0.945	0.978	0.991	0.996	0.998	0.999
4	0.275	0.453	0.577	0.667	0.734	0.786	0.826	0.858	0.920	0.968	0.987	0.995	0.998	0.999
5	0.000	0.246	0.417	0.541	0.634	0.704	0.760	0.804	0.890	0.956	0.982	0.992	0.997	0.999
6		0.000	0.227	0.391	0.514	0.608	0.681	0.739	0.854	0.941	0.976	0.990	0.996	0.998
7			0.000	0.212	0.371	0.493	0.588	0.663	0.811	0.924	0.969	0.987	0.995	0.998
8				0.000	0.202	0.356	0.477	0.572	0.760	0.904	0.960	0.983	0.993	0.997
9					0.000	0.194	0.344	0.464	0.699	0.879	0.950	0.979	0.991	0.996
10						0.000	0.187	0.335	0.627	0.850	0.938	0.974	0.989	0.996
11							0.000	0.182	0.541	0.816	0.924	0.968	0.987	0.994
12								0.000	0.439	0.775	0.907	0.961	0.984	0.993
15									0.000	0.599	0.835	0.931	0.971	0.988
20										0.000	0.588	0.829	0.928	0.970
25											0.000	0.584	0.826	0.927
30												0.000	0.582	0.825
35													0.000	0.581
40														0.000

For Mortgages with an Interest Rate of 17.75% and an Original Term of:

Age of Loan in Years	5 Years	6 Years	7 Years	8 Years	9 Years	10 Years	11 Years	12 Years	15 Years	20 Years	25 Years	30 Years	35 Years	40 Years
1	0.864	0.897	0.921	0.938	0.950	0.960	0.968	0.974	0.985	0.994	0.998	0.999	1.000	1.000
2	0.701	0.775	0.826	0.863	0.891	0.912	0.929	0.942	0.968	0.987	0.995	0.998	0.999	1.000
3	0.507	0.629	0.714	0.775	0.821	0.856	0.883	0.904	0.947	0.979	0.991	0.996	0.999	0.999
4	0.276	0.455	0.579	0.669	0.736	0.788	0.828	0.860	0.922	0.969	0.987	0.995	0.998	0.999
5	0.000	0.248	0.419	0.543	0.636	0.707	0.762	0.806	0.892	0.957	0.983	0.993	0.997	0.999
6		0.000	0.228	0.393	0.516	0.611	0.684	0.742	0.856	0.943	0.977	0.990	0.996	0.998
7			0.000	0.214	0.373	0.496	0.591	0.666	0.814	0.926	0.970	0.988	0.995	0.998
8				0.000	0.203	0.359	0.480	0.575	0.763	0.906	0.962	0.984	0.993	0.997
9					0.000	0.195	0.347	0.467	0.703	0.882	0.952	0.980	0.992	0.997
10						0.000	0.189	0.338	0.630	0.853	0.940	0.975	0.990	0.996
11							0.000	0.184	0.545	0.819	0.926	0.970	0.988	0.995
12								0.000	0.442	0.779	0.910	0.963	0.985	0.994
15									0.000	0.603	0.839	0.934	0.973	0.989
20										0.000	0.593	0.833	0.931	0.971
25											0.000	0.589	0.830	0.930
30												0.000	0.587	0.829
35													0.000	0.586
40														0.000

APPENDIX III
Seller's Property Disclosure Statement

NCR (No Carbon Required)

SELLER'S PROPERTY DISCLOSURE STATEMENT
(Including the main structure and any outbuildings)

This document provides disclosures with respect to the property known to the Seller as of the date of this statement. It is not a warranty of any kind and is not a substitute for property inspections by experts which the Buyer may wish to obtain. Buyer understands and acknowledges that the broker(s) in this transaction cannot warrant the condition of the property or guarantee that all defects have been disclosed by the Seller.

PROPERTY ADDRESS "SAMPLE ONLY NOT FOR REPRODUCTION"

SELLER'S NAME _____

1. TITLE AND ACCESS

a. Is the property currently leased? .... ☐ Yes ☐ No
b. Has anyone right of refusal to buy, option, or lease the property? .... ☐ Yes ☐ No
c. Do you know of any existing, pending or potential legal actions concerning the property or Owners Association? .... ☐ Yes ☐ No
d. Has a Notice of Default been recorded against the property? .... ☐ Yes ☐ No
e. Any bonds, assessments, or judgements which are liens upon the property? .... ☐ Yes ☐ No
f. Do you own real property adjacent to, across the street from, or in the same sub-division as subject property? .... ☐ Yes ☐ No
g. Any boundary disputes, or third party claims affecting the property (rights of other people to interfere with the use of the property in any way)? .... ☐ Yes ☐ No

2. ENVIRONMENTAL

Are you aware of the following with respect to the property?

a. Any noises from airplanes, trains, trucks, freeways, etc.? .... ☐ Yes ☐ No
b. Any odors caused by toxic waste, gas, industry, agriculture, animals, pets, etc.? .... ☐ Yes ☐ No
c. Formaldehyde gas emitting materials, especially urea-formaldehyde foam insulation? .... ☐ Yes ☐ No
d. Asbestos insulation or fireproofing? .... ☐ Yes ☐ No
e. Elevated radon levels on the property? .... ☐ Yes ☐ No
f. Elevated radon levels in the neighborhood? .... ☐ Yes ☐ No
g. Use of lead-base paint on any surfaces? .... ☐ Yes ☐ No
h. Contamination of well or other water supply? .... ☐ Yes ☐ No
i. Any past or present flooding or drainage problems? .... ☐ Yes ☐ No
j. Any past or present flooding or drainage problems on adjacent properties? .... ☐ Yes ☐ No
k. Any standing water after rainfalls? .... ☐ Yes ☐ No
l. Any sump pumps in basement or crawlspace? .... ☐ Yes ☐ No
m. Any active springs? .... ☐ Yes ☐ No
n. Is property located wholly or partially within Flood Hazard Zone, as determined by the National Flood Insurance Program? .... ☐ Yes ☐ No
o. Is the house built on landfill (compacted or otherwise)? .... ☐ Yes ☐ No
p. Is there landfill on any portion of the property? .... ☐ Yes ☐ No
q. Any soil settling, slippage, sliding, or similar problems? .... ☐ Yes ☐ No
r. Any sinkholes or voids on or near the property? .... ☐ Yes ☐ No
s. Any depressions, mounds, or soft spots? .... ☐ Yes ☐ No
t. Any pending real estate development in your area (such as common interest developments, planned development units, subdivisions, or property for commercial, industrial, sport, educational, or religious use)? .... ☐ Yes ☐ No
u. Any federal or state areas once used for military training purposes, within one mile of the property? .... ☐ Yes ☐ No
v. Traces of concrete, metal, or asphalt indicating prior commercial or industrial use? .... ☐ Yes ☐ No
w. Proximity of property to former, current or proposed mines or gravel pits? .... ☐ Yes ☐ No
x. Proximity of property to former or current waste disposal sites? .... ☐ Yes ☐ No
y. Ravines or earth embankment that may indicate former dumping? .... ☐ Yes ☐ No
z. Pipelines carrying oil, gas, or chemicals underneath or adjacent to the property? .... ☐ Yes ☐ No
aa. Existence of pipeline rights-of-way or easements over or adjacent to the property? .... ☐ Yes ☐ No
bb. Discoloring of soil or vegetation? .... ☐ Yes ☐ No
cc. Oil sheen in wet areas? .... ☐ Yes ☐ No

3. STRUCTURAL

a. Approximate age of the house: _____
b. Do you know of any condition in the original or existing design or workmanship of the structures upon the property that would be considered substandard? .... ☐ Yes ☐ No
c. Do you know of any structural additions or alterations, or the installation, alteration, repair, or replacement of significant components of the structures upon the property, completed during the term of your ownership or that of a prior owner without an appropriate permit or other authority for construction from a public agency having jurisdiction? .... ☐ Yes ☐ No
d. Do you know of any violations of government regulations, ordinances, or zoning laws regarding this property? .... ☐ Yes ☐ No
e. Do you know of any excessive settling, slippage, sliding, or other soil problems, past or present? .... ☐ Yes ☐ No
f. Any problems with retaining walls cracking or bulging? .... ☐ Yes ☐ No
g. Swimming pool out of level? .... ☐ Yes ☐ No
h. Do you know of any past or present problems with driveways, walkways, sidewalks, patios (such as large cracks, potholes, raised sections)? .... ☐ Yes ☐ No
i. Any significant cracks in any of the following: .... ☐ Yes ☐ No
☐ foundations, ☐ exterior walls, ☐ interior walls, ☐ ceilings, ☐ fireplaces, ☐ chimneys, ☐ decks, ☐ slab floors, ☐ garage floors?
j. Any slanted floors? .... ☐ Yes ☐ No
k. Any distorted door frames (uneven spaces between doors and frames)? .... ☐ Yes ☐ No
l. Any sticking windows? .... ☐ Yes ☐ No
m. Any sagging exposed ceiling beams? .... ☐ Yes ☐ No
n. Any structural woodmembers (including mudsills) below soil level? .... ☐ Yes ☐ No
o. Crawl space, if any, below soil level? .... ☐ Yes ☐ No
p. Any structures (including play structures, tree house, etc.) that could be hazardous? .... ☐ Yes ☐ No

Seller(s) Initials [_____] [_____]

FORM 110.11 (10-91) COPYRIGHT © 1991, BY PROFESSIONAL PUBLISHING CORP. 122 PAUL DR. SAN RAFAEL, CA 94903 (415) 472-1964

PROFESSIONAL PUBLISHING

NCR (No Carbon Required)

Property Address "SAMPLE ONLY NOT FOR REPRODUCTION" _____

4. ROOF, GUTTERS, DOWNSPOUTS

a. Type of roof: [ ] Tar and Gravel, [ ] Asphalt Shingle, [ ] Wood Shingle, [ ] Tile, [ ] Other _____. Age of roof: _____

b. Has roof been resurfaced? _____ If so, what year? _____

c. Is there a guarantee on the roof? _____ For how long? _____ By whom? _____

d. Has roof ever leaked since you owned the property? _____

If so, what was done to correct the leak? _____ [ ] Explanation attached.

e. Are gutters and downspouts free of holes and excessive rust? _____

f. Do downspouts empty into drainage system or onto splash blocks? _____

g. Is water directed away from structure? _____

5. PLUMBING SYSTEM

a. Source of water supply: [ ] Public, [ ] Private Well. If well water, when was water sample last checked for safety? _____

Result of test: _____ [ ] Explanation attached.

b. Well water pump: _____ Date installed: _____ Condition: _____ Sufficient water during late summer? _____

c. Are water supply pipes copper or galvanized? _____

d. Are you aware of below normal water pressure in your water supply lines (normal is 50 to 70 lbs.)? _____

e. Are you aware of excessive rust stains in tubs, lavatories and sinks? _____

f. Are you aware of water standing around any of the lawn sprinkler heads? _____

g. Are there any plumbing leaks around and under sinks, toilets, showers, bathtubs, and lavatories? _____ If so, where? [ ] Explanation attached.

h. Pool: Age: _____ Pool Heater: [ ] Gas, [ ] Electric, [ ] Solar. Pool Sweep? _____ Date of last inspection: _____

By whom? _____ Regular maintenance? _____

i. Hot Tub/Spa: _____ Date of last inspection: _____ By whom? _____

j. [ ] City Sewer, [ ] Septic Tank: [ ] Fiberglass, [ ] Concrete, [ ] Redwood. Capacity: _____ Is septic tank in working order? _____

6. ELECTRICAL SYSTEM

a. 220 Volt? . . . . [ ] Yes [ ] No

b. Is the electrical wiring Copper? . . . . [ ] Yes [ ] No

c. Are there any damaged or malfunctioning receptacles? . . . . [ ] Yes [ ] No

d. Are you aware of any damaged or malfunctioning switches? . . . . [ ] Yes [ ] No

e. Are there any extension cords stapled to baseboards or underneath carpets or rugs? . . . . [ ] Yes [ ] No

f. Does outside TV antenna have a ground connection? . . . . [ ] Yes [ ] No

g. Are you aware of any defects, malfunctioning, or illegal installation of electrical equipment in or outside the house? . . . . [ ] Yes [ ] No

7. HEATING, AIR CONDITIONING, OTHER EQUIPMENT

a. Is the house insulated? . . . . [ ] Yes [ ] No

b. Type of Heating System: _____

c. Is furnace room or furnace closet adequately vented? . . . . [ ] Yes [ ] No

d. Are fuel-consuming heating devices adequately vented to the outside, directly or through a chimney? . . . . [ ] Yes [ ] No

e. Heating Equipment in working order? . . . . [ ] Yes [ ] No

f. Solar heating in working order? . . . . [ ] Yes [ ] No

g. Air Conditioning in working order? . . . . [ ] Yes [ ] No

h. Does Fireplace have a damper? . . . . [ ] Yes [ ] No

i. Provision for outside venting of clothes dryer? . . . . [ ] Yes [ ] No

j. Water Heater in working order? . . . . [ ] Yes [ ] No

k. Is heater equipped with temperature pressure relief valve, which is a required safety device? . . . . [ ] Yes [ ] No

l. Electric garage door opener in working order . . . . [ ] Yes [ ] No

m. Burglar alarm in working order? . . . . [ ] Yes [ ] No

n. Smoke Detectors in working order . . . . [ ] Yes [ ] No

o. Lawn Sprinklers in working order? . . . . [ ] Yes [ ] No

p. Water Softener in working order? . . . . [ ] Yes [ ] No

q. Sump pump: in working order? . . . . [ ] Yes [ ] No

r. Are you aware of any of the above equipment that is in need of repair or replacement or is illegally installed? . . . . [ ] Yes [ ] No

8. BUILT-IN APPLIANCES

a. Are you aware of any built-in appliances that are in need of repair or replacement? . . . . [ ] Yes [ ] No

9. CONDOMINIUMS — COMMON INTEREST DEVELOPMENTS

a. Please check the availability of copies of the following documents: [ ] CC&Rs, [ ] Condominium Declaration, [ ] Association Bylaws, [ ] Articles of Incorporation, [ ] Subdivision Report, [ ] Current Financial Statement, [ ] Regulations currently in force.

b. Does the Condominium Declaration contain any resale restrictions? _____

c. Does the Homeowners Association have the first right of refusal? _____

d. Please check occupancy restrictions imposed by the association, including but not limited to: [ ] Children, [ ] Pets, [ ] Storage of Recreational Vehicles or Boats on driveways or in common areas, [ ] Advertising or For Sale signs, [ ] Architectural or decorative alterations subject to association approval, [ ] Others: _____

e. In case of a conversion, have you an engineer's report on the condition of the building and its equipment? _____

f. Monthly/annual association dues:$ _____ What is included in the association dues? _____

g. Has your association notified you of any future dues increases or special assessments? _____

If so, give details: _____ [ ] Explanation attached.

h. Are all dues, assessments, and taxes current? _____

i. I shall provide a statement from the Condominium Homeowners Association documenting the amount of any delinquent assessments, including penalties, attorney's fees, and any other charges provided for in the management documents to be delivered to Buyer. _____

j. Security: [ ] Inter-com, [ ] Closed circuit TV, [ ] Guards, [ ] Electric gate, [ ] Other: _____

k. Parking: Does each unit have its own designated parking spaces? _____

l. Sound proofing adequate? _____ Are there noisy trash chutes? _____

m. Property Management Co. _____

Seller(s) Initials [_____] [_____]

FORM 110.12 (10-91) COPYRIGHT © 1991, BY PROFESSIONAL PUBLISHING CORP. 122 PAUL DR, SAN RAFAEL, CA 94903 (415) 472-1964 **PROFESSIONAL PUBLISHING**

NCR (No Carbon Required)

Property Address _"SAMPLE ONLY NOT FOR REPRODUCTION"_____

10. OWNERSHIP

a. Are you a builder or developer? .... ☐ Yes ☐ No

b. Are you a licensed real estate agent? .... ☐ Yes ☐ No

c. Have all persons on the title signed the listing agreement? .... ☐ Yes ☐ No

d. Please list all persons on the title who are not U.S. citizens: _____
_____

11. PERSONAL PROPERTY INCLUDED IN THE PURCHASE PRICE

a. The following items of personal property are included in the purchase price: _____
_____

b. Are there any liens against any of these items? _____ If so, please explain: _____

12. HOME PROTECTION PROGRAM

a. Do you want to provide a Home Protection Program at your expense? .... ☐ Yes ☐ No

13. REPORTS

a. Have you received or do you have knowledge of any of the following inspection reports or repair estimates made during or prior to your ownership?

REPORT	YES	NO	BY WHOM?	WHEN?	REPORT AVAILABLE?
Soils/Drainage					
Geologic					
Structural					
Roof					
Pest Control					
Well					
Septic					
Pool/Spa					
Heating					
Air Conditioning					
House Inspection					
Energy Audit					
Radon Test					
City/County Inspection					
Notice of Violation					

14. OTHER DISCLOSURES

a. In addition to the disclosure statements made herein, the following facts are known or suspected by me/us which may materially affect the value or desirability of the subject property, now or in the future: _____ ☐ Explanation attached.

The foregoing answers and explanations are true and complete to the best of my/our knowledge and I/we have retained a copy hereof. I/we herewith authorize _____ **, the agent in this transaction, to disclose the information set forth above to other real estate brokers, real estate agents, and prospective buyers of the property.**

Seller agrees to hold harmless all brokers and agents in the transaction and to defend and indemnify them from any claim, demand, action or proceedings resulting from any omission or alleged omission by Seller in this Disclosure Statement.

Dated: _____ Seller: __SAMPLE_____ Seller: __SAMPLE_____

The undersigned Buyer understands that this document is a disclosure of Seller's knowledge of the condition of the property as of the date signed by the Seller. It is not a warranty of any kind and is not a substitute for property inspections by experts which the Buyer may wish to obtain. Buyer understands and acknowledges that the brokers in this transaction cannot warrant the condition of the property or guarantee that all defects have been disclosed by the Seller.

I/we acknowledge receipt of this SELLER'S PROPERTY DISCLOSURE STATEMENT, including additional explanations, if any, attached hereto.

Dated: _____ Buyer: __SAMPLE_____ Buyer: __SAMPLE_____

I am satisfied with the above SELLER'S PROPERTY DISCLOSURE STATEMENT.

Dated: _____ Buyer: __SAMPLE_____ Buyer: __SAMPLE_____

I am NOT satisfied with the above SELLER'S PROPERTY DISCLOSURE STATEMENT and herewith rescind my offer to purchase above property.

Dated: _____ Buyer: __SAMPLE_____ Buyer: __SAMPLE_____

I reserve the right to have the property inspected by the following professional(s) _____
_____

and to submit a copy of the inspection report(s) to Seller's agent on or before _____.

Dated: _____ Buyer: __SAMPLE_____ Buyer: __SAMPLE_____

FORM 110.13 (10-91) COPYRIGHT © 1991, BY PROFESSIONAL PUBLISHING CORP. 122 PAUL DR., SAN RAFAEL, CA 94903 (415) 472-1964

PROFESSIONAL PUBLISHING

Reprinted by permission of the copyright owner: Professional Publishing Corporation, 122 Paul Dr., San Rafael, CA 94903. Phone: 800-288-2006 Fax: 415-472-2069.

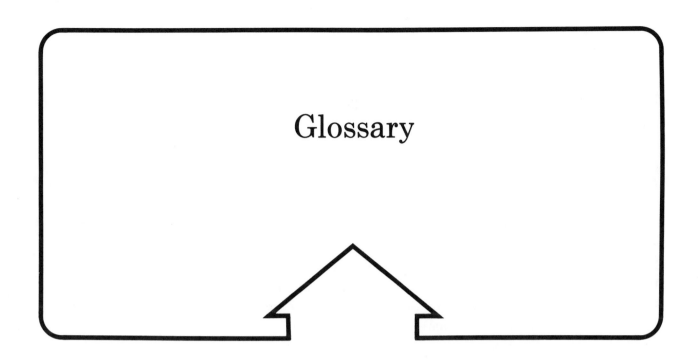

Glossary

Abstract of Title (Abstract). History of a parcel of real estate, compiled from public records, listing transfers of ownership and claims against the property

Acceleration Clause. Provision in a mortgage document stating that if a payment is missed or any other provision violated the whole debt becomes immediately due and payable

Acknowledgment. Formal declaration before a public official that one has signed a document

Acre. Land measure equal to 43,560 square feet

Adjustable Rate Mortgage. Loan whose interest rate is changed periodically to keep pace with current levels

Adjusted Basis. Original cost of property plus any later improvements and minus a figure for depreciation claimed

Adjusted Sales Price. Sale price minus commissions, legal fees and other costs of selling

Agent. Person authorized to act on behalf of another in dealings with third parties

Agreement of Sale (Purchase Agreement, Sales Agreement, Contract to Purchase). Written contract detailing terms under which buyer agrees to buy and seller agrees to sell

Alienation Clause (Due-On-Sale, Nonassumption). Provision in a mortgage document stating that the loan must be paid in full if ownership is transferred, sometimes contingent upon other occurrences

Amortization. Gradual payment of a debt through regular installments that cover both interest and principal

Appraisal. Estimate of value of real estate, presumably by an expert

Appreciation. Increase in value or worth of property

"As Is." Present condition of property being transferred, with no guaranty or warranty provided by the seller

Assessed Valuation.   Value placed on property as a basis for levying property taxes; not identical with appraised or market value

Assignment.   Transfer of a contract from one party to another

Assumable Mortgage.   Loan that may be passed to the next owner of the property

Automatic Renewal Clause.   Provision that allows a listing contract to be renewed indefinitely unless canceled by the property owner

Balloon Loan.   Mortgage in which the remaining balance becomes fully due and payable at a predetermined time

Balloon Payment.   Final payment on a balloon loan

Bill of Sale.   Written document transferring personal property

Binder.   Preliminary agreement of sale, usually accompanied by earnest money (term also used with property insurance)

Broker.   Person licensed by the state to represent another for a fee in real estate transactions

Building Code.   Regulations of local government stipulating requirements and standards for building and construction

Buydown.   The payment of additional points to a mortgage lender in return for a lower interest rate on the loan

Buyers' Market.   Situation in which supply of homes for sale exceeds demand

Cap.   Limit (typically about two percent) by which an adjustable mortgage rate might be raised at any one time

Capital Gain.   Taxable profit on the sale of an appreciated asset

Caveat Emptor.   Let the buyer beware

Ceiling.   Also known as lifetime cap, limit beyond which an adjustable mortgage rate may never be raised

Certificate of Occupancy.   Document issued by local governmental agency stating that property meets standards for occupancy

Chattel.   Personal property

Client.   The broker's principal, to whom fiduciary duties are owed

Closing (Settlement, Escrow, Passing Papers).   Conclusion of a real estate sale, at which time title is transferred and necessary funds change hands

Closing Costs.   One-time charges paid by buyer and seller on the day property changes hands

Closing Statement.   Statement prepared for buyer and seller listing debits and credits, completed by the person in charge of the closing

Cloud (on Title).   Outstanding claim or encumbrance that challenges the owner's clear title

Commission.   Fee paid (usually by a seller) for a broker's services in securing a buyer for property; commonly a percentage of sales price

Commitment (Letter).   Written promise to grant a mortgage loan

Common Elements.   Parts of a condominium development in which each owner holds an interest (swimming pool, etc.)

Comparable.   Recently sold similar property, used to estimate market value

Comparative Market Analysis.   Method of valuing homes using study of comparables, property that failed to sell, and other property currently on the market

Conditional Commitment.   Lender's promise to make a loan subject to the fulfillment of specified conditions

Conditional Offer.   Purchase offer in which the buyer proposes to purchase only after certain occurrences (sale of another home, securing of financing, etc.)

Condominium.   Type of ownership involving individual ownership of dwelling units and common ownership of shared areas

Consideration.   Anything of value given to induce another to enter into a contract

Contract.   Legally enforceable agreement to do (or not to do) a particular thing

Contract for Deed (Land Contract).   Method of selling whereby the buyer receives possession but the seller retains title

Conventional Mortgage.   Loan arranged between lender and borrower with no governmental guarantee or insurance

Curtesy.   In some states, rights a widower obtains to a portion of his deceased wife's real property

Customer.   Typically, the buyer, as opposed to the principal (seller)

Days on Market (DOM).   Number of days between the time a house is put on the market and the date of a firm sale contract

Deed.   Formal written document transferring title to real estate; a new deed is used for each transfer

Deed of Trust.   Document by which title to property is held by a neutral third party until a debt is paid; used instead of a mortgage in some states

Deed Restriction (Restrictive Covenant).   Provision placed in a deed to control use and occupancy of the property by future owners

Default.   Failure to make mortgage payment

Deferred Maintenance.   Needed repairs that have been put off

Deficiency Judgment.   Personal claim against the debtor, when foreclosed property does not yield enough at sale to pay off loans against it

Delivery.   Legal transfer of a deed to the new property owner, the moment at which transfer of title occurs

Depreciation.   Decrease in value of property because of deterioration or obsolescence; sometimes, an artificial bookkeeping concept valuable as a tax shelter

Direct Endorsement.   Complete processing of an FHA mortgage application by an authorized local lender

Documentary Tax Stamp.   Charge levied by state or local governments when real estate is transferred or mortgaged

Dower.   In some states, the rights of a widow to a portion of her deceased husband's property

Down Payment.   Cash to be paid by the buyer at closing

DVA.   Department of Veterans Affairs. Formerly VA, Veterans Administration

Earnest Money.   Buyer's "good faith" deposit accompanying purchase offer

Easement.   A permanent right to use another's property (telephone lines, common driveway, footpath, etc.)

Encroachment. Unauthorized intrusion of a building or improvement onto another's land

Encumbrance. Claim against another's real estate (unpaid tax, mortgage, easement, etc.)

Equity. The money realized when property is sold and all the claims against it are paid; commonly, sales price minus present mortgage

Escrow. Funds given to a third party to be held pending some occurrence; may refer to earnest money, funds collected by a lender for the payment of taxes and insurance charges, funds withheld at closing to insure uncompleted repairs, or in some states the entire process of closing

FHA. Federal Housing Administration (HUD), which insures mortgages to protect the lending institution in case of default

FHA Mortgage. Loan made by a local lending institution and insured by the FHA, with the borrower paying the premium

Fee Simple (Absolute). Highest possible degree of ownership of land

Fiduciary. A person in a position of trust or responsibility with specific duties to act in the best interest of the client

First Mortgage. Mortgage holding priority over the claims of subsequent lenders against the same property

Fixture. Personal property that has become part of the real estate

Foreclosure. Legal procedure for enforcing payment of a debt by seizing and selling the mortgaged property

Front Foot. Measurement of land along a street or waterfront—each front foot is one foot wide and extends to the depth of the lot

Grantee. The buyer, who receives a deed

Grantor. The seller, who gives a deed

Index. Benchmark measure of current interest levels, used to calculate periodic changes in rates charged on adjustable rate mortgages

Joint Tenancy. Ownership by two or more persons, each with an undivided ownership—if one dies, the property goes automatically to the survivor

Junior Mortgage. A mortgage subordinate to another

Lien. A claim against property for the payment of a debt: mechanic's lien, mortgage, unpaid taxes, judgments

Lis Pendens. Notice that litigation is pending on property

Listing Agreement (Listing). Written employment agreement between a property owner and a real estate broker, authorizing the broker to find a buyer

Loan Servicing. Handling paperwork of collecting loan payments, checking property tax and insurance coverage, handling delinquencies

Maintenance Fees. Payments made by the unit owner of a condominium to the homeowners' association for expenses incurred in upkeep of the common areas

Margin. Percentage (typically about 2.5 percent) added to *Index* to calculate mortgage rate adjustment

Marketable Title.   Title free of liens, clouds and defects; a title that will be freely accepted by a buyer

Mechanic's Lien.   Claim placed against property by unpaid workers or suppliers

Meeting of the Minds.   Agreement by buyer and seller on the provisions of a contract

Mortgage.   A lien or claim against real property given as security for a loan; the homeowner "gives" the mortgage; the lender "takes" it

Mortgagee.   The lender

Mortgagor.   The borrower

Multiple-Listing Service (MLS).   Arrangement by which brokers work together on the sale of each other's listed homes, with shared commissions

Negative Amortization.   Arrangement under which the shortfall in a mortgage payment is added to the amount borrowed; gradual raising of a debt

PITI.   Abbreviation for principal, interest, taxes and insurance, often lumped together in a monthly mortgage payment

Plat.   A map or chart of a lot, subdivision or community, showing boundary lines, buildings and easements

PMI.   Private mortgage insurance

Point (Discount Point).   One percent of a new mortgage being placed, paid in a one-time lump sum to the lender

Prepayment.   Payment of a mortgage loan before its due date

Prepayment Penalty.   Charge levied by the lender for paying off a mortgage before its maturity date

Principal.   The party (typically the seller) who hires and pays an agent

Procuring Cause.   Actions by a broker that bring about the desired results

Prorations.   Expenses that are fairly divided between buyer and seller at closing

Purchase-Money Mortgage.   Mortgage for the purchase of real property, commonly a mortgage "taken back" by the seller

Real Property.   Land and the improvements on it

Realtist.   Member of the National Association of Real Estate Brokers

Realtor®.   Registered name for a member of the National Association of Realtors®

Redlining.   The practice of refusing to provide loans or insurance in a certain neighborhood

RESPA.   Real Estate Settlement Procedures Act, requiring advance disclosure to the borrower of information pertinent to the loan

Restrictive Covenant.   See *Deed Restriction*

Sellers' Market.   Situation in which demand for homes exceeds the supply offered for sale

Settlement.   See *Closing*

Survey.   Map made by a licensed surveyor who measures the land and charts its boundaries, improvements and relationship to the property surrounding it

Time is of the Essence.   Legal phrase in a contract, requiring punctual performance of all obligations

Title.   Rights of ownership, control and possession of property

Title Insurance.   Policy protecting the insured against loss or damage due to defects in title: the "owner's policy" protects the buyer, the "mortgagee's policy" protects the lender; paid with a one-time premium

Title Search.   Check of the public records, usually at the local courthouse, to make sure that no adverse claims affect the value of the title

VA.   Veterans' Administration, now the Department of Veterans Affairs, which guarantees a veteran's mortgage so that a lender is willing to make the loan with little or no down payment

Vendee.   The buyer

Vendor.   The seller

Warranty Deed.   Most valuable type of deed, in which the grantor makes formal assurance of title

Zoning.   Laws of local government establishing building codes and regulations on usage of property

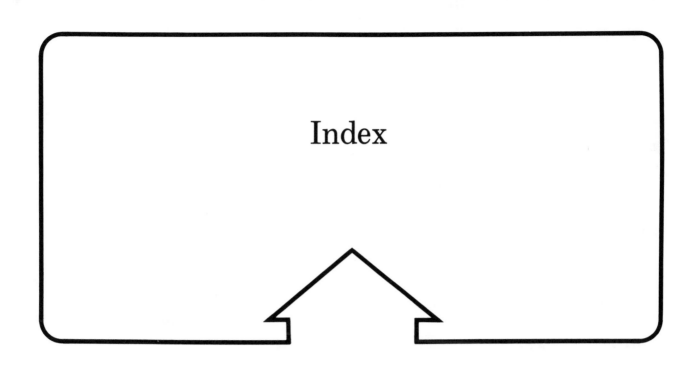

Index

Get the **Performance Advantage** on the job...*in the classroom*

	Order Number	**Real Estate Principles and Exam Prep**	Qty.	Total Price	Amount
1.	1510-01	Modern Real Estate Practice, 12th edition	_____	$34.95	_____
2.	1510-02	Study Guide for Modern Real Estate Practice, 12th edition	_____	$13.95	_____
3.	1961-01	Language of Real Estate, 3rd edition	_____	$28.95	_____
4.	1610-07	Real Estate Math, 4th edition	_____	$15.95	_____
5.	1512-10	Mastering Real Estate Mathematics, 5th edition	_____	$25.95	_____
6.	1970-04	Questions & Answers To Help You Pass the Real Estate Exam, 4th edition	_____	$21.95	_____
7.	1970-06	Real Estate Exam Guide: ASI, 3rd edition	_____	$21.95	_____

Advanced Study/Specialty Areas

8.	1560-08	Agency Relationships in Real Estate	_____	$25.95	_____
9.	1978-03	Buyer Agency: Your Competitive Edge in Real Estate	_____	$25.95	_____
10.	1557-10	Essentials of Real Estate Finance, 6th edition	_____	$38.95	_____
11.	1559-01	Essentials of Real Estate Investment, 4th edition	_____	$38.95	_____
12.	5608-50	Fast Start in Property Management	_____	$19.95	_____
13.	1551-10	Property Management, 4th edition	_____	$35.95	_____
14.	1556-10	Fundamentals of Real Estate Appraisal, 5th edition	_____	$38.95	_____
15.	1556-14	How to Use the Uniform Residential Appraisal Report	_____	$24.95	_____
16.	1556-15	Introduction to Income Property Appraisal	_____	$34.95	_____
17.	1556-11	Language of Real Estate Appraisal	_____	$21.95	_____
18.	1556-13	Exam Preparation for Residential Appraiser Certification	_____	$34.95	_____
19.	1556-12	Questions & Answers to Help You Pass the Appraisal Certification Exams	_____	$26.95	_____
20.	1557-15	Modern Residential Financing Methods, 2nd edition	_____	$19.95	_____
21.	1560-01	Real Estate Law, 3rd edition	_____	$38.95	_____

Sales & Marketing/Professional Development

22.	1913-04	Close for Success	_____	$18.95	_____
23.	1927-05	Fast Start in Real Estate	_____	$12.95	_____
24.	1913-01	List for Success	_____	$18.95	_____
25.	1922-06	Negotiating Commercial Real Estate Leases	_____	$34.95	_____
26.	1909-06	New Home Selling Strategies	_____	$24.95	_____
27.	1913-11	Phone Power	_____	$19.95	_____
28.	1907-05	Power Real Estate Advertising	_____	$24.95	_____
29.	1926-03	Power Real Estate Letters	_____	$29.95	_____
30.	1907-01	Power Real Estate Listing, 2nd edition	_____	$18.95	_____
31.	1907-02	Power Real Estate Selling, 2nd edition	_____	$18.95	_____
32.	1965-01	Real Estate Brokerage: A Success Guide, 2nd edition	_____	$35.95	_____
33.	1913-07	Real Estate Prospecting: Strategies for Farming Your Market	_____	$24.95	_____
34.	1913-13	The Real Estate Sales Survival Kit	_____	$24.95	_____
35.	1978-02	Recruiting Revolution in Real Estate	_____	$34.95	_____
36.	1926-02	Simplified Classifieds, 2nd edition	_____	$29.95	_____
37.	1903-31	Sold! The Professional's Guide to Real Estate Auctions	_____	$32.95	_____
38.	2703-11	Time Out: Time Management Strategies for the Real Estate Professional	_____	$19.95	_____
39.	1909-04	Winning in Commercial Real Estate Sales	_____	$24.95	_____

NEW! Audio Tapes

40.	1926-06	Power Real Estate Listing	_____	$19.95	_____
41.	1926-05	Power Real Estate Selling	_____	$19.95	_____
42.	1926-04	Staying on Top in Real Estate	_____	$14.95	_____

Book total _____

Tax _____

Shipping and Handling _____

Less $1.00 off if you fax order _____

Total Amount _____

810081

Place your order today! **By FAX: 1-312-836-1021**. Or call 1-800-437-9002, ext. 650.
In Illinois, call 1-312-836-4400, ext. 650. Mention code 810081. Or fill out and mail this order form to:
Real Estate Education Company 520 North Dearborn Street, Chicago, Illinois 60610-4354

YOUR SATISFACTION IS GUARANTEED!

All books come with a 30 day money-back guarantee. If you are not completely satisfied, simply return your books and your money will be refunded in full.

☐ Please send me the Real Estate Education Company catalog featuring your full list of titles.

Prices are subject to change without notice.
Also available in your local bookstore.

Fill out form and mail today!

Or Save $1.00 when you order by Fax: 312-836-1021.

Name_____

Address _____

City/State/Zip _____

Telephone (_____) _____

Payment must accompany all orders (check one):
☐ Check or money order (payable to Dearborn Financial Publishing, Inc., 520 North Dearborn Street, Chicago, Illinois 60610-4354)
☐ Charge to my credit card:
　☐ VISA　☐ MasterCard

Account No. _____ Exp. Date _____

Signature _____
(All charge orders must be signed.)　　8-91

Return Address:

_____

_____

_____

NO POSTAGE
NECESSARY
IF MAILED
IN THE
UNITED STATES

BUSINESS REPLY MAIL

FIRST CLASS　　　PERMIT NO. 88176　　　CHICAGO, IL

POSTAGE WILL BE PAID BY ADDRESSEE:

Real Estate Education Company

Order Department
520 North Dearborn Street
Chicago, Illinois 60610-9857

IMPORTANT · PLEASE FOLD OVER · PLEASE TAPE BEFORE MAILING

NOTE: This page, when folded over and taped, becomes a postage-free envelope, which has been approved by the United States Postal Service. It is provided for your convenience.

IMPORTANT · PLEASE FOLD OVER · PLEASE TAPE BEFORE MAILING